SWAP LS Engines into Camaros & Firebirds 1967-1981

Eric McClellan

CarTech®

CarTech®

CarTech®, Inc.
838 Lake Street South
Forest Lake, MN 55025
Phone: 651-277-1200 or 800-551-4754
Fax: 651-277-1203
www.cartechbooks.com

© 2013 by Eric McClellan

All rights reserved. No part of this publication may be reproduced or utilized in any form or by any means, electronic or mechanical, including photocopying, recording, or by any information storage and retrieval system, without prior permission from the Publisher. All text, photographs, and artwork are the property of the Author unless otherwise noted or credited.

The information in this work is true and complete to the best of our knowledge. However, all information is presented without any guarantee on the part of the Author or Publisher, who also disclaim any liability incurred in connection with the use of the information and any implied warranties of merchantability or fitness for a particular purpose. Readers are responsible for taking suitable and appropriate safety measures when performing any of the operations or activities described in this work.

All trademarks, trade names, model names and numbers, and other product designations referred to herein are the property of their respective owners and are used solely for identification purposes. This work is a publication of CarTech, Inc., and has not been licensed, approved, sponsored, or endorsed by any other person or entity. The Publisher is not associated with any product, service, or vendor mentioned in this book, and does not endorse the products or services of any vendor mentioned in this book.

Layout by Monica Seiberlich

ISBN 978-1-61325-520-9

Item No. SA245P

Library of Congress Cataloging-in-Publication Data

McClellan, Eric.
 Swap LS Engines into Camaros & Firebirds 1967–1981 / by Eric McClellan.
  pages cm
 ISBN 978-1-61325-031-0
 1. General Motors automobiles--Motors--Modification. 2. General Motors automobiles--Customizing. I. Title.

TL215.G4M36 2012
629.25--dc23

2012019702

Title Page: *This LS engine was installed in Mary Pozzi's 1973 Camaro. Mary competed extensively with this Pro Touring Camaro and achieved quite a bit of success. (Photo Courtesy Mary Pozzi)*

Back Cover Photos

Top Left: *The new subframe and suspension has been assembled and is ready for installation. The front subframe requires six main body bolts that are very strong, lining up the frame is a snap with the two alignment holes in the frame, which line up with corresponding holes in the body at the base of the firewall, but the sheet metal needs to remain in great shape. The frame alignment may need to be fine-tuned once the front sheet metal has been installed. Some Camaros have been damaged over the years and/or had floorpans replaced by people who lack attention to detail.*

Top Right: *Here, the body is separated from the frame. I used a jack and a block of wood to move each side of the body at a time. I then used a series of strategically placed jack stands to keep the car body level and give me room to slide the new frame into place. Although it may seem that the body is stable, you don't want the jack stands to slip and safety to be compromised.*

Middle Left: *The ATS LS swap mount kit includes all the hardware and polyurethane bushings made by Energy Suspension. ATS had to make a small modification to the bushings, so these aren't exactly off-the-shelf parts. The engine mounts are on the right and the black mount plates are in the middle. In addition, these mounts can be installed upside down if necessary, but installing them upside down changes the positioning of the engine slightly.*

Middle Right: *Most passenger-side headers are similar and do not have component clearance issues. Therefore, I only show you a driver-side comparison because often there are steering rod and other component clearance issues. Stainless Works specifically makes a version for the SpeedTech subframe (top). A universal version (bottom) is made by Hooker (PN 2288). Notice how the number-3 cylinder exhaust port is placed up and away from the steering components.*

Bottom Left: *This is a good close-up of the transmission crossmember that comes with the Speed Tech front subframe. It has a lot of front-to-back movement that allows me to place the engine and transmission virtually anywhere I choose. Using Grade-8 bolts, the crossmember just sits in place on top of the frame and is bolted in.*

Bottom Right: *The upper and lower radiator hoses will now need to be run. This typically isn't an off-the-shelf part so I have to come up with a better idea.*

CONTENTS

Acknowledgments 4
Foreword by Steven Rupp 5
Introduction 6

Chapter 1: Choosing an LS Engine 8
Selection Process 8
GM LS Engine Architecture 10
Gen III Engines 11
Gen IV Engines 13
Gen IV Vortec Engines 15
Chevrolet Performance Engines 17
Other LS Engine Builders 18
Sourcing from a Junkyard or Salvage Yard 19
Sample Junkyard Pull and Buildup: A Turbo 5.3L 20

Chapter 2: Engine and Subframe 26
Front Clip Sheet Metal 27
Stock Subframe 29
Engine Mounts 34
Oil Pans 38
Oil 41

Chapter 3: Chassis and Suspension 42
Removing the Subframe 42
Front Suspension 47
Rear Suspension 50
Wheels 52
Tires 54
Installing Mini-Tubs 56
Brake Systems 56

Chapter 4: Front-Drive Accessories 59
Camaro, Corvette, Truck and GM Kits 60
Balancers and Dampeners 63
Aftermarket Options 65
Helpful Hints 70

Chapter 5: Fuel System 71
Proper Planning 72
Fuel Pump 72
Filter 74
Hose and Fittings 75
Stock Fuel Tank Replacement 76
Tank Replacement Sources 78
AN Line Fabrication 87
Gas Pedal 88

Chapter 6: Cooling System 89
Radiator 90
Radiator Hose Location 93
Coolant Steam Line 95
Heater Outlets 95
Coolant Temperature Sensor 95
Electric Fan 95
PCV System 96

Chapter 7: Transmission 97
T56 Install 99
New-Style Transmissions 108
Classic Transmissions 108
Crossmembers 109
Bellhousing 110

Chapter 8: Wiring 111
Gauges 112
Wiring Harness 117
Adapting an LSX Wiring Harness 123
ECM Calibration 130

Chapter 9: Exhaust and Induction 131
Headers 131
Oxygen Sensors 136
Catalytic Converters 137
Induction 138

Chapter 10: Initial Start-Up 140
Systems Checks 141
Leaks 141
Nut and Bolt the Car 142
Engine Break-In: First Firing and Test-Drive 142

Source Guide 143

DEDICATION

To my son Max:
Some day you'll have all I can teach you.

ACKNOWLEDGMENTS

I owe a big thanks to everyone who helped me complete this book. It is a very true statement that nothing great can be done alone. It's all due to the good nature and knowledge of the following people and companies that this project was possible. For that I am eternally grateful.

Scott Parkhurst; Roger, Blake, and Jay of Speed Tech Performance; Horace, Chris, Damon, and David of Mast Motorsports; my UPS guy, Jeff; Nate Shaw of One Guys Garage; Chad Vancura; Ryan Christianson; Robert Rierson; Jim, Clay, and Myron of TPIS; David Schardt of Forgeline; Rick Elam of Baer Brakes; Ross McCombs of QuickTime; Blane, Liz, and Bill of Holley; Nick Strohbeen of Norm's Tires; Joe Rode of Eddie Motorsports; Nathan Tovey of TREMEC; Tom Fuehrer; Nick Licata and Steve Rupp of *Camaro Performers* magazine; Mary Pozzi; Mark Stielow; Scott Parker of *GM High-Tech Performance* magazine; Wayne and Ken of KWiK Performance; Kris Carlson of Auto Meter; Paul Grabowski of Stainless Works; Kevin of Bear's Performance; Todd of MSD; Mike Weinberg of Rockland Standard Gear; Carl Casanova of VaporWorx; Hector and Rick of Rick's Tanks; Mike Copeland of Diversified Creations; Karen and Jim of AutoRad Radiators; Jimi Day of Optima Batteries; Marc of Hedman; Jamie Meyer of General Motors; Kim Gossett of Matt's Classic Bowties; Rick and Mark of Street & Performance; Dennis Warhurst; Scott Hughes of American Autowire; Bret and everyone at RideTech; Eric Blakely and "Smitty" of Edlebrock; Kurt Anderson of Autokraft; Mike Norcia of Ram Clutches; Robb of RobbMc Performance; J.C. of Strange Engineering; Nick Fowler of Scoggin-Dickey Chevrolet; Kevin Stearns of Pacific Fabrication; Clif of LSXTV.com; LS1TECH.com; Lateral-G.net; and Pro-Touring.com.

FOREWORD

THE UBIQUITOUS LS ENGINE SWAP

Swapping LS engines into older cars has been going on for quite some time now. I don't remember who did it first, but I do remember my first introduction to what has become commonplace in hot rodding.

The Y2K bug had just turned out to be a bunch of hype, and I had just bought a 2000 SS Camaro, replete with a sweet factory-installed LS1 under the hood. I loved that car and before long I was down at Hotchkis Performance asking about their bolt-on suspension products. As fate would have it, the gearheads at Hotchkis were just starting the process of swapping an LS1 into their 1971 "F71" Camaro. Next thing I knew, they were taking measurements from my 2000 to help them along the path of developing a swap kit for the fourth-generation Camaro.

Back then doing a swap like this was nothing like it is today. Computer tuning options were extremely limited, and there were few aftermarket parts to make it easier. But, Hotchkis got it done and they fried the tires of the 2000 SS for the December 2000 cover of *Hot Rod* magazine.

Seeing that Camaro got me thinking. I loved the smooth power and reliability of my 2000 SS, but it lacked the soul of classic muscle. A couple of years later, I bought a 1969 Camaro and an LS1 from a junkyard to do an engine swap. By then there was a bit more aftermarket support, but swapping still involved a lot of trial, error, and fabrication. When the car was finished, the combination of classic style and modern technology was as sweet as I thought it would be. Looking around, I could see that I wasn't alone as LS engines were now being grafted into just about every car you could imagine, but the favorite seemed to be first-gen Camaros.

Soon after slotting the LS1 into the 1969 Camaro, I landed a magazine tech editor gig and moved on to my current, and seemingly never ending, project "Bad Penny," a 1968 Camaro that has consumed a handful of various LS engines culminating in a 461-inch RHS block 700-hp monster. Every time I do a swap, I learn something new or find some cool new product.

Fast forward to 2012 and LS swaps have sort of become my thing. I get asked a lot of questions, and the most common one is: "How much does an LS swap cost?" I typically answer with a question of my own: "How long is a piece of string?" You see, an LS swap can be as expensive, or as inexpensive, as you want it to be. Find a scrapyard 5.3L truck engine for 500 bucks, rework a wiring harness, fabricate some engine plates, put in a load of sweat equity, and you can get it done on surprisingly little coin. If you decide you want a boutique-built Gen IV LS7 with internals made from unobtanium along with cutting-edge electronics, and the budget skyrockets into low earth orbit. Today, thanks to the aftermarket, dropping an LS engine under any hood, and running it, is easier than ever, and even more so if that hood belongs to a first-gen Camaro. In fact, you could do a soup-to-nuts install without ever having to touch a welder, plasma cutter, or mill. Off-the-shelf swap headers are available to fit just about any subframe, and many have matching engine mounts plates.

Many companies offer programming software for GM computers, and some, such as Holley and FAST, offer completely aftermarket computer and harness packages. Aftermarket oil pans for any subframe abound and fuel systems are readily available. These installations used to be a royal pain, but today they have become nearly commonplace because of the many oil pans and EFI-ready tanks. Radiators, throttle bodies, pulley systems and other parts needed for a swap can be found in some company's catalog of widgets. And for those with an awesome set of tools, and the desire to go old school, a swap can still be done by digging up just the right set of factory parts from retired GM cars and trucks. Best of all, since the LS engine platform has been around for nearly 14 years, they are easy to find and relatively cheap on the secondary market.

Either way you go, I'm pretty sure that you'll find (just as I did) it's hard to go back once you've experience just how much better a modern LS engine can make your classic F-Body.

Steven Rupp, Technical Editor
Camaro Performers magazine

INTRODUCTION

Your first step should be to define your performance goals and budget. You need to honestly and accurately determine how your F-Body will be used. Therefore, you need to select the best engine and setup according to a particular application. An engine's common application is typically street, street/strip, drag racing, auto crossing, or road racing. Each engine design and setup is suited for a particular application. Do you want a torquey high-performance street engine? Do you want to just cruise? Do you want to race? How much will be street and how much will be racing? What type of racing will you do? A top-performing street engine produces exceptional torque from 1,500 to 5,000 rpm for potent stoplight-to-stoplight torque, not high-RPM horsepower. Drag race cars need to pull hard off the line but operate at high RPM, so high RPM is the target rather than low-RPM torque. A street/street engine must combine exceptional low-RPM torque with high-RPM output, so this combination becomes particularly challenging because you often need to compromise with induction, head, and cam design to arrive at the best compromise.

LS Engine History

The LS engine was a clean-sheet type of build for General Motors. This meant that they used a similar design from the original pushrod small-block V-8 designed by Ed Cole in 1944 and 1945, but that's about where the similarities end. General Motors then knocked everyone's socks off when, in 1997, the LT engine was knocked off its pedestal and a new king was crowned. The first appearance of the venerable Gen III or LS1 engine appeared in the 1997 Corvette. At the time, no one but the clairvoyant could have predicted that in four short years, the LS engine would completely dominate the market.

Over the years, GM LS engines have been some of most efficient and compact pushrod V-8 engines on the market, producing copious amounts of horsepower. You can install one into about any car that has four wheels and even a few things that don't. The LS shares absolutely no parts with the Gen I small-block. One obvious difference is that all LS engines have six-bolt main caps as opposed to the two- or four-bolt main caps in first-generation small-block.

The LS series of engines comes in two basic variants: aluminum block and iron block. Soon after the LS1 was released in 1997, it became prolific throughout GM's lineup. Aluminum-block LS engines were installed in most V-8 cars while a typical truck version was an iron block. A few SS trucks, such as the TrailBlazer, were exceptions to this rule. In the later years, aluminum blocks were introduced into trucks, such as the Yukon and Silverado. Finding a 6-liter aluminum-block LS truck engine is fairly common now and I've rou tinely seen them at local junkyard for $500 for a complete engine.

My Engine and Car for this Build

A 1968 Camaro is the LS swap car featured in this book. It origi nally came with an inline 6-cylinde engine and a Powerglide with col umn shift. The test Camaro started life meekly but was rebuilt between 2002 and 2006. I knew the platform was ripe for an LS swap. This wa not a big-block car that had a high collector value; it was a pedestrian 6-cylinder car with nothing fancy, so I wasn't cutting up something rare. The car was built with a small-block 350 and backed with a T56. It was a decent street car, but as with every car project, it was never done.

When I bought my LS engine and performed the engine swap in the Camaro, I considered these factors and thought very hard about the answer: The car would be a street-legal Camaro that would see a considerable amount of track time. I wanted to be able to turn as well as clock fast quarter-mile times. I wanted the reliable and lightweight LS platform to power our build.

I chose Mast Motorsports to build me a killer LS3 that could handle the abuse of a road course but could also be tame enough to handle the most crowded of shopping malls. Mast offers a wide selection of engines that can be built for virtually any budget

INTRODUCTION

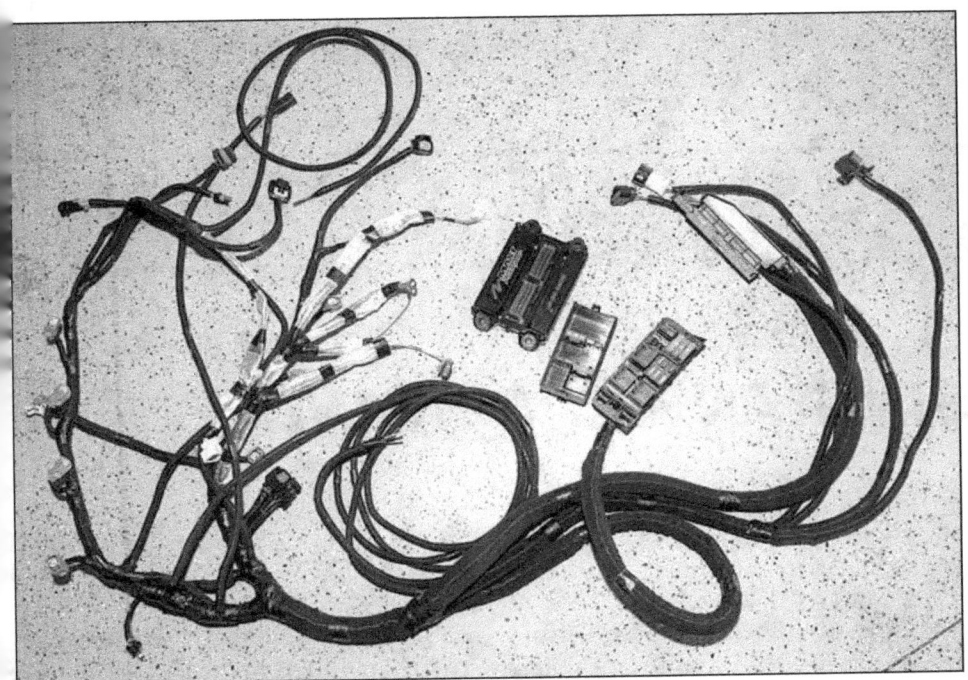

Make sure you have the correct wiring harness so your swap project is successful. Mast makes a proprietary wiring harness that works extremely well and takes all the guesswork out of the process. The harness fits tight against the block and is almost invisible when complete.

To mate an engine and harness requires the correct PCM or ECU. When buying a used engine, you need to buy the original ECU and other controls, so you don't have to buy these expensive accessories later.

Let me introduce the car that's the subject of my build. This 1968 Camaro originally came with an inline-six and a Powerglide transmission. The former owner installed a warmed-up 350 and a T56.

and power range. Once again, I had to consider my goal for the project: road racing. I had to pick something that would work well for the street and for the track.

During a call to Mast, they suggested an LS3 (PN 000-2T2) with a 4.070-inch bore and 4.000-inch stroke that increased displacement to 416 ci. The LS was equipped with a Callies forged crank, Scat H-beam rods, a set of diamond pistons, a Mast custom three-bolt core cam, and CNC LS3/L92 heads. Up top, I have a Holley Modular High-Ram intake that was made for the track. However, the stock LS3 carries a stock intake manifold that flows very well. It's been used on many pro-touring high-end builds, so it's not an impediment for producing horsepower. Mast also installed one of its own proprietary oil pans, which is designed for a carbureted engine. The pan contains baffling so the engine can perform under racing conditions. I bought the M-90 Mast controller and wiring kit to make it all work smoothly. This engine package dyno'd at 600 hp and 505 ft-lbs of torque. Quite an improvement over the 430 hp a stock LS3 comes with!

CHAPTER 1

Choosing an LS Engine

Many choose iron blocks rather than aluminum versions because they are inexpensive and are easily stroked. They are cheaper and can handle bigger power loads and this is why you see iron-block versions juiced to the hilt with nitrous. However, to be fair to the aluminum versions, I've seen some twin-turbo versions of the aluminum block handle power well into the four-digit range.

The first cathedral-port head version of the LS1 engine ruffled some feathers. General Motors has since added a square-port design on the LS3. This means that the intakes on the LS1 and LS3 are not interchangeable. With the typical cathedral-port LS6 intake (interchangeable with the LS1) making roughly 320 cfm, the stock LS3 version flows 365 cfm right from the factory. That's more than your average big-block of days gone by.

Selection Process

Cathedral- and square-port LS engines both have impressive architecture and equipment. Over the years the engines have been relatively compact, able to be stuffed in just about any car that has four wheels and even a few things that didn't have four wheels. The LS was also extremely reliable; the amount of abuse these engines can take is sometimes just plain astonishing. They are easily repaired; General Motors made millions of these engines and just about everyone has a few 305 blocks lying around as lawn ornaments. Most important, however, to the guys who just can't leave well enough alone, is that you can easily modify them; the aftermarket

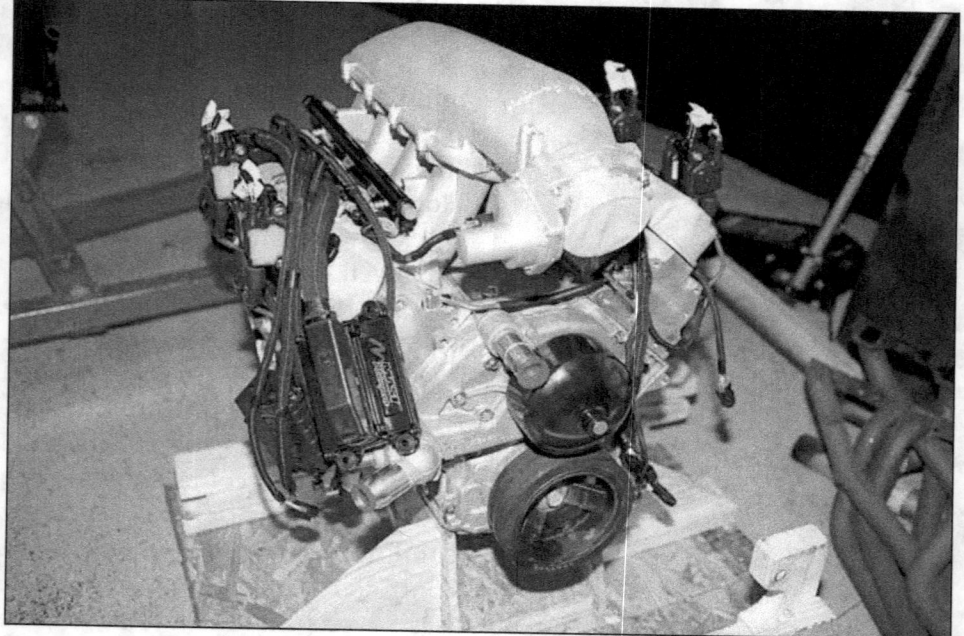

In the crate, my wiring harness was attached to the new engine with all the equipment to get it up and running. My engine had a respectable 592 hp and 505 ft-lbs of torque even in really humid and hot air. I expect that number to easily reach 600 hp or more with cooler air.

CHOOSING AN LS ENGINE

or the small-block Chevy is magnificently huge.

Okay, so you're asking yourself, "So what?" How could this engine really replace almost 45 years of the iron, four-bolt-main small-block that you've come to know and love so dearly? Let me count the ways! For starters, the profile of the engine is quite low, allowing it to be stuffed into some very tight spaces and a wide variety of cars. Second, the engine is easy to build and upgrade. It touts a six-bolt main block that can take far more abuse than your granddad's old iron-block engine, and it does it while weighing 40 pounds lighter. The short-block has been proven to be very reliable up to and beyond 500 hp. Finally, the LS provides excellent potential fuel economy in today's four-dollar-a-gallon world, so it's a god-send for guys who like to have plenty of juice on tap but also enjoy a leisurely highway cruise. With a 6-speed T56 tranny, it's not unheard of to get 25 mpg with an LS engine and a light foot.

The cylinder heads were a massive leap forward and provided an immense boost in power and efficiency. The heads incorporated technology and combustion chamber design from NASCAR SB-2 358-ci race engines. The valve size is roughly the same as a high-performance small-block head (2.165 intake/1.59 exhaust for the LS3 head versus a 2.20 intake/1.60 performance small-block head). The valve angle was changed slightly and the heads were given a much larger flow rate. More air in equals more power! Now companies, such as Mast Motorsports and West Coast Racing Cylinder Heads, can build you a set of heads for any setup or power level you are trying to achieve. Companies have offerings up to and sometimes beyond the naturally-aspirated 650-hp range from an LS combination and well over 800 hp in a boosted application. General Motors has since upgraded its LS lineup with a host of new engine combinations, each one getting better than the last.

There are of course iron-block versions of the LS engine. However, those were lower compression and mostly put into trucks and SUVs, such as the Silverado and Escalade. If you want a big bore engine and want some forced induction, these are a great way to go. A naturally-aspirated engine can make big power, but it tends be a little more difficult than a forced-induction engine with a supercharger or turbocharger. Many iron-block versions of the LS engine are out there and are by far the most plentiful and the most economical. Up until recently, the LS iron-block engines were the most affordable LS engines for building a potent and powerful stroker combination until General Motors came out with the LS3. This power plant features thicker walled cylinders and easily accepts a stroker kit more readily than the previous LS1 and LS2 short-blocks. It also has the largest bore of the entire lineup at 4.00 inches versus 3.78 of the other blocks, except of course the LS7, which has a 4.125-inch bore. This block (PN 12623967) is nearly equivalent to prepping and machining an iron block for the same purpose. If you choose an iron block, you must realize these are 75 pounds heavier than a similar aluminum-block engine.

Installing an LS engine in your F-Body is often more inexpensive and produces more performance than rebuilding the Gen I small-block that came in your car. With an LS engine, you can ditch that timing light and use a laptop computer to extract a few extra ponies by precisely tuning the ignition curve of the EFI system. No more fiddling with finicky carburetors. On an LS engine, the computer is so efficient and so intelligent that you can

This is Mast Motorsports' truck version of an LS engine. You need to determine your application because that helps you select the best engine for your performance goals. In addition, you need to set your budget and ideal weight for the engine. Aluminum-block engines are lighter but tend to be more expensive than the heavier and less-expensive iron blocks. All LS engines share the same basic dimensions. (Photo Courtesy Mast Motorsports)

set an accurate tune for your engine and you don't have to be concerned with reliability. A suitable ignition program on your engine can add a lot of horsepower to your build. Finding the right tuner can be a challenge, but suffice to say, it's important to dyno tune any engine to not only get the most power out of it but also to keep it as reliable as possible. A bad tune can ruin an engine very quickly. Swapping any LS engine into your F-Body can be a breeze if you have the right information, but please do not expect this to be cheap. A typical budget build runs about $10,000 or more. A build, such as this, includes the engine, transmission, and bare-minimum parts, such as a stock oil pan, stock intake, injectors, and the standard stock parts. Of course, this depends upon on how effectively you use your hard-earned dollars.

GM LS Engine Architecture

You should ask yourself, "What is the goal of my build?" That's an important factor when selecting a block, whether it's aluminum or iron. That goal should guide you through the course of the entire build. This also applies to the type of block you want to run if you choose to build your own or have the choice between aluminum and iron blocks. There are advantages and drawbacks to iron and aluminum blocks.

The most affordable and economical LS engine version is the iron block. While these blocks can support a lot of horsepower, they are often 100 pounds heavier than their aluminum siblings in the LS lineup. The 5.3L truck block is the most common block found at junkyards these days. Typically, these are inexpensive, but they are also roughly 80 pounds heavier than the aluminum 5.3L block. An iron block's biggest advantage is that the block itself can withstand higher loads and therefore more horsepower than a comparable aluminum block. For example, if you planned to add forced induction to your engine and expect to make more than 1,000 hp or greater, sticking with the iron block is suitable. You might be tempted to go straight for the 6.0L block because of the price. If you find that the price is similar, the extra cubes do help, but don't make that much of a power difference in the long run. You can add more power with a good set of heads and a well-suited cam than you can with cubic inches alone.

The aluminum block has advantages and disadvantages as well. While the block itself is considerably lighter at approximately 80 pounds, you have to spend a few more dollars to buy one, especially if you want an LS3 version of the block. At the time of this writing a new bare LS3 block is about $1,300, while a used aluminum 5.3L long block costs about $500 to $750 depending on accessories and condition. In my experience testing with aluminum-blocked LS engines I've found that the aluminum versions are typically good up to 1,000 hp but not much more. If I want more than that or I'm trying to introduce a lot of boost with forced induction or nitrous, I want to step up to an iron block because it's stronger than aluminum. My feeling is that if you really do make more than 1,000 hp, the extra weight of the iron block is truly negligible. I've found that the 6.0L versions can fetch a hefty price tag; a recent search for them netted me a few finds in the $1,200 to $1,500 range for the short-block alone.

It must be said that all of these engines share design and component similarities but can be vastly different. Many LS parts are interchangeable, but many are not. If you have questions about which parts interchange with particular engines, you need to do some research before purchasing parts. A complete GM LS engine parts interchange guide would fill an entire book so I provide the most important interchange aspects.

To date, General Motors has released more than two-dozen iterations of the LS-series engine. A lot of the engines and parts can be found at salvage yards or more easily through the Chevrolet Performance Parts catalog. The biggest difference between Gen III and Gen IV LS engines is the Gen III has a 24x (26 minus 2) crank reluctor wheel while the Gen IV engine has a 58x (60 minus 2) reluctor wheel for greater computer power and more computing power; this means that the computer has more data points to draw from and can make more accurate timing adjustments to the fuel and air mixture. The easiest way to tell the two engines apart is the Gen III engines have the cam sensor at the top rear of the engine and the Gen IV iterations have the cam sensor closer to the timing cover.

All GM LS engines have similar dimensions or in other words, the length, width, and height of all LS engines is the same. In addition, the engine mounts are located in the same position for almost all engines. Therefore, these compact engines are easily swapped into a first- or second-generation F-Body. In fact, the GM LS engine is little smaller than the small-block Chevy but it often sits farther back in the chassis and closer

CHOOSING AN LS ENGINE

to the firewall. As a result, most LS engines are suitable for swap into an F-Body car. Your choice of an LS engine depends upon your budget, performance goals, and intended use. In this chapter, I provide key information on the major LS engines on the market so use the information to make a wise buying decision. I went to Mike Copeland, one of the gurus of the LS swap for expert information when I did the research for this book. He rose to the rank of project manager of the Concept and Vehicle Integration department in the GM Performance Division and now he is managing operations at Lingenfelter Performance. He taught me just about everything there is to know about these engines and how to make them fit. Throughout this book you find his knowledge and ingenuity sprinkled from cover to cover. Mike provided the follow information.

Below are the basics on most of the LS engines that you come across in today's market. I hope that this data helps you choose the best engine for your project. General Motors has a few crate engines available if you don't want to go routing through the scrap yard for picked over cars, those are covered at the end of this chapter.

Gen III Engines

As you well know the GM LS took over for the LT engine, so when the LS1-equipped Corvette was launched in 1997, it ushered in the Gen III LS era. As a guideline, Gen III engines were offered in aluminum block for cars and iron block for trucks. The Gen III line ran concurrently with the Gen IV line from 2005 to 2007. These engines are distinguished by the cathedral-port design heads, which produced excellent low-RPM port velocity.

LS1

Installed in the 1997 Corvette, the LS1 engine was first LS engine ever released to the public. This power plant produced 345 hp and 350 ft-lbs of torque, which for the day wasn't too shabby coming out of the smog-choking 1970s and 1980s era that brought about the K-car. The LS1 features an all-aluminum block and aluminum heads. It featured 15-degree cathedral-port heads that flowed very well. It has a modest compression ratio of 10:1, which works well with a supercharger or other types of power adders. Within a few short years, General Motors installed the LS in a wide range of cars and trucks. General Motors made many of these engines so they're relatively easy to find. There are many variations in block and head castings.

The first block (PN 12550592), made from 1997 through 1999, had a crossover passage that supplied oil to the right side of the engine. In addition, a small hole drilled through the main webs further promoted "bay-to-bay breathing," which reduced oil vapor from getting trapped between the main caps.

The 1999–2004 blocks changed little, and the two casting numbers for these years are 12559378 and 12560626. The only thing you might notice is the extra reinforcement on the right front corner and a deep oil slot that improved oil flow to the right side of the engine.

In 2001 and 2002, General Motors changed a few things. At that time, General Motors had a shortage of LS1 blocks and this shortage meant that a few LS6 blocks snuck their way into production. The LS6 (PN 1256118) was the official block for the Corvette in 2001, but it was also installed in some 2001–2002 Camaros. Keep in mind that this did not change anything else on the engine; only the block was different and just because you have one doesn't always mean that it's an LS6 right off the bat.

These engines produced 295 to 405 hp, depending on the vehicle in which it was installed. Of course, the Corvette received the 405-hp LS6. Firing order is the same at 1-8-7-2-6-5-4-3.

As previously mentioned, the LS1 has thin cylinder walls. According to General Motors, the LS1 block should only be limited to .004 inch of cylinder boring for the early blocks and

Mast allows the coils to be located behind each head to create a clean look that's a little reminiscent of small-block days. (Photo Courtesy Mast Motorsports)

a paltry .010 inch for the later versions. As a result, it's virtually impossible to obtain big cubes from this engine because of the thin cast-iron sleeves. Without a resleeve of an LS1 block, the maximum stroke is 4.125 inches with a 3.905-inch bore, which calculates to about 393 ci. If you're searching for larger displacement, I highly recommend finding a suitable iron block or another aluminum version that can be overbored to your requirements. If you want big cubic inches, this isn't the block for you.

Models: You can find these engines in 1997–2004 Corvettes, 1998–2002 Camaro/Firebird, and 2004 GTOs.

LS6

The LS6 engine is essentially an updated LS1 fitted with bigger and better heads. It has a bigger cam and better flowing heads and intake. The LS6 has more compression than the LS1 at 10.5:1. The LS6 also has slightly better 243 casting heads with sodium-filled exhaust valves and hollow intake valves. The 204/218 cam is also better than the LS1 and carries the obvious LS6 intake over the stock LS1 version. Other than those small pieces and a couple of small-block designs, the LS1 and LS6 are virtually the same. The heads and cam flow very well. Installed in the Corvette Z06, these engines produced a respectable 385 hp and 380 ft-lbs of torque. This was a significant increase from the previous LS1. In 2002, the LS6 (casting number 12551358) saw a bump to 405 hp and 400 ft-lbs, which was a 5-percent increase in output. By the mid-2000s, the LS6 was getting dated, and in 2004, the LS2 replaced it.

This block is similar to the LS1 in the respect that it has a cast-aluminum block and heads. It was built with 10.5:1 compression and has the standard 1-8-7-2-6-5-4-3 firing order.

Models: 2001–2004 Corvette Z06s and 2004–2005 Cadillac CTS-Vs.

LQ4/LQ9

The iron-block LQ4 and the LQ9 (Vortec 6000) share similar architecture with the LS6, but the difference is that it came in the trucks and SUVs of the GM lineup. Essentially these are the iron-block version of the LS6. It has a 4-inch bore that makes it compatible with the much more desirable L92 and LS7 heads. The heads have a larger combustion chamber than the LS6 head. The LQ9 has a 10.1:1 compression ratio while the LQ4 has a lower 9.4:1 in a 364-ci package. The LQ9 cranks out 345 hp and 385 ft-lbs of torque, while the LQ4 produces a much lower 300 hp and 360 ft-lbs of torque.

Clearly, the LQ9 makes a better starting point for any build and can be bored and stroked to make even more power. Of course, the downside of this combo is that the block adds some weight. That fact may be negligible when considering the power potential. The LQ9 gets bragging rights for being the most powerful engine in the Vortec lineup.

Chevrolet Performance sells this engine through its dealers. Bottom line: If you are looking for a truck LS engine, this is the one to buy.

Models: 1999–2004 Silverado, Suburban, Yukon, and Hummer H2 (LQ4). The LQ9 engine is found in 2002–2006 Escalades and 2003–2007 Silverado SSs and Sierras.

LR4

The LR4 is the 4.3-liter 4800 Vortec. It was rated from 255 hp to 285 hp and 280 to 295 ft-lbs, depending on the year and model of the vehicle you find. These have a small bore and stroke, and are not suitable for high-performance applications.

Models: 2007 Sierra, Savana, Silverado, and Express.

L59/LM7

More than five million LM7, LM4, L33, and the LH6 engines were sold in North American alone. These models are by far the most plentiful of the Gen III and Gen IV engines available. The LM7 is an iron-block version. The cast-iron L59 blocks were built from 1999 to 2007 while the aluminum block was made from 2003 to 2007. The LM7 is basically the same as the

The Vortec 6.0L VVT engine is more commonly known as the L96, which is found on the GMC Savana. Truck LS versions have this tall-style intake and the alternator placed in the 1 o'clock position. This is one of the most affordable engines to find in a salvage yard. (Photo Courtesy General Motors)

CHOOSING AN LS ENGINE

LM4 but uses an iron-block. The L59 is available in either 4.8- or 5.3-liter iterations, so verify the casting number to properly identify the displacement of the engine. The 4.8-liter cast–iron block casting number is 12551358. The 2003–2004 models feature the drive-by-wire throttle control system, while earlier models are fitted with a mechanical throttle linkage. The LM7 versions are rated roughly between 285 and 295 hp and 330 ft-lbs of torque depending on model and year. The L59 is a flex-fuel version of the LM7, just be aware when picking an engine.

Models: 2002–2005 Cadillac Escalade 2WD, 2002–2006 Avalanche, 2003–2007 Chevrolet Express/Savana, 1999–2007 GM C/K trucks, 1999–2007 GMC Sierra 1500, 1999–2006 Suburban/Yukon XL, and 1999–2006 Tahoe/Yukon.

LM4

In 2003 the LM4 was the first Vortec 5300 in the GM lineup to use an aluminum block. This version of the Vortec 5300 is 100 pounds lighter than the LM7 version and has what General Motors calls a "pan-axle," which allows room for front differential to bolt right onto the oil pan for four-wheel-drive applications. If you plan on a four-wheel-drive swap, this engine just might be the ticket. Rated at 285 and 295 hp and 325 and 335 ft-lbs of torque, again based on model and year.

Models: 2004-and-later Trail-Blazer (extended wheel base), 2004 Envoy, and 2004 SSR.

L33

This all-aluminum 5.3-liter truck engine is more commonly found in the extended-cab versions of GM's C and K lines. This engine is a slight bump up from the LM4 in horsepower to 310, but a decrease in torque to 300 ft-lbs. This Gen III engine was replaced by the Gen IV system. The cylinder heads are based on the LS6 design, which produce more power. These are good finds if you are looking for an all aluminum engine for your swap.

Models: 2005–2007 Silverado and Sierra.

GEN IV Engines

In 2005, General Motors launched a new updated version of the LS engine in the form of the Gen IV. While engine architecture and most of the engine features remain the same on Gen IV engines, there are some key differences. These include the relocated knock sensor (to the outside of block), relocated MAP sensor, longer head bolts (check), and a drive-by-wire throttle body. Most important, these engines feature rectangular ports, generally have better flow characteristics than the Gen III, and therefore produce more power than the earlier Gen III engines.

LSA

Considered the Cadillac version of the LS9, this supercharged 6.2-liter V-8 is installed in the CTS-V, which many call a "family sedan." The LSA is rated at 556 hp and 551 ft-lbs of torque. The LSA is slightly different than the LS9 in the respect that it has a slightly lower capacity supercharger, 9.0:1 compression compared to the LS9s 9.1:1, a single unit heat exchanger and cast pistons, all of which add up to a little brother version of the LS9. If you've had the pleasure of driving one, you know that having one in no way makes for buyer's remorse for not stepping up to the LS9.

Models: 2009-and-later Cadillac CTS-V and 2012-and-later Camaro ZL1.

LS2

The LS2 is the Gen IV version of the LS1 and LS6 engines. While it uses the same LS6 heads and camshaft, it has a larger 4-inch bore. The compression ratio and power has been bumped up a tad to 10.9:1 and 400 hp/400 ft-lbs of torque with the standard 364 ci. This engine had a limited run before General Motors ushered in the LS3 engine so the LS2 has been superseded.

Models: 2005–2007 Corvette, 2005–2006 SSR, 2005–2006 GTO, 2006–2007 CTS-V, and 2006–2009 TrailBlazer SS.

LS4

The LS4 is a 5.3L engine installed in the Pontiac Grand Prix GXP, Impala, and Monte Carlo. This is the first V-8 to make its way, transversely, into a front-wheel-drive vehicle since 1955. General Motors had to shorten the crank 13 mm, 3 mm from the front and 10 mm from the rear, so it is a bit of an oddball. It features a displacement on demand system and makes 303 hp and 323 ft-lbs of torque. These engines share the same main-cap design and deep skirt model as other LS engines in this series.

Models: 2006–2009 Chevrolet Impala SS, 2006–2007 Chevrolet Monte Carlo SS, 2005–2008 Pontiac Grand Prix GXP, and 2008 Buick LaCrosse Super.

LS7

The LS7 has the largest bore (4.125-inch), and therefore the largest displacement in the LS family. The LS7 is 7.0 liters of pure General

CHAPTER 1

The LS7 is almost indistinguishable from any other LS engine, but the key to telling it from the rest is its dry-sump oil delivery system. You may need to examine the engine from below to spot the dry sump system. (Photo Courtesy General Motors)

Motors fury. I imagine that if General Motors unleashed its most feral engineers and gave them free reign to release their aggression on anything they saw fit, they would come up with this engine. The block has been sleeved so it can be stroked for more cubic inches and boasts a forged crankshaft and main caps. The rods are titanium and pistons are hypereutectic for high-performance service. It has titanium intake and sodium-filled exhaust valves that allow this engine to rev up to and beyond 7,000 rpm. This engine is a perfect plug-'n'-play engine for those who just want to drop in an easy 505 hp and 470 ft-lbs of torque and be done with it. As General Motors designed it, this is indeed the ultimate small-block engine.

Models: 2006–2013 Chevrolet Corvette Z06.

LS3

An upgraded and punched-out LS2, the LS3 6.2-liter block replaces the 6.0-liter LS2. Serving as the base engine for the 2008 and newer Corvettes, the new block has a 4.06-inch bore and displaces 376 ci. The all-aluminum engine has 10.7:1 compression and 47-pounds per hour injectors pump out 430 hp and 424 ft-lbs of torque. The extra power comes from the CNC heads, new LS7 injectors, larger bore, new piston, and tweaking of the valvetrain. This engine loves to rev and usually tops out right around 6,600 rpm. These engines are going to be fairly tough to find as they are highly sought after. You might as well order one from Chevrolet Performance or from a builder, such as Mast Motorsports.

Models: 2008-and-later Corvette, 2009 G8 GXP, and 2010-and-later Camaro SS.

LS9

The LS9 is the king of all LS engines at this time. Currently, it is the most powerful American production engine ever made. A supercharged 376-ci engine that bellows out 638 hp and 604 ft-lbs of torque makes this one screaming monster of an LS engine. General Motors decided to forgo the larger LS7, 7.0-liter block due to the internal pressures of the supercharger. They instead went for the LS3 block for its thicker cylinder walls being able to handle the greater pressure. If you are reading this carefully, you've noticed I mentioned the LS3 block multiple times. The LS3 at the time of this writing is the only block to go with if you want to make big power and want it to be light. Even General Motors thinks so as proof by this engine build. These engines only came in the 2009 and newer Corvette ZR1s, so finding one is going to be impossible. You're better off buying one from

The downside to having all the engines look and operate the same is that it makes it tough to tell the high-performance engines apart from the average ones. The LS3 for the Corvette produces a healthy 430 hp from the factory. While it's hard to tell, the accessory drive setup hugs the front of the engine more than with any other kit. (Photo Courtesy General Motors)

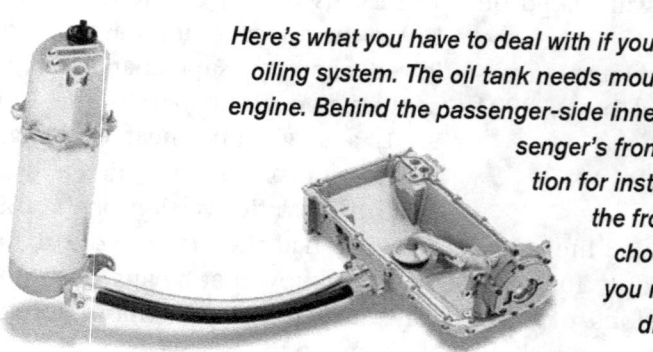

Here's what you have to deal with if you go with the LS7 dry-sump oiling system. The oil tank needs mounting somewhere near the engine. Behind the passenger-side inner fender or inside the passenger's front fender is a popular location for installing the oil pump. Notice the front crankshaft drive: If you choose to use a stock oil pan, you need to plan for this major difference. (Photo Courtesy General Motors)

CHOOSING AN LS ENGINE

At 640 hp and 604 ft-lbs of torque, the supercharged LS9 is the most powerful production LS engine. In fact, it's the most powerful production engine from any American manufacturer. If you order one of these just be aware that the front accessory kit cannot be easily changed; the supercharger belt makes that readily apparent. The intercooler is compact enough to fit under the plastic engine cover, which means less work for you when plumbing the engine. (Photo Courtesy General Motors)

The LS9 front accessory kit comes with all you see here. The LS9 fits into the stock F-Body frame with a significant notch in the subframe. The clear difference is the beefy blower belt. (Photo Courtesy General Motors)

This is a front view of the LS9 drive kit. The alternator and A/C pump are run off a separate belt. This is a complicated piece of automotive art. The A/C pump doesn't clear the lower frame support on an F-Body and requires the front frame to be notched. (Photo Courtesy General Motors)

Gen IV Vortec Engines

Gen IV Vortec engines are fairly plentiful at the time of the writing, although finding one might be a bit more challenging. They use Variable Valve Timing and Active Fuel Management (also called Displacement on Demand, by General Motors), and therefore are most complex LS engines.

L76

The L76 is an all-aluminum 6.0-liter Gen IV engine. It uses what General Motors calls Active Fuel Management, which is just another name for its Displacement on Demand system. In essence, what AFM does is it allows the engine to deactivate certain cylinders (under light loads) so they do not fire, thus giving better fuel economy while still retaining the power of 361 hp and 386 ft-lbs when it is needed for heavy engine loads. It also shares a structural oil pan with the Pontiac G8. This engine uses an electric throttle control system that allows the ECM to directly control the throttle engine.

Models: 2007–2009 Chevrolet Suburban, 2007–2009 Chevrolet Avalanche, 2007–2009 Chevrolet Silverado, 2007–2009 GMC Sierra, and 2007–2009 GMC Yukon XL.

L92

The 6.2-liter L92, an all-aluminum engine, is also known as the Vortec 6200. It features variable valve timing and produces a solid 403 hp and 417 ft-lbs of torque. Typically variable valve timing has been reserved for overhead-cam engines, but Chevy figured out a way to make it work with a pushrod setup, making this engine a first of a kind.

Models: 2007-and-later Cadillac Escalade, 2009 Chevrolet Tahoe, 2007 to present GMC Yukon Denali/Denali XL, 2007 to present GMC Sierra Denali, 2008 to present Hummer H2, 2009 to present Chevrolet Silverado 1500 Vortec Max, 2009 to present GMC Sierra 1500 Vortec Max.

Chevrolet Performance as a crate engine and getting yourself a factory warranty.

Models: 2009-and-later Corvette ZR1.

LC9

The LC9 has a compression ratio of 9.9:1 and uses regular unleaded fuel as well as E85. Make sure you grab the ECM to go with the LC9 so it knows that you might run E85 from time to time. Just like its brothers, it uses Active Fuel Management and a returnless fuel-injection arrangement. These engines are found in AWD SUVs and are rated at 302 hp and 330 ft-lbs.

Models: 2007–2013 Chevrolet Avalanche, 2007–2013 Chevrolet Silverado 1500, 2007 to present Chevrolet Suburban 1/2 ton, 2007–2013 GMC Sierra 1500, and 2007 to present GMC Yukon XL 1/2 ton.

LFA

This all-aluminum engine was fitted into a few specialty vehicles for General Motors. It touted 6.0 liters and made a respected 332 hp and 367 ft-lbs of torque. It has all the bells and whistles of all the Gen IV engines including Variable Valve Timing and Active Fuel Management.

Models: 2008 to present Chevrolet Tahoe Hybrid, 2008 to present GMC Yukon Hybrid, 2009 to present Cadillac Escalade Hybrid, 2009 to present Chevrolet Silverado Hybrid, and 2009 to present GMC Sierra Hybrid.

LH6

The LH6 is an upgrade from the LM4 for the Gen IV engines. The LH6 is employed with Active Fuel Management and is aluminum, whereas the brother version, the LY5 has an iron block. This is a 5.3-liter block and was the first put into production from the Vortec line. Output is decent at 300 hp and 330 ft-lbs of torque.

Models: 2004–2009 Chevrolet TrailBlazer, including EXT (through 2006), 2005–2009 GMC Envoy Denali, 2005–2006 GMC Envoy XL, 2005 GMC Envoy XUV, 2005–2007 Buick Rainier, 2005–2009 Saab 9-7X, 2007 Chevrolet Silverado 1500, and 2007 GMC Sierra 1500.

LH8

The LH8 is yet another 5.3-liter variant; it was designed for the Hummer H3 and other trucks in GM's lineup. The difference here is the exhaust that includes a quad catalytic converter system that is compact enough to fit the limited space and fit the EPA's emissions standards.

Models: 2008 to present Hummer H3 Alpha, and 2009 to present Chevrolet Colorado/GMC Canyon.

LMG

Consider this version the 5.3-liter equivalent of the LY5, except this version can accept flex fuels, such as E85. E85 has grown in popularity due to its cheap price and high-octane rating, which is great for racers looking to make big power on cheap fuel. The downside is that flex fuels, such as E85, are less efficient and while they make better power, they also burn a lot more fuel much more quickly. Expect a conservative loss in fuel mileage between 10 and 20 percent, depending on driving habits.

A 2011 5.3L Vortec engine has the same basic shape as every other LS engine, but the intake, oil pan, and accessory drive are the main differences. The intake is usually taller and flows less efficiently than some of the car versions. (Photo Courtesy General Motors)

Models: 2007–2013 Chevrolet Avalanche, 2007–2013 Chevrolet Silverado 1500, 2007 to present Chevrolet Suburban 1/2 ton, 2007 to present Chevrolet Tahoe, 2007 to present GMC Sierra 1500, 2007–2013 GMC Yukon, 2007 to present GMC Yukon XL 1/2 ton.

LY2

The LY2 was new in 2007. It featured a 4.8-liter cast-iron block and aluminum heads. This engine uses the E38 ECM for the system controls. Due to the low displacement, this might be worth a pass when digging through the boneyard.

Models: 2007–2013 Chevrolet Silverado 1500, 2007 to present Chevrolet Tahoe, 2007–2013 GMC Sierra 1500, and 2007 to present GMC Yukon.

LY5

The LY5 is the iron-block version of the LH6. It has a 9.9:1 compression ratio and aluminum heads. It was made from 2007 to the current day. Horsepower is measured at 320 and the torque comes in around 340 ft-lbs.

Models: 2007–2013 Chevrolet Avalanche, 2007–2013 Chevrolet Silverado 1500, 2007–2013 Chevrolet Suburban 1/2 ton, 2007 to present Chevrolet Tahoe, 2007 to present GMC Sierra 1500, 2007 to

CHOOSING AN LS ENGINE

present GMC Yukon, and 2007 to present GMC Yukon XL 1/2 ton.

LY6

The LY6 is a Gen IV-version of the iron-block version LQ4 and LQ6 engines. While this engine is still using the iron block, it has a few surprises that the previous version did not. This engine has a variable valve time engine management system that really bumps up the output to 353 hp and 373 ft-lbs of torque. It might be wise to snag a few of these if you see them in the boneyards, as I suspect these will be hard to find in the near future. The iron block in combination with the low 9.67:1 compression ratio is literally begging to be super or turbo charged.

Models: 3/4-ton 2007 to present Silverados, Sierras, Suburbans, and Yukons.

Chevrolet Performance Engines

Installing a crate engine offers many advantages over a home engine rebuild. You're starting with a brand-new factory engine with a warranty. The Chevrolet Performance catalog offers just about any power level and wallet level that you could want. Many of its engines come with generous warrantees and fit great in any vehicle. I mention crate engines because they are readily available and can be built to suit any need. Most of all, they provide performance versions of the popular LS series engines, which really caught my attention.

E-Rod Engines

The E-Rod engine lineup from Chevrolet Performance is Chevrolet's answer to the growing demand for "green" engines and emissions standards. Chevrolet Performance offers several of its famous engines, such as the LSA, LS3, LS7, and the LS5.3L. These engines are emissions compliant in virtually every state, but it wouldn't hurt to check your local emission laws to make sure this option is available for you. These engines come with a set of catalytic converters that you add to the current exhaust system and still deliver excellent power.

LS327 (PN 19165628)

This 5.3-liter Chevrolet Performance engine features an iron-block, Grafal-coated pistons, and a performance cam that bumps the power up to 325 hp and 347 ft-lbs. This combination is great for budget conscience rodders, but this engine combo is several thousand bucks cheaper than the LS6 or the newest LS3.

LS376 (PN 19244549)

Call this the souped-up LS3; it is based on the LS3 engine with one major difference: the cam (measuring 112 with 219 intake, 228 exhaust, 1.7 rocker, and 525 intake and exhaust), which you can get via Chevrolet Performance (PN 88958733). With that modification alone, the power jumps to a whopping 480 hp and 475 ft-lbs of torque, just from a cam swap! The power comes in earlier than the stock LS3 due to the cam lobe design.

LSX454 (PN 19244611)

All LS engines have the same external dimensions, including the LSX454. General Motors carved out 454 ci, the famous moniker from the Mark IV big-blocks, all

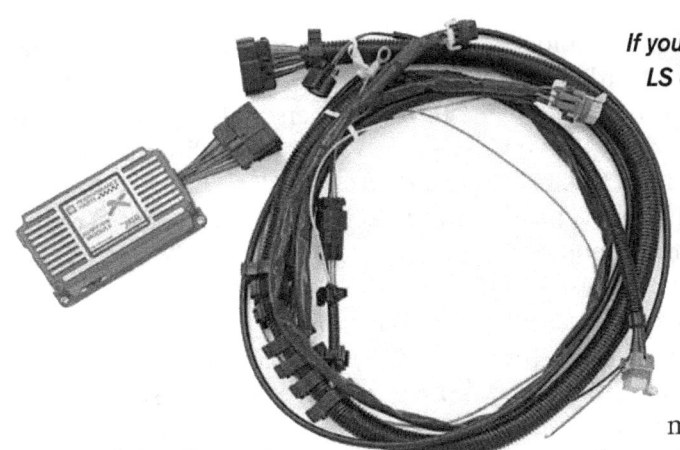

If you install a carburetor on an LS engine, you need to install this external module to help the engine run with ease. Some additional wiring is required and a good tune on your carb is also helpful. (PhotoC ourtesy General Motors)

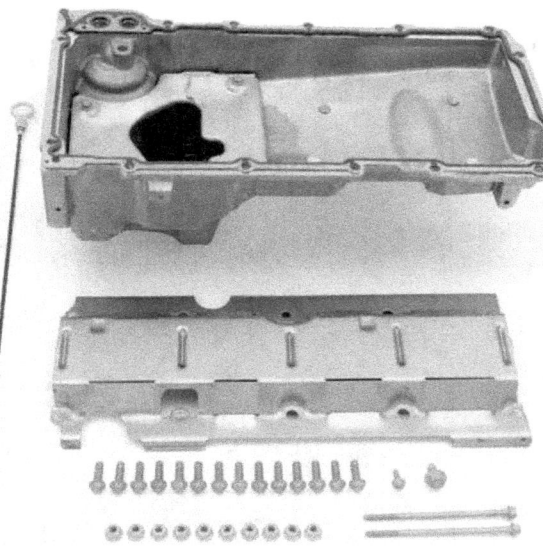

Here's General Motors' answer to the 1955 to mid-1980s LS swap. This pan combination fits most vehicles. More important, it fits the first- and second-generation-F-Body. (Photo Courtesy General Motors)

SWAP LS ENGINES INTO CAMAROS & FIREBIRDS 1967–1981

within the confines of the LS block. It is a fully forged engine that has the new LSX six-bolt heads that breathe ultra well. General Motors even throws in a set of fancy "LSX454" orange valve covers that look great at a car show with the hood up. This engine is shipped without any accessories, oil pan, or intake as it's designed to run EFI or a carb. This engine is rated for a carburetor setup at 620 hp and 600 ft-lbs or 580 hp and 600 ft-lbs with EFI. Just think, with this engine you don't have to change your fender emblems!

Other LS Engine Builders

You've read my reasons for choosing the engine I did after much consideration. Below are a few other options that you may want to look into if you choose to have someone else build your engine. The popularity of LS engines is booming and there's no shortage of companies willing to build you virtually any power level you desire.

TPiS

Myron Cottrell founded TPiS in 1988. Cottrel has been in the engine sports industry since the 1950s. He taught the art of precise machine work and engine building at a vocational school during the 1970s. TPiS is a proponent of complete engine swaps and, therefore, is providing complete engines and individual components for the LS enthusiast.

TPiS doesn't just build engines; they race them too. They not only offer tight tolerances and longevity in street and race applications, they use their race knowledge and experience to translate into a better product.

A member of the Engine Masters Challenge, Cotrell's engines have shown strong results at each competition with a very competitive field. I have had personal experience with this shop and can confidently recommend it as a solid choice for an LS build as well as almost any engine project.

ERL Performance

ERL is probably most well-known for its 500-ci LS short-block, which makes the small-block-sized LS more like an old-school big-block Rat engine. ERL offers a great performance line of short-blocks, long-blocks, and stroker kits for the do-it-yourself builder. For example, the company offers a long-block that allows for 427 or 454 ci and promises 680 hp and 580 ft-lbs of torque.

ERL also specializes in sleeving LS blocks and claim these sleeved engines can handle upward of 1,500 hp. To get the 500 ci previously mentioned, they obtain a 4.200-inch bore and a 4.500-inch stroke through the use of an aluminum deck plate and iron sleeves. They call this the LS Superdeck II. All I know is that if I were looking for a solid-performance LS engine, I'd start with an ERL short-block.

Lingenfelter Performance Engineering

Started by John Lingenfelter more than 30 years ago, Lingenfelter has been an established leader in engine sports for three decades. It offers a wide variety of services and products for LS engines and other engine sport endeavors. These products include fuel, exhaust, suspension, electrical, and various other LS components.

Lingenfelter doesn't simply offer Chevrolet Performance crate engines but rather the company builds high-performance crate engines based on Chevrolet Performance LS engines. These crate engines are outfitted with premium speed parts, such as Lingenfelter hydraulic roller cams, Lingenfelter heads, Comp Cams double valvesprings, and titanium retainers. Equipped with premium parts, these crate engines command premium prices starting at just over $10,000. For comparison, the Lingenfelter LS3 550-hp crate engine retails for $10,236 while the Chevrolet Performance engine sells for $7,570.

Currently, Lingenfelter offers five different versions of the LS engine in 550-, 575-, 605-, and 650-hp iterations for a variety of applications and

Here's the typical used LS1 engine you find at most junkyards. I bought the entire engine, ECU, and ancillary equipment, and had it all shipped to my house for less than $2,000! I asked the junkyard to be careful with the wiring loom and to throw it in with the engine so the related equipment was included. This particular engine came from a 2000 Camaro. Unfortunately the car met with a tree and was totaled in the process. This LS1 has a cable-operated throttle body, an F-Body oil pan, and an aluminum block.

CHOOSING AN LS ENGINE

budgets. In addition, it offers LS2 road race engine. Lingenfelter also has three versions of the LS7 in 630-, 650-, and 750-hp versions. Finally, if the stock 638-hp LS9 isn't enough, Lingenfelter offers its LS9, the King Kong of LS engines, in a 750-hp version.

Sourcing from a Junkyard or Salvage Yard

If you source an engine from a salvage yard, the health of the engine cannot be precisely determined. You can take the risk and install the engine in your F-Body car, but you don't know how well or poorly it will perform. Or how long it will last; you know that it could fail. It may be a running engine. You don't know if the engine has 200,000 miles on it or if it has a substantially worn valvetrain or, on the other end of the spectrum, a fresh engine with 20,000 miles on it.

You need to closely consider the source of the engine. If you can verify its mileage, source vehicle, and overall condition before it was, you can transplant a salvage yard engine into your F-Body car without a rebuild, and you can do it with a large measure of confidence. To be absolutely certain of the condition of the engine, you need to perform a complete rebuild. While that may not be necessary for all salvage yard engines, I recommend a complete rebuild for these engines.

While that's a lot of work, it's the only certain way to ensure the engine will be reliable and perform at its best. Besides, it allows you to upgrade pistons, rods, cam, and valvetrain for more torque and horsepower. You could also build the engine to accept a power adder. Once you have an idea of how the engine will be used, it is a lot easier to match the build to your needs. Matching reliability and power is always a major consideration. The bigger the power output, the more you need more stout parts.

If you are having an engine built for you, it's best to have a detailed conversation with the builder about major components and the major machining phases. You need to specify your performance goals, application, and budget. If you're rebuilding an engine, you can easily install a stroker package without a lot of additional expense. You need to select a suitable rotating assembly for your block and have the block machined to attain the proper clearances. The final cubic-inch size is just as major a consideration as the head and cam package. All of the parts have to work as a matched system and weak links need to be weeded out.

If you choose to source your engine from a local salvage yard, you need to choose your engine wisely. Most important, you need to provide precise instructions to parts pickers, so you get the entire engine and all the essential accessories to run the engine. You need a couple of key phrases for your proprietor so you can speak the lingo. Typically, parts pickers at junkyards aren't very careful when they grab parts you ask for. Most often, they won't be as careful and prefer to remove parts with an oxyacetylene torch rather than a wrench. To ensure you get an entire engine with all the accessories you need, you want to ask for a "pull-out." This means that it includes the front-drive accessories and anything physically bolted onto the engine, such as a starter. Before handing over any money, you should clarify exactly what you want to buy because sometimes things get lost in the transaction.

You need to ask that they carefully and cautiously remove the wiring harness, so that they don't haphazardly remove it with wire cutters. It's imperative that you ask them for the ECM and/or TCM unless you're going to use an aftermarket system. Without the ECM, an engine cannot run and integrating a different ECM to your engine requires reflashing the ECM, so now you know why it's imperative. It takes more time to remove this and may cost you a couple extra dollars to have it happen, but it can save you a lot of extra money in the long run if you have a little patience with the junkyard.

Now that you have a "new to you" engine, you want to inspect and evaluate it for any major problems. First and foremost, visually inspect the engine itself. Make sure the block doesn't have any exterior cracks or obvious signs of damage. A crack in the block could mean a thrown rod.

Second, before you purchase it, make sure the crankshaft turns over. If you buy a seized engine, you won't be sure of the extent of the damage or problems until you disassemble the engine. You may be into an expensive rebuild.

Then check all the sensors to make sure they haven't been broken off and that the wiring hasn't been cut or tampered with. Typically, the fuse block does not come with a pull-out because the LS fuse block is integrated with the rest of the vehicle; it's not practical to have this included with your purchase.

A complete visual inspection should include the intake for obvious signs of damage because it is a plastic piece and they have been known to crack.

An inspection of the accessories should be next. Make sure the correct accessories are in place, that they spin freely, and the bearings aren't worn out. Using a breaker bar to spin the crank also suffices, assuming there's a belt to run the accessories.

Finally, check the casting number to make sure you got the correct engine.

Engine Disassembly

Once you're satisfied with the exterior inspection, it's time to dive into the engine itself. I strongly recommend that you rebuild any used engine because you have no idea how the engine has been maintained or operated. If you want to ensure that you have a strong and reliable engine, it's best to rebuild the engine before it's installed in the chassis. It's better to spend the time, effort, and money now so that you don't have to do it later with some unknown surprise.

At this stage, disassemble the engine carefully and mark each part as you take it off for further reference. The plastic intake should be thoroughly inspected to make sure it isn't cracked or broken around the throttle body and the intake ports. From there, carefully disassemble and inspect the heads, making sure to look at each spring and valve that you take out for any bends or broken pieces. You need to have the head or block casting parts Magnafluxed to identify any crack or problem. The process exposes cracks, defects, and other imperfections that you cannot see with the naked eye.

With any junkyard engine, you need to go through the short-block. Remove each of the main caps to check the crank bearings to see if the engine has ever been abused or starved of oil. Leave one main cap on and remove all the piston and connecting rod assemblies. Check again for any abuse or oiling problems. If there's any deep scarring of the crankshaft or a spun bearing, you can quickly identify the problem. In the case of the crankshaft, you have to determine if you can turn down the journal; if there is not enough material and oversized bearings cannot be used, you may need to replace the crank. If the bearings are damaged, have a machinist press them off and replace them. After you've pulled the pistons and checked them for damage, look inside the piston bores and check for scarring or other signs of damage to the cylinder walls.

After you've completed the disassembly process, take your heads and block to a local machine shop for cleaning in a hot tank and Magnaflux crack inspection of the heads. If you're building your own engine, it may be helpful to have the machine shop install the cam bearings for you as they can be tricky to get seated properly. Expect a couple of weeks worth of time for turnaround and a couple of bucks out of your pocket.

I always recommend new bolts for any rebuild because bolts deteriorate over time and the clamping force decreases. Your bolts must be able to hold the correct amount of clamping force or the fasteners will be out of spec. That means the engine could suffer a failure. Many engines, mine included, come with a torque-to-yield style of bolts. Therefore, when the bolt has been properly torqued for the first time, it cannot be re-used as it most likely stretched. It's cheap insurance to buy new bolts. Always use plenty of assembly lube and Loctite where applicable.

Basic rebuild kits can be had for a couple hundred bucks and often come with pistons and other wearable parts. It's best to talk about your options with your machine shop as they can help you choose the right rebuild parts for your engine. This is especially true if you changed any of the parameters of the engine, such as the bore and stroke. Planning is the key to a long and healthy engine life.

Sample Junkyard Pull and Buildup: A Turbo 5.3L

When building your LS engine, a lot goes into determining the level of the build, the parts, and the process. You ask yourself, "How much power can a stock long block take?" Well, when I chatted with Nate Shaw of One Guys Garage and he told me of his plan to build a budget corn-fed 5.3L LS engine, I decided I needed to find out for myself.

Nate allowed me to tag along with him as he took his engine to the dyno for fine-tuning at TPiS in Chaska, Minnesota. Nate said that he started with a virtually untouched 5.3L all-aluminum long block from a 2005 Silverado that landed in a junkyard with 130,000 miles on it. Nate then replaced the head gaskets with an LS9 set because they have more layers than the stock LS gaskets. The LS9 set of gaskets provides more strength over stock LS1 head gaskets, especially in boost applications. Nate used ARP head studs, replaced the timing chain, and installed dual valvesprings with new pushrods to increase his odds of reliably pushing the engine hard. The only other piece that Nate changed at the beginning was adding a stock

Sample Junkyard Pull and Buildup: A Turbo 5.3L *continued*

-body oil pan to clear the subframe in his vehicle. Beyond that Nate tells me the rest is bone stock and untouched. In this case, the subframe is from Nate's Nova, but the chassis for the 1967–1969 Camaro and the 1968–1974 Nova are virtually identical.

When it comes to purchasing decisions, Nate said, "Money could be saved on the intercooler as people have proven that the $100 eBay specials do work well. I chose a higher end unit as it fits my car better and has a little better overall performance. Also, the turbo is a name-brand unit; it's a perfect combination of power capabilities and size."

Nate added, "E85 is the fuel of

5.3 Vortec Build-Up List

Engine Part	Source	Cost
2005 L33 5.3 (aluminum block with 799 LS6-style heads, 9.9:1 compression)	AAA Auto Salvage	$550
ARP head studs, used	LS1tech	$150
LS9 head gaskets, new (12622033)	Partstaxi.com	$99.67
Cam (custom ground for TTPerformance)	N/A	$175
Lunati dual-valvespring kit	N/A	$213.95
Water pump, used	LS1tech	$50
Exhaust manifolds, used	N/A	$180
Exhaust gaskets, intake gaskets, crank dampener (Corvette), oxygen sensors, IAT sensor, belt tensioner	Rock Auto	$273.28
LS1 intake	N/A	$35
Throttle body	NA	$10
3-bar map sensor, new (12223861)	eBay	$40.95
Exhaust manifold and turbo V-bands	eBay/Racing Parts Depot	$53
F-Body oil pan, used	Local	$100
LS3 dipstick	eBay	$24.94
160-degree Thermostat and IWIS timing chain	Lingenfelter	$65
Stock truck ECM (HP Tuners 3-bar speed density)		$25
Modified truck wiring harness	N/A	$100
Holley valve covers, used	N/A	$100
LS2 coils, used	TPIS	$175
Knock sensor, new	TPIS	$25
ARP crank bolt	TPIS	$25
5.3L Comp Cams 7.4 pushrods	N/A	$75

Turbo Parts	Source	Cost
Precision 7675 CEA, used (76-mm billet compressor wheel, 75-mm turbine wheel, .96AR T4 flange)	eBay	$1,150
Turbosmart Hypergate 45 wastegate, new		$275
Treadstone vertical flow A/A intercooler, new		$438.27
Intercooler piping, CX Racing	eBay	$79
Throttle-body 90-degree silicone adapter		$26
Manual boost controller	eBay	$25
T4 weld flange	eBay	$20
Mild steel mandrel bends for crossover, downpipe, wastegate, flex connector, exhaust wrap		$175
Knockoff blowoff valve, new, Race Parts Solutions	N/A	$100
Oil pressure feed and drain hoses, fittings	Jegs	$81

Fuel Parts	Source	Cost
Aeromotive 13101 boost reference regulator, used	eBay	$121
2 Walbro 255 external fuel pumps		$245
Delphi 95-pound injectors, new	eBay	$261.95
Versafueler low-impedance driver box, used	LS1tech	$185
Misc. fuel lines and fittings	N/A	$125

Total Cost: $5,578.01 without valve covers
$5,853.01 with valve covers (not required)

CHAPTER 1

Sample Junkyard Pull and Buildup: A Turbo 5.3L *continued*

choice due to its higher octane rating, cooling properties, and is easily available in Minnesota." Another area that Nate addressed is the injectors. He says, "I used low-impedance 95-pound Delphi injectors simply due to cost, but high-impedance injector prices are coming down. They do make things a little more simple as there isn't any wiring when installing a driver box between the PCM and injectors."

The first pull of the engine was, in short, disappointing and was far short of the horsepower targets. Even after fiddling with some of the tuning parameters, the guys at TPIS and CJ Tunes were frustrated at seeing the power leveling off at 5,000 rpm. A cam swap proved to be a much-needed improvement in all areas of the dyno curve. The engine finally came alive and made a very healthy 824 hp and 718 ft-lbs of torque. That was all on a stock long block.

According to Nate, the key to reliability in LS engines is "E85 and a good tune. People really underestimate the strength of the stock parts when you have those two things. Naturally, it won't last forever, but it works well when compared dollar for dollar to other higher-end engines. Carl from CJ Tunes is my guy and he works magic. I don't trust anyone else to tune my engines."

E85 hasn't been around for long. Actually, it's been around just long enough for the ingenious to see the potential for big power. Although I've heard some wild octane ratings ranging from 95 to 115, I have yet to find the definitive answer to that question. The problem with ethanol as it sits right now is that it's not all that easily definable as gasoline. E85 that's 85 percent ethanol and 15 percent gasoline could be equated as "race fuel," which you cannot find at your average fill-up station. Ethanol (E85) allows for lower combustion chamber temperatures, which then allows for more fuel to be fed into the chamber and to be able to more safely run higher compression ratios. All of this equates to more power and longer use out of the long block. The downside is that due to the stoichiometric ratio, because more fuel is needed to run a engine when compared to gasoline, the fuel mileage you'll notice is significantly reduced.

The original plan for the engine was to run roughly 20 psi and knock out around 900 hp, but as with all plans, they don't always turn out. The sun set too early and Nate ran out of dyno time. Nate assures me that even though he wasn't able to fully tune it to its full potential the 3,200-pound donor car is propelled into the 9s in the quarter-mile.

As far as future plans for the engine, Nate says an LS6 intake might gain a few more ponies, maybe as many as 20 to 30, but he's fairly happy with the results and is pretty confident that this combination is a lot more fun than that old Silverado that was its first home. I couldn't have imagined a better way to be put out to stud.

This 5.3L aluminum long-block became my test engine. It came out of a 2005 Chevy Silverado with 130,000 miles for the paltry price of $550, complete from oil pan to intake, minus front-drive accessories. I haven't touched the short-block itself and have replaced only the timing chain and the oil pan with an F-Body pan to fit the application where it will rest later in its life.

I kept the set of stock GM heads with the casting number 799. The 799 head is modeled after the LS6, which is the 243 head. However, it does not have the sodium-filled valves. Most 2005 and newer 5.3L engines come with this 799 head so chances are you might already have it. In 2005 to 2007 extended-cab Silvarados, the L33 5.3L came with the better 799 heads and stronger connecting rods. They also have the benefit of the 24X reluctor crank that's compatible with the older LS computers that can be had for a pittance.

Sample Junkyard Pull and Buildup: A Turbo 5.3L *continued*

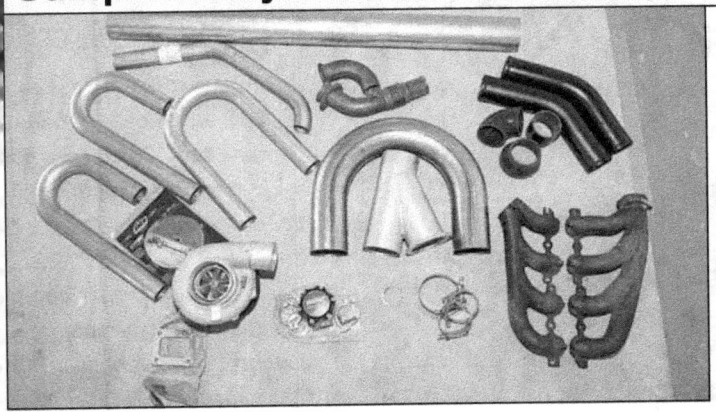

Before building the tubing, all the pieces need to be assembled and arranged: the necessary pipes, turbo, and exhaust manifolds.

My engine is all set on the dyno and is ready for its first pull. When everything was said and done, I was fairly impressed with performance of a mostly stock engine.

I hung the air-to-air intercooler in a likely location using a spare set of ratchet straps as a crude temporary bracket.

The TurboSmart Hypergate-45 wastegate controls the amount of boost. I started off with a 7-pound spring and worked my way up to 14 pounds using the manual controller. Eventually this wasn't enough and I went to a stronger 14-pound spring, which netted roughly 16 psi and a very healthy 824-peak hp at 6,100 rpm and 718 ft-lbs of torque at 5,900 rpm.

I bought a Precision 7675CEA turbo from eBay for $1,150. I chose this turbo because it had the best combination of small size and power for the application. It's rated for up to 1,200 hp and has a .96AR.

CHAPTER 1

Sample Junkyard Pull and Buildup: A Turbo 5.3L *continued*

The blowoff valve I chose is a TIAL knock-off 50-mm job from racepartsolutions.com.

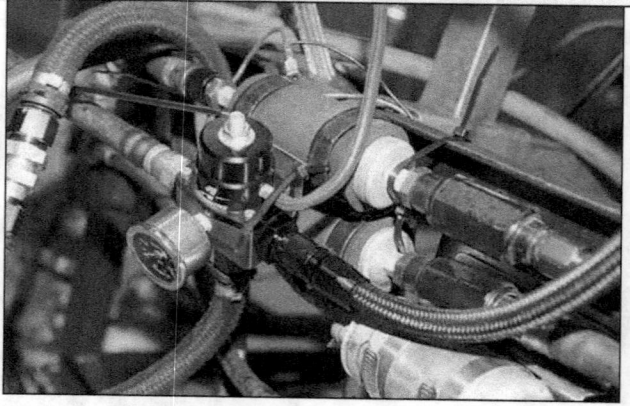

I had to install a pair of 255 ltr/hr pumps to increase fuel delivery and meet the fuel demands of E85 so I did not cycle too much fuel through the engine. To keep the heat down I went with this instead of one bigger pump because these pumps are external of the fuel cell. The Aeromotive fuel pressure regulator (PN 13101) is set to 43.5 psi and pressure matched 1:1 after that.

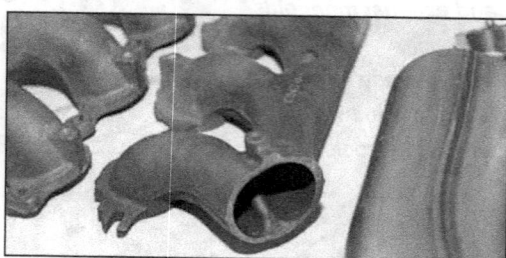

The driver-side exhaust manifold is a stock piece from a 2003–2005 Trail-Blazer with a V-band clamp welded on to allow better positioning. The manifold is installed reversed for the obvious reason to feed the turbo with its unyielding thirst for more power.

The passenger-side exhaust manifold is borrowed from a 2005–2009 Grand Prix GXP. This is the forward-positioned manifold and it allows a good way to pipe the tubing toward the turbo.

Nate hand-built this crossover tube out of mild steel measuring 2¼ inches to connect the two exhaust manifolds.

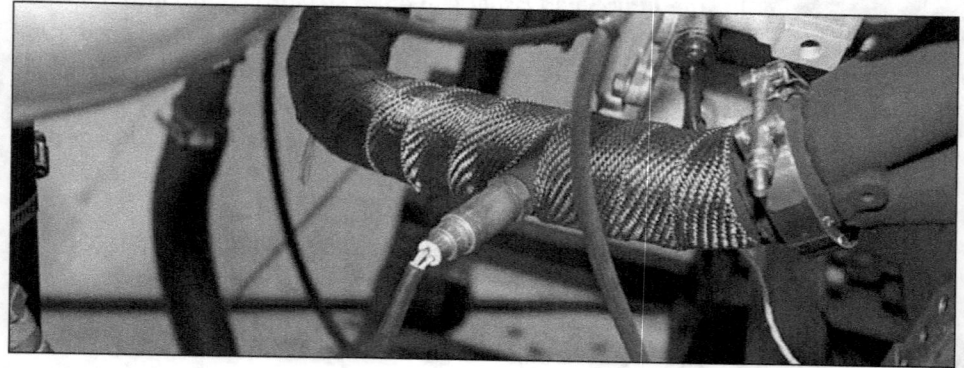

Nate welded bungs into the tube to affix the oxygen sensors. The sensors can be welded just down the exhaust system. Orientation isn't as important as the location in the system. Both of these were added after the header and before any turbo mechanicals.

Choosing an LS Engine

Sample Junkyard Pull and Buildup: A Turbo 5.3L *continued*

The throttle body is just as stock as the rest of the build; it's the 75-mm stock factory piece with a stock LS1 intake.

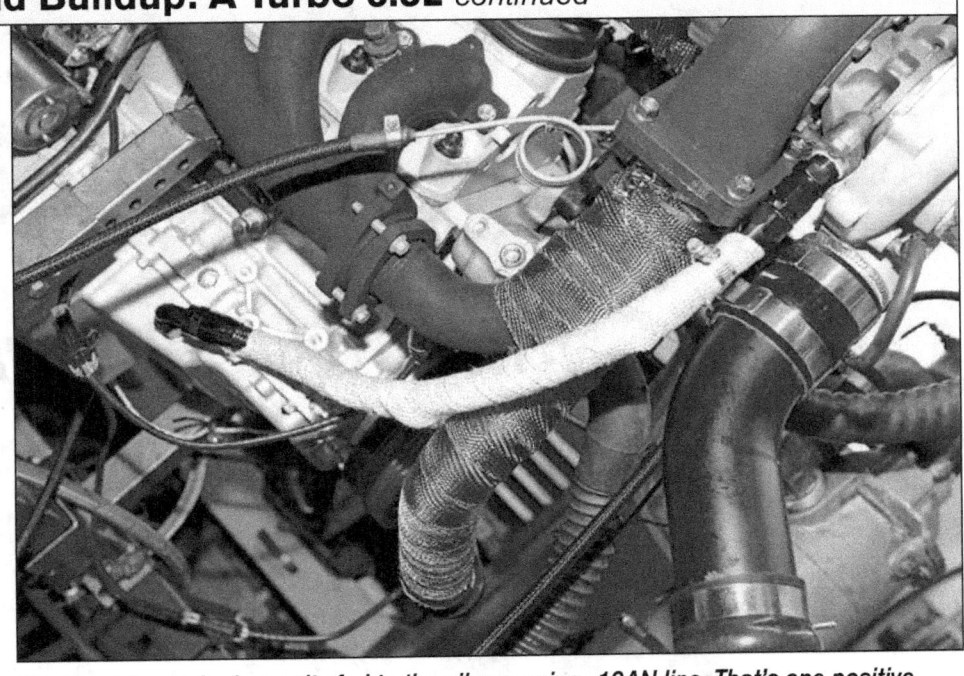

The Precision turbo is gravity fed to the oil pan using -10AN line. That's one positive advantage to mounting the turbo up high; I don't have to run a scavenge pump.

Safe behind the glass, we fired up the turbo LS and let her rip.

I swapped out the old stock 5.3L cam with another Internet special from LS1tech.com for $150. The new cam measures 224/228 with an intake of .552 and exhaust of .565 and a lobe separation of 114 degrees. With this cam timing, I corrected the power stagnation problem at 5,000 rpm. (Photo Courtesy Jim Hall)

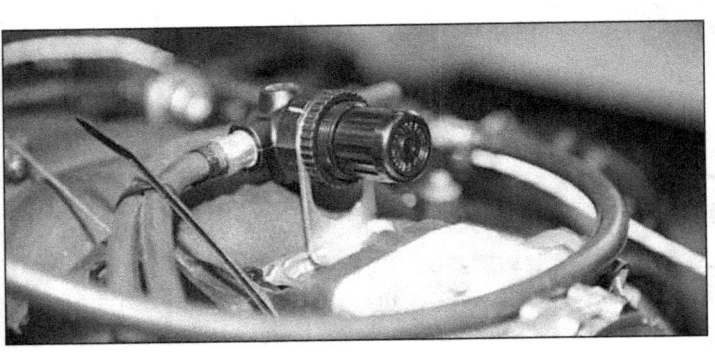

This manual boost controller was just used for dyno purposes. For the final install Nate plans to use an electronic AMS500 boost controller.

CHAPTER 2

ENGINE AND SUBFRAME

Years ago, installing an LS engine between the front fenders of first- or second-generation F-Body car was a challenging endeavor. That is no longer the case because aftermarket engine mounts, transmission crossmembers, and peripheral equipment are now readily available for about any combination. When swapping an LS engine into a 30- to 45-year-old F-Body, you're integrating some of the latest GM engine technology into a vintage car, so it's not just bolting the engine to the subframe. An LS engine swap into an F-Body goes far beyond that. It's installing a complete performance package that's compatible with F-Body chassis. As a result, the LS engine, transmission, suspension, brakes, wheels, and tires all have to be *compatible* at the minimum; and *complementary* for maximum performance.

Before you mount the engine on a hoist and prepare to install it, also select the engine mounts, adapter plates, transmission crossmember, headers, and oil pan because these are part of a package. Although experienced swappers can use parts from multiple brands and essentially piece together their own engine mount kit, I recommend you purchase a complete swap kit from a single manufacturer. By doing it this way, you have compatible parts and make the install much easier because you won't have fitment issues from mixing and matching parts. Holley, Street & Performance, Energy Suspension, Autokraft, and Turn Key Engine Supply offer kits for LS engine swaps into early F-Bodies.

The installation of an LS engine can be done in the typical garage with jack stands, a solid and reliable engine hoist, and a host of typical hand tools. I recommend that you use a load balancer because it's easier to position the engine while installing it on the frame rails. A load balancer is particularly helpful when keeping the front sheet metal, which includes fenders, front fascia, and grille. It's needed especially if you are installing the transmission and engine together as one unit, as I

Mary's LS3 drops right in as if it were meant to be there all along. (Photo Courtesy Mary Pozzi)

ENGINE AND SUBFRAME

This LS engine was installed in Mary Pozzi's second-generation Camaro. (Photo Courtesy Mary Pozzi)

Mary prefers to install her engines without the transmission. It makes for a lot more wiggle room up front and reduces dings and other costly errors. (Photo Courtesy Mary Pozzi)

chose to do. It's cheap and safe insurance for your well-being and to keep your investment.

At this stage, you've carefully considered and determined your application, so you've selected your engine and determined the setup. Now you need to figure out which transmission you're going to use. Virtually any one on the market is compatible with an LS, so you have to narrow it down. The good news is that you won't have to modify the transmission tunnel in most cases. I say "most cases" because many first- and second-generation F-Body cars are close in specification, but the operative word is "close." The tolerances can vary widely from one body to the next. The only exception that I am aware of is the 4L80E transmission; it is typically quite large and in most cases needs a transmission tunnel adjustment.

Front Clip Sheet Metal

When swapping an LS engine into your first- or second-generation F-body, remove the front clip sheet metal so you have easier access to the front subframe for mounting the engine. In addition, won't risk damaging the valuable sheet metal when installing your new LS power plant. While removing the sheet metal isn't a requirement to install the LS, it has many advantages as discussed, and I had my own reasons. For one, I did this for demonstration purposes as detailed later. Also, I removed the front sheet metal because I'm going to change the subframe in the near future, and it makes the install much easier in the long run if I do this step first. Keep in mind that if you remove the front end, you need to realign

Every project has to start with a first step. As with any engine-swapping project, you need to remove the hood before the real work begins.

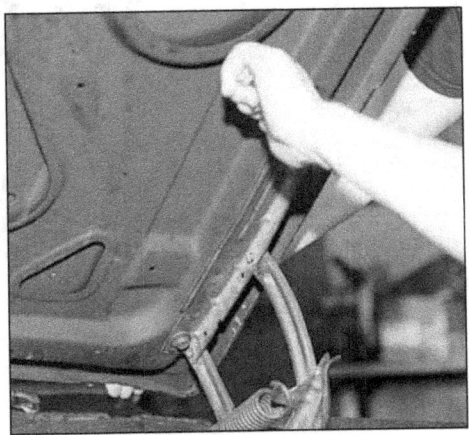

All you do is remove four bolts and have an extra pair of hands to help take off the hood.

all the panels for gap and proper fit when the parts are reinstalled.

Several bolts secure the front sheet metal to the frame, and you need to remove the bolts and carefully support the front fenders when removing them. To remove the front sheet-metal bodywork, use a simple socket set with a fair amount of WD-40 and a couple of buddies who can help you lift the front clip off.

When it comes time to separate the bodywork from the frame, get some friends to help lift off the sheet metal. You need to carefully and methodically remove the sheet metal because you don't want to damage it. When you're performing a swap project, you don't want the expense or hassle of performing bodywork because the sheet metal was tweaked or damaged during removal. Although the liftoff procedure can be done with three people, a fourth person makes the job easier to complete because that person can help resolve any unforeseen snags and hang-ups, such as removing missed bolts or disconnecting wiring and hoses. Often times, the "spotter" is the vehicle owner, as was the case here.

Spend the time to make sure all the bolts and fasteners that connect the sheet metal to the chassis have been removed, so you save on the frustration and hassle. Remove a few bolts so the front end can be separated from the rest of the chassis. Several bolts hold the front clip to the subframe and firewall. In fact, several bolts connect to the firewall and the inner fender well bolts. Use a 9/16- and 1/2-inch socket and ratchet to remove these bolts.

Be sure to disconnect important components, such as the front wiring, ground wires, hoses, and anything else that might get in your way. I found it easier to disconnect the front wiring harness at the firewall, which is just under the brake booster and held in by a solitary bolt.

After removing the battery tray, you see one of the six main body mount bolts that hold on the sheet metal. Removing the battery tray and body mount bolts is a simple procedure using the appropriate sockets and wrenches. In this case I had to cut one of them off with a reciprocating saw due to rust. I had the misfortune of running into a seized bolt that rounded off when I took an impact gun to it. I took this opportunity to buy new tools and cut the bolt off. Another body mount bolt is located on the driver's side. While performing this procedure, it's wise to replace the stock body mounts with either stock replacements or, in this case, solid aluminum mounts that work together with the Speed Tech subframe. These mounts keep the body securely supported and work just as well on the aftermarket subframe as they do on a stock subframe. They are the same size and shape as the stock versions but are completely solid.

Two bolts fasten the two fenders to the firewall. These are easier to access if you remove the hood hinges.

Two 1/2-inch bolts hold the core support to the front subframe. As you can see here, mine suffered under years of rust so it had to be cut out with a reciprocating saw. This is just one aspect of working on rusty old cars. Unfortunately, the massive body bolt was in a hard-to-reach location. The fastener lubricant didn't help budge the bolt and eventually I rounded off the head, leaving only one option: cut the bolt out.

You and a couple of buddies can quickly and easily pull the entire front sheet metal off the car. I used simple sockets to remove the bolts. Most of them are 1/2- or 9/16-inch so keep a couple of those sockets handy. Carefully remove the bolts. While you don't have to support the bodywork as it's being removed, you need to have help when doing this work. Make sure all the electrical harness connections, such as the headlamp, marker, horn, relay, etc., have been removed before lift off. The front fenders and front valance can be removed (and then re-installed) in one piece, making access very easy. This is the best way to make your Mustang friends jealous.

ENGINE AND SUBFRAME

As you can see, the engine mounts fit nicely inside the stock frame. This location is for the stock small-block location.

The A/C pump location can present a major problem clearance problem with frame and/or body. I can either remove the A/C bracket and pump or notch the frame. I chose to relocate the A/C unit. You can jump to the chapter on front-drive accessories and see how I fixed the problem. When presented with this issue, Mark Stielow chose to notch his frame to make room for his LS9.

In addition, you need to remove the bolts that hold the inner fender wells in place. The mounting bolts on the passenger's side were accessed through the engine compartment while the driver's side was less complicated if I removed the bolts from the inside of the fender. In addition, there are two lower bolts holding the front fenders to the body. These are located just in front of the rocker panels and are underneath the car held on with J-clips.

At this stage, the front-end sheet metal should be removed from your F-Body. When you're disassembling the body, bag and label all the bolts and spacers you have removed. It saves time and reduces hassle during reassembly and when aligning the body panels. The front tires should be removed before lifting off the front clip because it allows plenty of legroom and enough room to guide the fenders off. One key tip: Make sure the lower part of the fender has enough clearance to release itself; this is a good job for the spotter as it's his paint job.

Stock Subframe

You can certainly retain the stock subframe for an LS swap in your first- or second-gen F-Body. If you choose to use the stock subframe, you need a few special parts to make it work properly, so don't let that deter you from making a clean install. These parts include special engine mount adapters, a new location for the transmission crossmember, and a set of headers designed for the LS series of engines in either the first- or second-generation F-Body.

Before installing the LS engine in an F-Body subframe, carefully and methodically remove the wiring harness from the chassis because you don't want to leave it connected to the chassis and damage it when installing the engine. While it is entirely possible to install the engine with the wiring harness in position, it's best just to remove it to avoid any possible damage.

A slight issue I had was the clearance of the sway bar. It didn't touch but this is certainly too close for comfort. You may have to purchase an aftermarket sway bar or carefully bend yours to make it fit better. An alternative method is to add spacer blocks between the inboard sway bar bushings and the subframe. This drops the front of the sway bar for clearance. If you use the stock subframe, you have to purchase a suitable aftermarket sway bar with more clearance. Some installers notch the sway bar but that's usually not a good idea unless you are very confident in your welding and fabrication skills. Instead, using a dropped pitman setup is often a much better choice.

CHAPTER 2

Without a distributor the engine has a lot more breathing room. You may find that you have more room between the firewall and the engine than you anticipated. This is a common problem that can be solved with relocating the mounts and moving the engine forward enough from the firewall. Adjustable mounts can be helpful but aren't always necessary.

My new slim brake booster and master cylinder from Matt's Classic Bowties provides ample line pressure and does not contact the new engine. I finished off the brake system with a pre-bent stainless kit from Speed Tech that is a simple bolt-on and screw-in type of setup. These pre-bent lines need some finesse as are maneuvered around parts such as the frame and steering components. The lines are sensitive so do not force them while routing; if you do, they can kink. Brake lines aren't paramount to an LS swap as stock ones work just fine.

When the transmission is connected to the LS engine, its bellhousing sits much closer to the cylinder heads than in the Gen I small-block engines so your LS engine sits nearly flush with the firewall. As a result you have a few clearance issues to resolve. The valve cover clearance is very tight and often a valve cover interferes with the heater hose outlets on the firewall. Not only does this cause an issue with typical engine movement during normal operations, but it also makes it almost impossible to route heater hoses. To resolve this problem, you can install a 1969 Camaro big-block heater box and heater core because this repositions outlet fittings so the hoses clear the valve covers. Make sure to get the correct model for your application. The first-generation versions are all the same but the second-generation cars use a different design.

The stock brake booster is often too big and crowds the factory LS ignition coils on the valve covers. Replacing the brake booster with a smaller housing is another effective

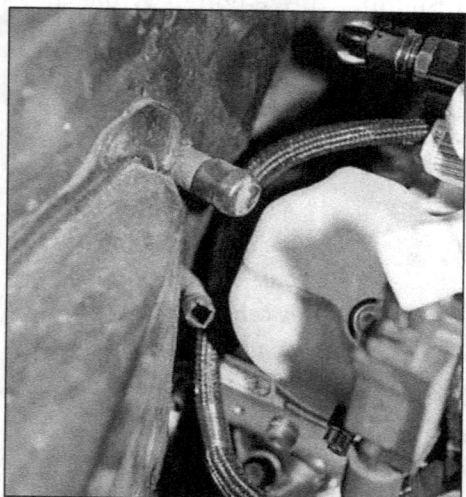

I noticed some pretty tight clearances with the heater outlets. If you are having issues with this, a quick fix is to get a heater core for a big-block. This is the simple and easy solution to this common problem. I recommend replacing the heater core because you have easy access to it at this stage.

As you can see, with the front sheet metal off, removing the old engine is a whole lot easier.

ENGINE AND SUBFRAME

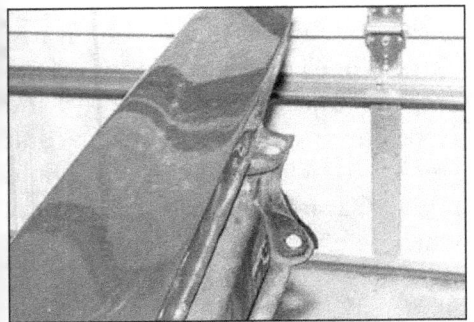

A series of bolts fastens the front fenders. These are the two that hold the inner and outer fender onto the firewall and cowl positions. The front upper and lower valance support the front fenders. The rear part of the assembly may be a bit wobbly, so make sure you have friends to help keep the front clip from twisting.

The driver-side and passenger-side fenders are a bit different and are asymmetrical in how they attach to the car. On the driver's side, three bolts and three large washers connect to an outstretched arm to the inside of the fender. These are relatively easy to access.

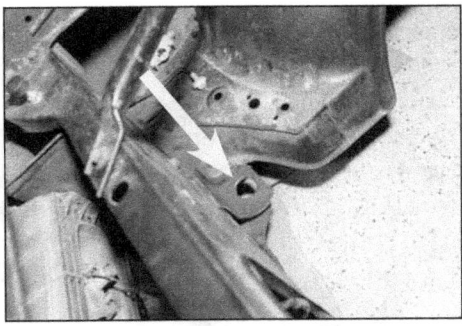

The arrow in the center of this image points to the body mount bolthole.

solution, especially if you are going to keep the stock or similar brake package.

Installing a coil-relocation kit and moving the coils is one option. Many companies offer relocation kits. In fact, ATS sells a kit that allows the coils to be moved to the underside of the engine, making them virtually invisible. It features a set of custom-made brackets that allow you to put the coils in any number of locations, including the back of the heads so you have many options for mounting the coils. This kit works with LS3 coils and gives the engine a clean, uncluttered look. Keep in mind what type of brakes you'll be using as a small booster generally means less brake assist. I was able to find a much smaller, 8-inch dual-diaphragm version that I sourced from Matt's Classic Bowties. I also used a 7/8-inch master cylinder that provides enough line pressure to provide the clamping force needed for the six-piston Baer calipers.

For my particular engine swap, the stock steering linkage was retained so maneuvering the engine into position under the hood and aligning it with the frame rails was a real challenge. I had to inch my way forward with the LS3/T56 transmission. If the T56 had not been mated to the engine, this procedure might have been a lot easier. A lot of finessing went into using the stock frame mounts and the ATS engine mounts. I often had to lower the engine a

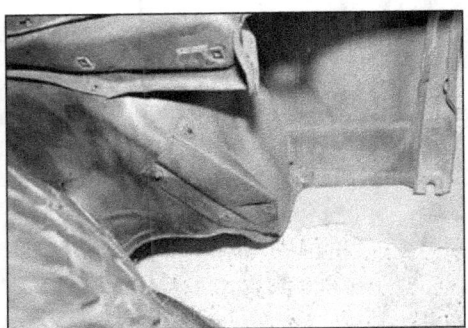

The inner passenger-side fender is a mirror image of the inner driver-side fender. On the passenger's side, it's easier to remove these two bolts than the three on the driver's side.

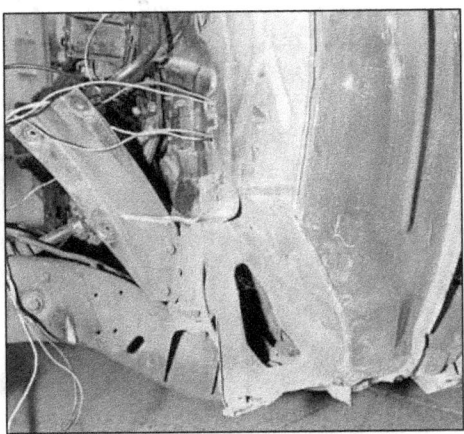

By now, you should have all the bolts for the front sheet metal removed. Double-check to see if any remaining parts are still attached and formulate a removal plan. Don't forget the little bolt on each side that holds the lower part of the outer fender onto the car, so it doesn't flap around in the wind.

The stock brake booster is way too big and doesn't clear the valve covers and coils so it needs to be replaced with a more compact aftermarket brake booster. I replaced mine with an 8-inch booster from mattsclassicbowties.com. I also have to run a smaller-bore master cylinder for the upgraded brakes. A popular Pro-Touring mod is to run a nonpower-brake master cylinder. They have a lot better pedal feel when under hard braking.

fraction of an inch then push it forward to make any progress.

The engine hoist securely supported the engine and transmission combination, but that can't be said for the chain-to-hoist link, which gave out at the last possible second. I had a friend help me with the procedure moving the engine down and back over and over again. You could in theory do this alone in your shop, as I had to do many times before. It helps to make the install go that much more smoothly with an extra pair of hands and eyes to guide things into place safely. This method had to be repeated many times to get it just right. While I didn't get a photo of the process, I did use a jack to support and guide the transmission into place. It seemed to help balance the load and provide a fair amount of stability when guiding the engine into place.

Aftermarket Subframe Installation

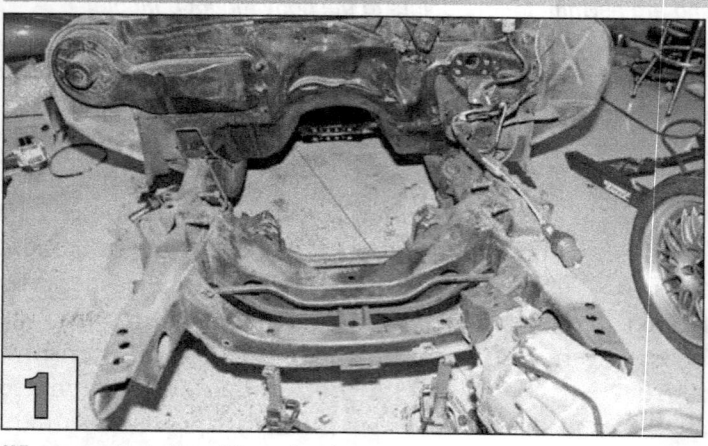

When you install an LS engine in a stock chassis, all the lines are out of the way and the transmission crossmember is in place for easier install. The crossmember needs to be relocated in most applications depending on your transmission choice. Therefore, you need to use aftermarket engine mounts.

My engine is about to be slotted into position. Removing the front sheet metal makes it a lot easier to install and get at things. It doesn't take up that much time when all things are considered. I was able to get it in place by alternately lowering it and then pushing it back inch by inch. I used an engine hoist and a buddy to help guide it into place. Repeated movements in small increments are required to get the engine into its final position.

My LS3 is safely and securely in place. I had to do this very carefully because of the transmission being in place; you may have to remove the transmission. The Mast oil pan fits quite well with the stock steering linkages. There are a number of other oil pans that may fit your needs.

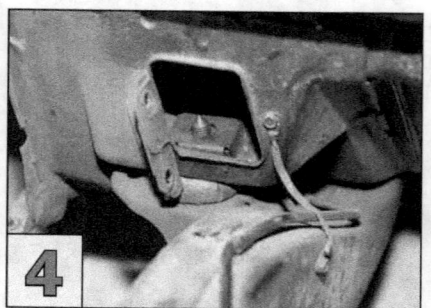

Here's the passenger-side frame bolt, fuel line, and ground strap. Make sure to clear these two objects when removing the bolt. This frame mount looks as if it has seen better days, so it should be replaced.

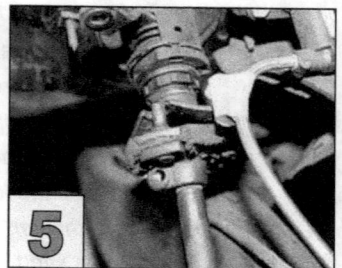

The steering rod's rag joint is often forgotten when separating the subframe from the body. The rag joint is held together by two bolts and should just come right apart. Mine is worn out and really needs a new one. (I will replace it with a solid joint later.)

ENGINE AND SUBFRAME

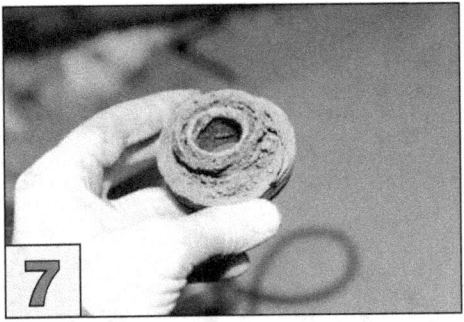

When using stock parts, it's best to just replace them. I cut out certain pieces, such as this brake line, because I planned ahead and knew I was going to replace them.

These body mounts are severely worn and must be replaced. If you haven't done this yet, it's a good idea not only for performance but for ride quality too. The new bushings install just like the old ones; put them in place before setting the body over the frame.

After you drag out the old subframe, you are left with really good access to the car. This is the best time to repair any holes and add a fresh coat of paint.

Support the body with jack stands and make sure the jack stands are securely positioned. Remove the four body bolts from the frame and separate the body. Do this slowly and carefully. I used a jack and a block of wood to move one side of the body at a time. I then used a series of strategically placed jack stands to keep the body level and give me room to slide the new subframe into place. Although it may seem that the body is stable, you don't want the jack stands to slip and compromise safety.

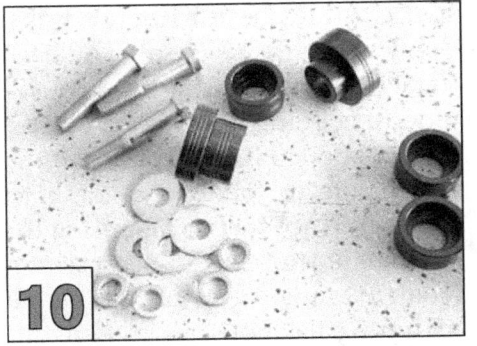

I followed Speed Tech's recommendation and installed their solid body mount kit. The body mounts install just like the stock ones: Place them in their location and drop the body onto the frame making sure to use the corresponding mount from the bottom of the frame. The little rings on the mounts ensure each one goes in the correct place. Speed Tech supplies all the Grade-8 hardware to complete the job. You could go with the stock rubber mounts, but considering the amount of work it takes to replace them, I felt it best to just use solid ones and be done with this project for life.

SWAP LS ENGINES INTO CAMAROS & FIREBIRDS 1967–1981

With the wheels mounted to the subframe, I was able to roll the frame under the car with the engine and transmission already attached. It allowed me to maneuver the subframe into place and square up the car. I then used a jack to tip the front of the car down enough to match the angle of the subframe. My brother-in-law Erik helped me align the frame and subframe. Using the alignment holes on the middle body mount, I made sure it was as square as possible before heading out to the alignment rack. A long screwdriver or a dowel helps align the frame fore and aft and you shouldn't need any special tools to get it square; these holes are sufficient.

Later at the alignment rack I found out that I was .1 degree within complete square of the car, so using this procedure is extremely accurate. Four massive frame bolts installed and the job was complete in less than half an hour with the aid of a good buddy.

You can see the lines on the frame mounts to indicate which is which. The lower half (far right) mates perfectly with the upper half (left and middle) to form a solid place to mount the car. The frame mounts have rings around them. In this case they match up to make the correct mate. For example, some have two rings, some have three, and the others have one ring.

Engine Mounts

An LS engine swap, in reality, starts from the bottom up and engine mounts are quite possibly the most important piece of the entire swap process. The correct positioning of the engine and fitment of the radiator, headers, exhaust, hoses, wiring, and other components is critical for performance and reliability. You need to select the engine mounts and adapter plates while taking the rest of the engine package into consideration. In other words, when you select the engine mounts and adapter plates, contact the manufacturer to make sure that the oil pan, headers, accessories, and other parts you plan to use are compatible with the engine mount package.

LS engine mounts are in exactly the same location on every engine block so you need to determine the location of the transmission mounts. If you choose to go with an adjustable or setback set of engine mounts, this obviously changes the location of your transmission mount. You need to select a compatible transmission crossmember for the transmission you install. As a result, you need to take transmission case design and mounting points as well as the crossmember design into account.

Be sure to follow the manufacturer's instructions for mounting the engine in the chassis because different manufacturers have different mounting locations for the engine. If the engine isn't correctly mounted on the frame, some of the parts, such as the exhaust, hoses, and steering rod may not fit. It may be difficult to correctly align the driveshaft for the rear axle assembly. The transmission crossmember location, the header fit, the amount of room for a radiator and fan combination, the clearance of your oil pan and the front-drive kit all rely on the correct mounting and placement of the engine. This highlights a major point that I make throughout this book, which is the importance of coordination and careful planning. A matching engine mount and header combination is your best ally when doing this swap.

Make Your Own Engine Mounts

Making your own engine mounts is a bit daunting. That used to be the only option when installing the LS engine into first- and second-generation F-Bodies. Thankfully, the aftermarket has come to the rescue to solve this simple, yet important part of the swap.

As mentioned previously, externally all LS engines are virtually identical, and this holds true for the

ENGINE AND SUBFRAME

engine mount location. The four bolts holding on the mount are all in the same spot and have the same spacing, so the same mounts you would use for an LS1 fit every other iteration in the LS family. The four mounting bolt locations are slightly forward of the engine centerline when viewing it from either driver's or passenger's side.

When swapping an LS engine into an F-Body car, often the transmission does not line up with the mounts while the stock engine aligns perfectly with the mounts when installed. One reason may be the engine mounts you just swapped in are not compatible. The Gen I small-block has a 1⅜-inch area that extends beyond the rear part of the passenger-side cylinder head where the transmission bellhousing bolts to the engine block. The Gen III/IV LS series has a scant .060-inch area that comes out of the same area where the bellhousing meets the block.

There are many types of engine mounts, but as a starting point, you need to determine the type of engine mounts you have on the engine and frame. Just because your F-Body came with a small-block, it doesn't mean the engine mounts and frame mounts are the same. Tall and short small-block frame mounts have been used. General Motors installed two different heights of mounts on F-Body cars. One type was designed for high-performance cars while the other was designed for common road cars. The high-performance versions, designed for the Z/28 and other cars, were left-hand 3⅜ inches and right-hand 3¾ inches. An engine-mount thickness of 2⅛ inch helps achieve the correct engine mount height. The common F-Body 4- and 6-cylinder mounts are 3¹¹⁄₁₆ inches for left-hand mounts and 3¹⁵⁄₁₆ inches for right-hand mounts. The mounts are 1⅝ inches thick. The difference between these two numbers is the height. To order the correct parts, be sure to select the correct size and shape of engine mounts for your chassis.

Many companies make engine mounts for an LS swap into 1967–1981 Camaros as well as a host of other vehicles. Motor mounts are relatively inexpensive and can be ordered in just about any combination and shape. Typically, a good quality set of engine mounts sells for about $150 and slightly more for higher quality sets so you shouldn't have to fabricate a set of your own but that is always an option.

You can fabricate your own out of 1/4-inch plate steel, but it's not worth the time and effort. Engine mounts are inexpensive and readily available. Most complete kits come with Energy Suspension polyurethane Chevy engine mounts. These mounts are the small-block standard of the three bolts. The major difference between manufacturers seems to be materials and finish of the engine mounts. Some are made of aluminum while others are plate steel.

For most LS engine swaps into F-Body cars, you can use the stock mounting locations. You should trial fit the engine in the frame. If the sheet metal has been removed, it makes the process much easier. With the engine on a cherry picker, align the engine mounts with the chassis mounts. If it properly aligns and clears the firewall, your job is much easier. However, it doesn't always work out that way. Sometimes the engine needs to be set back, forward mounted, or to have adjustable mounts. Because of inconsistent and inadequate quality control at the factory in the late 1960s and early 1970s, some cars can be as much as 1/2-inch off from another F-Body car. It means that not all parts are going to fit exactly as designed.

As I've been told, you "have to think like a hot-rodder," and that means you need to think and work through a problem. Sometimes that means having to tweak things to make them fit. So, with that said, there is no single engine mount I can recommend for all engines and F-Body chassis. As a result, you need to test fit, measure, and work out the correct engine mounts for your engine, car, and setup. However, if you know that you want to set the engine back an inch or more, you have already guaranteed yourself the need for a custom set of engine mounts and extra work.

Aftermarket LS Engine Mounts

Because engine mounts are only one piece of the engine swap system, you need to select engine mounts that correctly position your engine in the chassis with the oil pan and transmission crossmember, and allow adequate room between the valve covers and the firewall. Fortunately, all LS engines have the mounting bosses in the same location. The following are some of the sources that make high-quality engine mounts.

Dirty Dingo: Dirty Dingo Slider engine mounts provide a wide range of adjustability. According to the company, the mounts move the engine vertically up to 1/4 inch and allow mounting it 2 inches aft while being able to use the factor rubber mounts (in some cases). Double check that these measurements work with your application, so you don't run into problems. You might want to give them a call just in case.

CHAPTER 2

Holley: Holley made a push in 2010 to become one of the major LS aftermarket suppliers for swappers. I had to sit up and take notice at the advances Holley has made in its LS swap lineup. Holley offers a complete line of LS swapping accessories and products. Specifically, its catalog of engine mounts can cover nearly every possible swap known to exist. The company offers a mount plate for 1/2 inch forward, 1¼ inches and 1/2 inch up, stock, and 3 inches forward.

ATS: As mentioned previously, I chose a lot of the parts for my vehicle based on a *performance* aspect. ATS's engine mounts are made from aluminum rather than steel, and thus reduce weight. This weight saving might not seem like much, but when added to many other weight-saving procedures, it can add up to quite a bit. In the racing world, every little ounce is fodder for being chucked overboard.

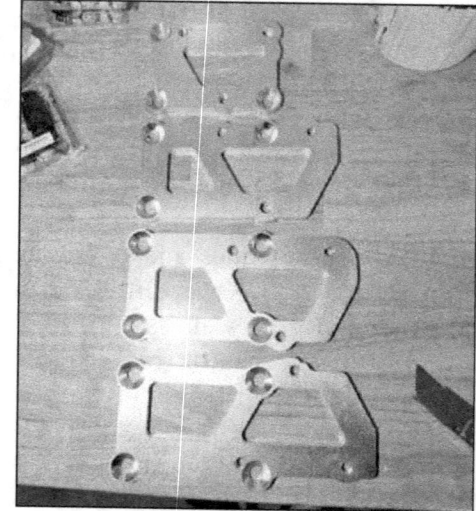

Holley makes a wide range of engine mounts for just about any LS engine project. The company has four sizes ranging from 3 inches forward of the stock location (top) all the way to the stock location (bottom) and everything in between. The zero-offset piece is often used for many F-Body swaps. There are lots of options that allow you to move the engine backward. Rarely does anyone want to move it forward because the front crossmember interferes with the oil pan. For anything greater than a 3-inch movement rearward, you will likely have to fabricate mounts.

Holley also makes mounts for the clamshell-style mount in the stock location. While many swappers do not opt for these mounts, some installers facing unique installation challenges may select them.

Engine Mount Installation

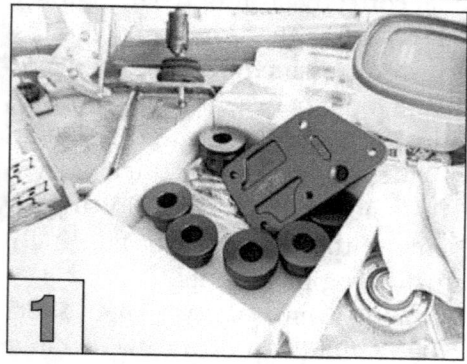

1 These are ATS engine-mount plates for LS engines and solid body mount bushings. (It's a nice touch that they match in color.) The LS engine does not have a multitude of engine mounts, so one size usually fits all. However, certain engines, chassis, and accessories create certain packaging challenges and you need to take this into consideration when selecting engine mounts.

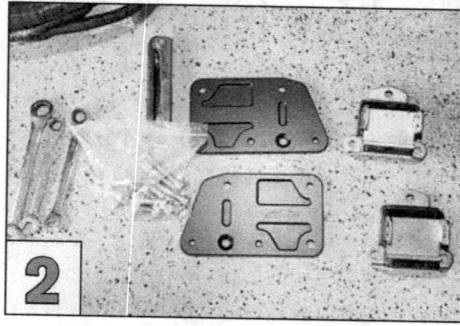

2 The ATS LS swap mount kit includes all the hardware and polyurethane bushings made by Energy Suspension. ATS had to make a small modification to the bushings, so these aren't exactly off-the-shelf parts. The engine mounts are on the right while the black mount plates are in the middle. In addition, these mounts can be installed upside down if necessary, but doing that changes the positioning of the engine slightly.

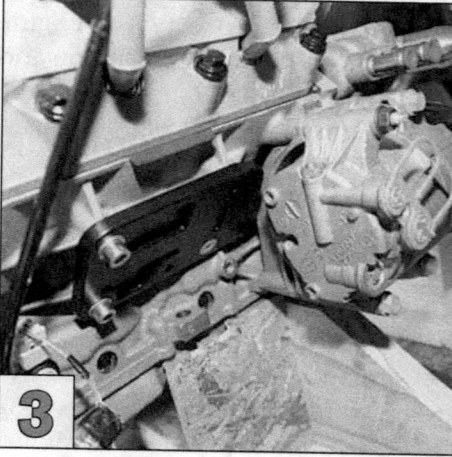

3 I checked the fitting of the mount plate for clearance and then installed the three bolts to secure it. I didn't have enough clearance between the Corvette-style front accessory kit and the A/C unit. I solved this problem by relocating the A/C pump to the upper side of the passenger compartment.

ENGINE AND SUBFRAME

4 The ATS mounting plates are labeled to properly identify each side, so there is no confusion on location. They also require installing some flush-mounted bolts from the back of the plate. While ATS did not supply torque specs, they recommended using a dab of blue Loctite on each bolt to keep them in place.

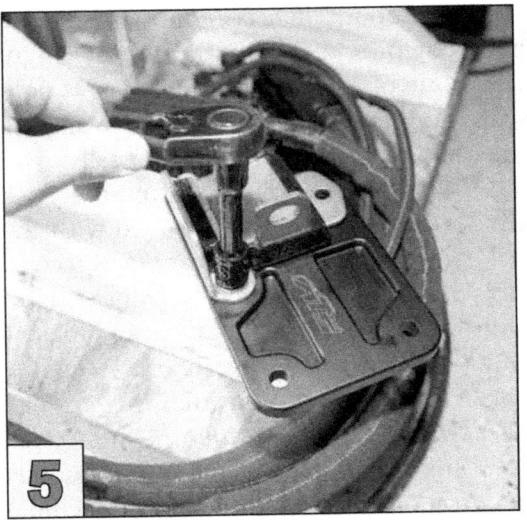

5 I used a ratchet and socket to install the mount on the plate. The plates can be attached in the correct orientation or upside down for slightly more clearance. Just make sure to use the correct bolts in the correct place per the instructions so you don't have interference with other components. It should be noted that I have heard of some people having issues with solid engine mounts tripping the knock sensors erroneously. I stuck with polyurethane because this car will see some serious street time and I'd like to keep all of the fillings intact.

6 The Corvette accessory kit creates a major packaging problem. The A/C bracket gets in the way of the engine mounts and, more important, the frame. I relocated the A/C pump to the upper passenger's side of the engine. The adapter plate bolts to mounting bosses on the block. The engine mounts fasten to the adapter plates.

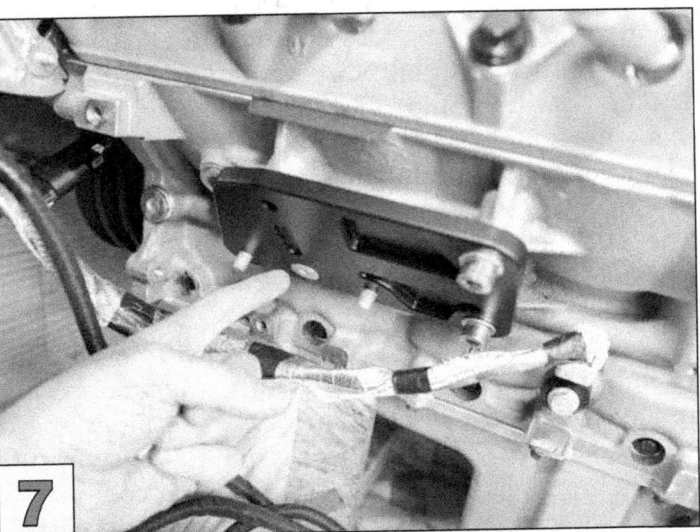

7 I missed this flush-mount bolt the first time I tried to install the engine mounts, so take note of this, and make sure it is installed.

8 The engine mounts have been correctly installed and the engine is ready for installation in the chassis.

SWAP LS ENGINES INTO CAMAROS & FIREBIRDS 1967–1981

CHAPTER 2

ATS engine mounts are reversible so they can be used to resolve special mounting problems. While ATS recommends the orientation based on the instructions, they can be mounted upside down on the opposite side of the engine to help with clearance issues in some instances. Not many mounts on the market can make that claim. Now, it must be said that doing this loses some height (it raises the engine) and possibly moves the engine forward, of course, depending on your application.

I had a major clearance problem with the stock air conditioning (A/C) compressor and bracket location that came with the kit from the Scoggin-Dickey GM dealership (see Chapter 4 for the solution). At this stage, I removed the compressor to get the mount to bolt to the engine block. The ATS engine mounts precisely fit the stock subframe as well as Speed Tech's brand-new subframe.

Just one quick word about the Energy Suspension polyurethane mounts that come with the ATS kit. You may notice the forward edges of the mount have been modified, so the engine and other parts precisely align. One of the ears is removed so it does not get in the way during the engine mounting procedure. Typically, you would be required to run the back metal plate that is provided with the kit. However, in this case, ATS recommends that to keep tolerances tight, you not run the metal backing plate.

Hedman: The Hedman engine mount kit is versatile so you can resolve special fitment issues when installing an LS engine in an F-Body car. The kit sells for $615 and includes engine mount pads, engine mounts, urethane bushings, and a transmission crossmember with Grade-8 hardware. Kit versions are available for manual and automatic transmissions.

This kit may offer a suitable solution if you don't have a crossmember and are having difficulty aligning your engine with the subframe engine mounts. Essentially, this kit comes with everything you need and it functions as a system. When selecting mounting components, be sure to use compatible components from one company to ensure the engine properly installs. I've seen several instances in which an owner buys a variety of parts from different manufacturers, runs into clearance issues, and then has to buy the compatible components. This wastes time and money. This kit works well with proprietary headers.

Autokraft: Autokraft makes a lot of products for LS swaps. Their LS swap adapter plates are specially designed to work with their proprietary oil pan. The mounts feature billet aluminum materials and include polyurethane mounts that come with the kit. Autokraft's current market price hovers right around $175 for a set of engine mounts.

Oil Pans

Selecting the correct oil pan for your particular LS engine swap can be difficult, but today there are many OEM and aftermarket options. Domestic LS engines have a rear sump placement while GTO and Holden cars have a front sump placement. With the many variables involved in an LS swap, such as engine mounts, crossmember, and exhaust, I cannot definitely determine the precise oil pan for a particular engine swap. As I cover

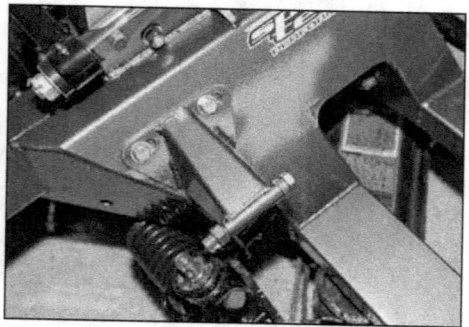

My subframe engine mounts have Grade-8 bolts measuring 1/2 x 4 inches. These hold everything tight. Three bolts fasten the subframe to the frame. I really like the adjustability in the frame mounts because it allows roughly 1 inch of play fore and aft in the engine bay. For improved weight distribution, I pushed these all the way rearward.

Make sure you move the steering along its full side-to-side travel (wheels on the ground) to ensure that everything clears. The LS pan is lower and protrudes in different places than a pan for the small-block Chevy. (Photo Courtesy Mary Pozzi)

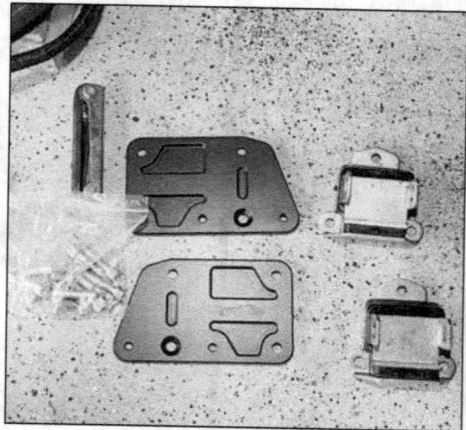

An engine mount kit typically includes the mount plates, brakes, fasteners, and related hardware.

ENGINE AND SUBFRAME

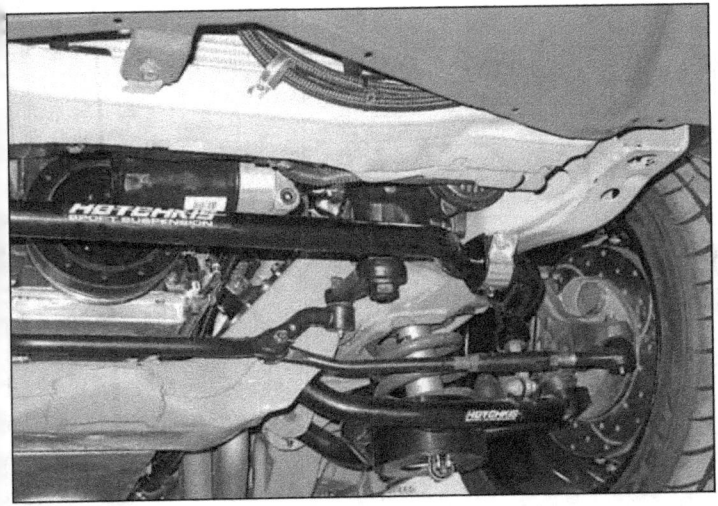

At the front of the Camaro, you can see the bottom of the oil filter and remote mount, and the lines to the oil cooler ahead of the radiator. (Photo Courtesy Mary Pozzi)

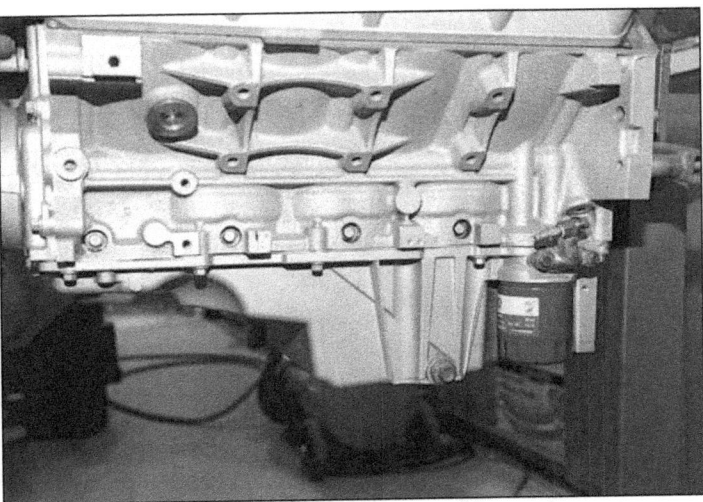

This profile shot of an F-Body pan shows the sharp cut-off point for making sure the steering linkage fits. This only works if the engine mounts are in the stock or farther rearward position.

later in this section the CTS V-and-later F-Body pans are suitable for certain engine swaps. However, if the OEM pan isn't compatible, Autokraft, Milodon, Mast, and others make special-application oil pans. After all, the stock first- and second-generation F-Body subframe isn't always the most hospitable place for engine swaps. In fact, some swappers have to notch the subframe to get a particular oil pan to clear it.

The plug on the bottom left of the oil pan is the oil level sensor. Most aftermarket harnesses don't use this plug, so you can keep it or do what I did and use it as an oil-temperature port. Simply use the wiring and oil-temperature sending unit that comes with your gauge cluster and plug it into the adapter.

Stock F-Body Oil Pan

A fairly inexpensive option is to run a stock LS F-Body oil pan because this pan fits F-Bodies with a variety of transmissions. You use the stock-location or set-back engine mounts. This pan may require modifications to it or to the suspension pieces including the power steering lines. I have seen instances in which some guys have gotten lucky using the combination of the F-Body LS1 pan and Hooker engine mounts and didn't have to modify the pan, but I haven't had much luck making that work. The suspension should go through its full range of travel, which is from full extension to full compression. You should then verify that the suspension components do not come in contact with one another, no binding, and no interference.

Stock pans sell for a premium at swap meets so it often makes sense to buy a new one. Currently, the price for a used one is around $150. For this price, you may opt for the GM conversion kit that is brand new and has all the correct parts. You have to remember to use the F-Body windage tray, dipstick, pickup tube, and gasket to make this work correctly.

LH8 Oil Pan

You might be thinking that the LH8 pan (usually found in Hummer H3s) would work just fine. It has the same basic shape and design of the F-body pan. However, this pan sits way too low in the frame, so it's not a viable option. To clear potholes, expansion joints, and other common road undulations you have to raise the car's ride height about an inch. The stock F-Body pan has a depth of 5.25 inches from the block to the bottom of the pan while the LH8 pan is a monumental 8.5 inches. That's well over 3 inches taller and doesn't afford adequate clearance for street

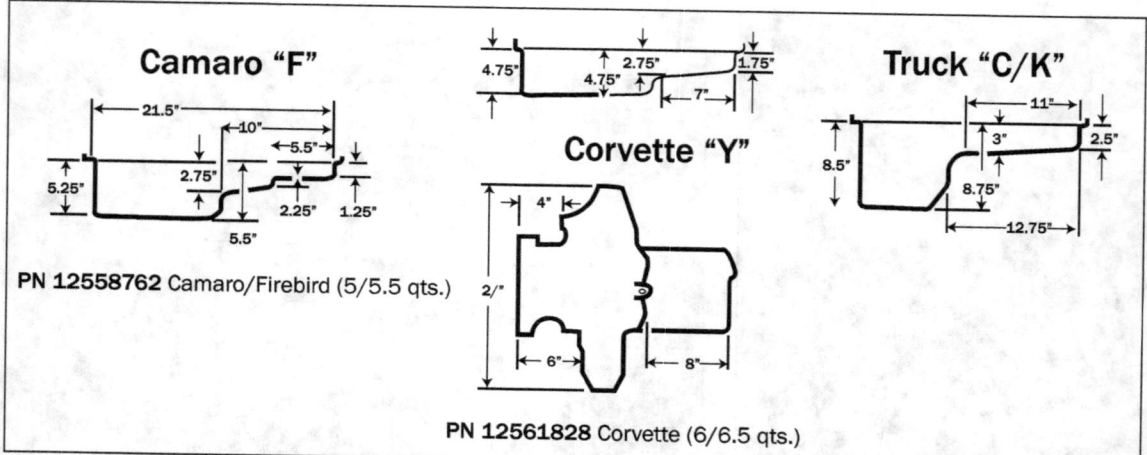

These are diagrams of the various GM stock oil pans that you can find in a junkyard. The Camaro is the best candidate because of the positioning of the rear sump farther back than the Corvette versions.

driving. I've heard horror stories of guys hitting speed bumps and cracking their pans.

CTS-V Oil Pan

There's a small caveat with this oil pan: You have to grab the older version. The newer ones have oil cooler bosses that can interfere with the crossmember on the subframe. This is a slightly nicer option as it can hold slightly more oil than the F-Body version. This pan is roughly 6¾ inches from block surface to the bottom of the oil pan. While deeper than the F-Body pan, it's certainly not as deep as the LH8 truck pan.

In a traditional rear sump layout:
- External sump max depth (from mounting flange), 6.75 inches
- External sump length (from bellhousing flange), 21.5 inches
- External sump width, 10.5 inches

Holley Oil Pan

Holley offers a wide selection of products for LS engine swaps but has been late to the game. Holley's cast-aluminum LS oil pan is machined to precise specs and has the traditional rear sump oiling system. It has been designed to fit a variety of GM cars and trucks from 1955 to 1987. (My first-generation Camaro certainly fits

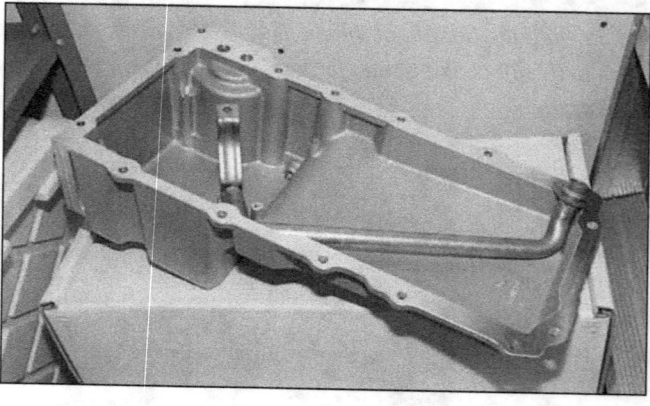

The Holley-machined aluminum LS swap oil pan (PN 302-1) comes with sump baffle, pickup tube, plug, oil passage cover, and oil filter stud. It is designed to work with the stock LS3 dipstick (GM PN 12634547) and tube (GM PN 12625031).

those requirements.) It allows for the OEM oil filter location and an OEM fit. The kit has everything needed, including the baffle, pick-up tube, and oil filter accessories to make it an easy job. Just provide the dipstick and you're good to go. These kits sell for just under $400.

In a traditional rear sump layout:
- External sump max depth (from mounting flange), 5.89 inches
- External sump length (from bellhousing flange), 7.65 inches
- External sump width, 9.75 inches

Autokraft Oil Pan

Autokraft claims that this pan clears all types of linkages from stock to a rack-and-pinion setup, and cutting the subframe is not necessary. This pan features four-corner internal baffling, a custom pickup tube that is ideally suited for road racing, and a stock oil filter location for easy access, so performing an oil change is easy. Autokraft machines a billet piece of aluminum to make it possible to run the filter in the correct location. This pan has a 5½-quart oil capacity and they recommend that you use a stock F-Body dipstick to make an accurate measurement. To get one of these, you have to shell out about $400.

In a traditional rear sump layout:
- Front half of pan, 1.75 inches
- Width of rear sump, 11 inches
- Length of rear sump, 9 inches
- Depth of rear sump, 5.5 inches

Mast Motorsport Oil Pan

This oil pan for LS swaps fits first- and third-generation F-Bodies and even some street rods and trucks. It has the factory oil filter location.

This is important because you don't want to move the oil filter location if space gets tight with other components, such as the headers (which can be tight) or steering components, depending on your particular build.

This pan uses the OEM pan gasket, so it seals tightly and is easy to find. This pan is unique because it has two -10AN fittings rather than an oil outlet for a temperature gauge or a pressure gauge. These fittings are designed for a remote oil filter if you choose to install one. When looking at the driver's side of the oil pan, the right side is the "out" or pressure side and the left side is the return. I don't have any current plans for a remote oil filter in the test vehicle but it would be nice to have. I drilled out the provision in the oil pan and installed a 1/8-inch NPT fitting to run the oil pressure switch from Stack. This way it stays hidden.

GM Conversion Oil Pan

The oil pan swap kit is ideal for just about any LS swap. General Motors calls it the "Muscle Car Oil Pan Kit" (PN 19212593). It fits almost all 1955–1995 rear-wheel-drive V-8 GM cars and trucks that use the traditional wet-sump-style oil pan. The kit includes an oil pan, dipstick, dipstick tube, bolts, gaskets, and pick-up tube with a windage tray. The pan's front valley measures a very thin 2.625 inches, and the entire unit is only 11 inches wide. After it clears the crossmember and steering linkage, the pan expands to 7.75 inches and tapers off to 6.75 by 7.75 inches for its base measurement. Currently, this LS swap oil pan kit is the most economical on the market at around $150 from your favorite speed parts vendor.

Oil

Oil has gone through many changes because of the 2004 federal law that required a reduction in engine oil's sulfur and zinc-phosphorus compounds, or ZDDP. ZDDP is an oil additive that's the primary anti-wear agent for internal-combustion engines. It protects against excessive camshaft and lifter wear, premature piston ring wear, and more than usual cylinder wall damage, also known as piston scuff. This change had significant impact on the performance automotive world, especially for those with forged components and flat-tappet camshafts.

In 2004 car and truck models, the federal government mandated that all auto manufacturers must warranty all catalytic converters to 120,000 miles. This is where the reduction in sulfur and ZDDP comes into play; sulfur and ZDDP are considered "harmful gasses" and therefore are caught in catalytic converters, which prevent their emission into the atmosphere.

All catalytic converters fail over time due to exhaust gases passing through the exhaust system, which is unavoidable. Another important factor to know is that all engines discharge oil through the exhaust.

While, it's typically a very small amount, it was decided that it was easier to alter oil make-up rather than rework the catalytic converters themselves.

Current oil mixtures are reduced in sulfur and ZDDP compounds by 20 percent and sometimes more. Mast has seen engines being torn down with barely 1,500 miles on the short-block and showing as much wear as an engine with more than 100,000 miles, all because improper oil was used. Therefore, it is crucial that you use the appropriate oil with a good amount of ZDDP.

Also, Mast recommends that performance engines with forged components use GM Engine Oil Supplement (EOS) for the first 90 minutes of the engine's life and a zinc and phosphorous ZDDP for the entire service life of the engine. They suggested I use Shell Rotella-T 15W40 API Specification CI-4 Plus or Valvoline NSL Racing Oil 10W30 (conventional engine oil). People have also had good luck using a half bottle of Comp Cams engine break-in fluid with every oil change as it has a high level of ZDDP.

Remember, this is cheap insurance for a very expensive piece of machinery. Invest in high-quality oil; it's vital protection for your engine.

Many companies offer a suitable oil pan for many LS swap projects. These include Holley, Mast, GM Performance, and other reputable places. You need to consider the placement of the K-member, steering components, and engine. Specifically, the engine is often placed far back in the chassis. I have yet to find any engine mounts that fit well more forward than the stock or "0" location. Moving it back toward the firewall is quite easy, as LS engines do not have a distributor to get in the way. Dirty Dingo adjustable mounting plates are suitable for this type of engine positioning.

CHAPTER 3

CHASSIS AND SUSPENSION

You need to upgrade the suspension and chassis to harness and fully utilize the power of an LS engine, While the Camaro's unibody frame and suspension were modern manufacturing technology for the 1960s, these are antiquated now. The stock stamped-steel suspension arms and multileaf rear springs cannot offer a modern level of performance for an LS engine developing 400 hp or more. You need to define your application, budget, and driving style. Then you need to select the chassis and suspension systems to fit those needs. Your LS engine is part of an entire system and therefore the suspension and chassis needs to be integrated into your car.

Removing the Subframe

This procedure may seem a bit daunting at times, because much of the car must be removed to complete the task. Yet, this can be done in your garage with several sets of jack stands and a little patience.

Four giant bolts hold the factory subframe to the chassis, so removing those bolts is all that's required. Sounds simple right? Well, it truly can be simple with some detailed planning and careful consideration for safety. The front subframe is awkwardly balanced, so I recommend making sure that everything is removed from the frame to make the process easier. I recommend making a check list of all the things that are still currently attached to the subframe and double-check that list to make sure they have been safely removed. These include fuel lines, brake lines, emergency brake cable, steering components, wiring, and

With swap components from Speed Tech, you get LS-specific engine mounts, body mounts, and energy suspension polyurethane engine mounts. All of which are designed to work with their subframe and the LS platform. The new subframe and suspension has been assembled and is ready for installation. The front subframe requires six main body bolts that are very strong. Lining up the frame is a snap with the two alignment holes in the frame; these line up with corresponding holes in the body at the base of the firewall, but the sheet metal needs to remain in great shape. The frame alignment may need to be fine-tuned once the front sheet metal has been installed. Some Camaros have been damaged over the years and/or had floorpans replaced by people who lack attention to detail.

CHASSIS AND SUSPENSION

The engine and transmission combination has been installed on the new front clip. The headers, engine mounts, and oil pan are all designed to work in harmony. With virtually limitless combinations of parts on the market, it's important to plan ahead by asking the makers if they have parts that work well with other parts.

This photo perfectly illustrates that an A/C compressor just simply doesn't fit in a stock or even aftermarket frame. Speed Tech can notch the frame for an extra fee if you simply cannot live without the compressor being in this location. If you wanted to notch the frame on your own, a cutoff wheel on a grinder is preferable to a torch or plasma cutter because it is more precise.

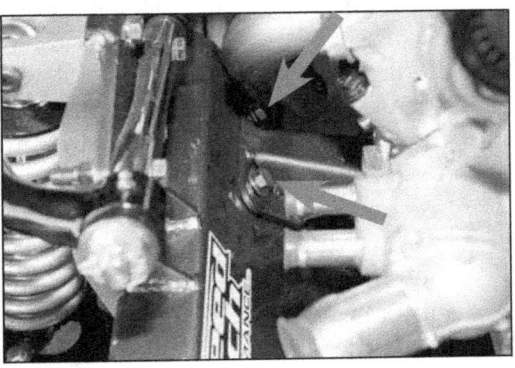

Three bolts hold the engine to the frame, also known as frame pads. A ratchet and socket are used to secure them into place. This allowed me to move the engine back far enough to retain the stock location.

When you select a certain manufacturer's system, all components are designed for proper fit and excellent performance so you don't have to deal with compatibility and fit issues. With my install, I have tons of room on the passenger's side of the exhaust and no interference whatsoever. The driver's side is another perfect example of how, when done right with the right amount of prep work, everything just goes in smoothly without having to modify it to make it work. Of course, with headers, planning is key. I have seen issues with headers hitting a steering box and need to be dimpled. Another option is to buy a new set of headers.

The frame has been lowered and all the components are closer to the ground. The oil pan has roughly 2 inches of ground clearance. If you are running a stock suspension, the car has a higher ride height and you have much more clearance. For many street cars, 2 inches is too low, which means you have to be very careful when hitting speed bumps. The headers are positioned higher off the ground than a typical small-block because of the Speed Tech system of parts working together. The ride height in the front is 3.5 inches off the ground when measured from the frame to the ground.

CHAPTER 3

The sway bar does not interfere with the crank pulley the way the stock suspension does. The sway bar is mounted after the K-member.

any other modifications that have been made to connect the frame to the body of the car.

You need to isolate the body from the frame. To do this, you must raise the car high enough to support the body and let the frame hang free. I use two jack stands with blocks of wood to distribute the load better on the inside of the existing frame. Then I raise the jack to put a small amount of tension on the frame so it doesn't come crashing down on me because of something silly and unforeseen. The four massive bolts are removed and the jack is slowly let down, allowing the body to rest on the jack stands. At this point the frame should be free and ready to be pulled away and chucked in the dumpster.

This is a great time to replace your old and worn-out body mounts with something a bit more sturdy. It might also be worth cleaning up the underside and adding some fresh paint to prevent rust. You may have to cut out the old body mounts, as they tend to rot from age. Pulling them out is straightforward and they typically fall apart if they are old and cracked. This is a good time to check for rust under the body and apply a coat of rust-resistant paint. Installing a new subframe is just as easy with some careful planning. You need to determine whether to remove the sheet metal, all the hoses, wiring harness connections (bellhousing to transmission), and all the other odds and ends. Make sure four jack stands are supporting the body. I place two jack stands on the frame rails behind the firewall and two jack stands under the rear axle. If you have access to a car lift, it makes this procedure much easier.

If the subframe is completely assembled and wheels and tires are attached to the hubs, you can simply roll the new subframe into position and easily align it with the body mounts. It's much easier to install the engine and transmission on the subframe when it's not attached to the body. Then with the wheels on the frame, you can move the subframe into place under the car. The wheels take all of the weight while you maneuver the frame under the car. Then, using a jack or your lift, lower the car onto the subframe, which is supported by jacks.

I chose to keep the wheels on the new subframe to make it easier to maneuver under and around the body. I also did this with the engine and transmission installed but in retrospect it would have been easier to do without the engine and tranny combo. Weight in this instance isn't a factor as the front suspension holds the weight of the engine and transmission. I was able to move the front subframe and drivetrain combination by lifting it from the transmission mount. With all the weight on the front wheels, anyone with a modicum of strength can lift the rear drivetrain.

Lining up the new frame is a bit tricky and once the four bolts are snugly in place with new body bushings you can consider this part of the job complete. Four large bolts fasten the front subframe to the unibody. When you purchase new body mounts, they typically come with new Grade-8 bolts. If yours doesn't, make sure to replace your old rusty bolts with high-quality new ones. After all, you've invested a tremendous amount of time and money so don't cut corners at this stage.

Lining up the four bolts takes some time to get it correct. To properly align the subframe, you often need to move it back and forth and carefully line it up below the car body. Once you find a good location for the frame below the body, the shell can be lowered onto the frame. Be extra careful as the body may be a bit precariously balanced. (I was able to tip the body down at a sharp angle and lift the frame using a jack to mate the frame to the body.) The

The engine mounts have about an inch of play and this allows the rack-and-pinion steering system to clear the engine. In this photo, the steering and engine are too close to each other. I was able to push it back farther and have plenty of room. The fasteners were not tightened down so I was able to move everything back and then retighten all the bolts. You can use a jack to relieve some weight so you can push the engine farther back.

CHASSIS AND SUSPENSION

The engine/transmission assembly on top of the new subframe has been fitted to the body. Now, the new LS engine has been installed in my old-school muscle car.

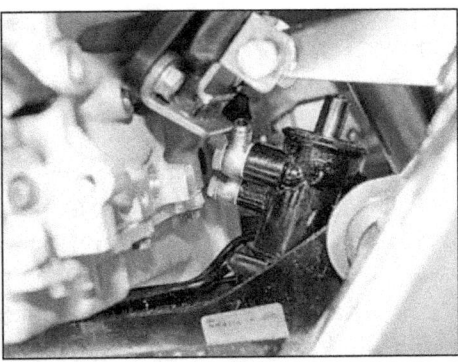

The engine sits very close to the rack-and-pinion steering. To install the fittings that allow me to run the power steering hose to the pump, I had to raise the engine slightly. Much later, I learned that these two fittings must face the front of the engine. Pay particular attention to this so you don't make the same mistake.

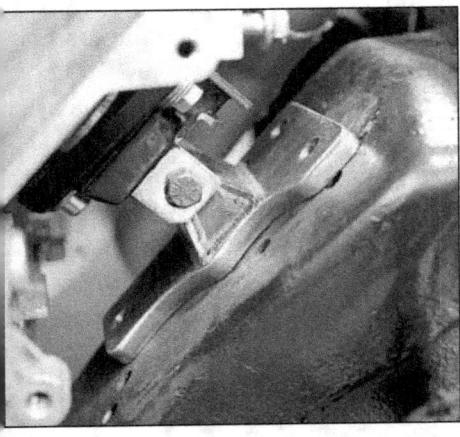

The engine needs to be positioned and the level checked several times. This is critical for transmission tunnel fabrication and position of the shifter. It's also critical for position of the engine relative to the steering linkage movement and header clearance. Having the engine positioned too far back can cause heat buildup on the floorpan and sides of the tunnel.

Make sure there's sufficient clearance between any hot surfaces and the body panels of the car. You should have 3/8-inch air gap for sufficient air movement. Plenty of heat-wrap and heat protection products are available to assist in the battle against heat. (Photo Courtesy Mary Pozzi)

frame and body come predrilled with alignment holes. Use a long dowel to line up the holes to make sure the frame is square.

After I took the car to the alignment shop, my method was within .1 degree. It is laser aligned, so I know it's accurate.

Buying the suspension as a system certainly has its advantages. When you buy a complete system you are also buying the engineering that went into it. It's all designed to

Make sure the engine is level before securing it to the mounts. Placing a carpenter's level on the intake, you can make sure it's true side to side and fore to aft. I made new solid engine mounts for this build. (Photo Courtesy Mary Pozzi)

work together in perfect harmony. A system uses parts that are engineered to effectively function together and enhance performance. The upside to using a system is that you know the parts are meant to go together. This means the headers, engine mounts, and transmission mounts are all aligned properly and any interferences are minimized.

I've seen a few instances where headers don't quite fit well with the engine mounts and hit the steering box or even the frame. The Speed Tech front subframe has been designed to work together with all the other components and this leaves me with less hassle in the long run. Not to mention the powder-coated gunmetal gray. That's my favorite color!

A final word on aftermarket subframes. Regardless of manufacturer or subframe model, whether it's Detroit Speed, Heidts, ChassisWorks, Speed Tech, it's beneficial to buy the entire system. Most aftermarket suppliers, including Holley, ATS, and others, have their own version of the LS swap engine mounts and transmission

CHAPTER 3

Installing an LS7 or LS9 in an Early F-Body

For the following information, I went to the king of all things Camaro and LS9, Mark Stielow. He shared with me his secrets for putting this monster engine inside the confines of his 1969 Camaro.

The LS7 makes a very respectable 505 hp on pump gas and even more with a good set of headers and a cam swap. If you can get your hands on one of these, you'll be sitting pretty. Now, with that said, the LS7 does have a few key features that make it different from the rest of the LS family of engines.

First off, the LS7 has an exceptional dry sump oiling system that's designed for cars that regularly see high cornering g-forces that can rob an engine of oil, thus causing massive internal failures. This system can be swapped onto other LS platforms, such as the LS1, LS2, and LS3. However, there is a giant "but" with that statement. You have to make drastic changes to your front cover, crankshaft, reluctor wheel, oil pump, and many other major components. I have seen swap kits for these go for as much as $3,500! At that price, it might be worth it to just buy an LS7 outright.

The stock LS7 oil pan is not compatible with the Camaro subframe so an alternative must be found. You can either buy an aftermarket version that is made to fit or replace the exotic oiling system with an F-Body oil pan and run a standard oil filter. At the time of this writing, no oil pans are available for retaining the original dry sump oiling system in the LS7 and fit it into a first- or second generation Camaro.

You also need to determine the mounting location for the 8-quart oil tank. This large oil tank needs to be installed in an upright position. You can mount it in many locations under the hood; often it's on the passenger's side of the engine close to the firewall. In many F-Bodies, there is adequate clearance on this side of the body. You can find aftermarket companies that make external tanks of differing sizes, so making it fit into a crevice might not be all that difficult.

Finally, the front-drive accessory kit needs some modifying to make it compatible with the subframe. One way to make this work is to notch the frame, which can be quite time consuming. Another way is to relocate the A/C compressor to the upper passenger's side of the engine using an aftermarket kit.

Either way, it's important to have the A/C system installed on this car. Since it's a passive system when not in use, it really doesn't put a lot of drag on the engine like the old A/C compressors used to. As I always say, if you got it, use it!

Here's Mark Stielow wedging in his LS9. He also prefers the tranny-less option for dropping in a new engine. (Photo Courtesy Mark Stielow)

If you want to run A/C or want to install an LS9, you need to notch your frame, regardless of where it comes from. Lots of measurements are needed to pull this off well. To do so, you must be able to cut the frame out using any variety of cutting tools, such as a reciprocating saw, plasma cutter, and cutoff wheel. After that you need to fabricate plates out of 1/8-inch plate and weld them into place. (Photo Courtesy Mark Stielow)

CHASSIS AND SUSPENSION

Here's what a notched frame looks like after it's been cut and re-welded. Several small pieces of flat stock are beat and shaped into the proper size then perimeter welded for strength. (Photo Courtesy Mark Stielow)

crossmember. Each manufacturer has spent a considerable amount of time researching and engineering its own specific setups. Some companies even make their own version of headers, which is also designed to work with their subframes and accessories. I highly recommend that regardless of the aftermarket subframe you select, you should buy or stick with one company's entire system. This prevents having to solve compatibility issues among systems and parts. Have confidence in the fact that the system you are working with is well designed and made to work right without interference in major components.

Various subframes are installed using the same method, but some of the details may be a little different. To make sure yours works properly, it's important to consult the manufacturer. They ask you important questions, such as which engine you are using and what transmission you plan to run. These questions, along with suspension style and brake considerations, are all part of planning a solid build.

Front Suspension

Many complete subframe assemblies are available on the market today, and most bolt up to the stock mounting holes, so a great amount of fabrication isn't necessary. Popular high-performance or pro-touring subframes, from companies such as Speed Tech, Heidts, Chassis Works, and Detroit Speed and Engineering, conveniently and easily bolt up to the stock chassis.

Art Morrison Enterprises

Art Morrison is a long-time builder of high-performance suspension and chassis systems. It has been offering a variety of suspension and chassis parts for some time. This premium-quality subframe bolts to the unibody Camaro like other leading units. Using designed finite element analysis the GT Sport front clip provides excellent strength and rigidity while tipping the scales at a paltry 105 pounds.

The subframe itself features mandrel-formed 2 x 4-inch frame members, coil-over shocks, power rack-and-pinion steering at a 20:1 ratio, adjustable transmission crossmember, and anti-roll bar. The subframe carries specially modified C6 spindle and front suspension parts, including forged-aluminum control arms. The power rack-and-pinion steering is positioned 2 inches lower in the frame for increased handling agility.

In fact, the subframe readily accepts all LS engines and the transmission crossmember is compatible with popular high-performance transmissions, such as the Tremec T56, TH350 and 400, 700-R4 and 4L60E, Muncie

4-speeds, and Richmond 5/6-speeds. It can be fitted with stock C6 brakes or Wilwood brakes with 13- or 14-inch rotors. Other optional equipment includes custom headers and an adapter for the stock steering column. However, Morrison recommends an aftermarket column.

Detroit Speed and Engineering

Detroit Speed and Engineering (DSE) front subframes have proven themselves in competition throughout the country. Most notably Mark Stielow's *Mayhem* won the 2012 Optima Ultimate Street Car Challenge using the DSE front subframe. This direct bolt-in subframe features premium tubular upper and lower A-arms, coil-over shocks and tuned springs, power rack-and-pinion steering at 12:1 ratio, splined anti-roll bar, steering knuckles with late-model sealed bearings, and C6 Corvette steering knuckles with hubs.

The frame tubes are constructed using hydroforming technology in which a hydraulic press forces water through the frame rails. It creates a piece with uniform wall thickness for greater strength and rigidity. This process doesn't require welding so the strength of the frame rails is retained. The assembly comes with stamped-steel main and secondary crossmembers that provide greater strength and stability.

The LS engine fits cleanly on the subframe. DSE's front subframe can accommodate a 10-inch-wide wheel with 335-series profile, but before you buy wheels, you must measure your particular F-Body to be sure it can accept that wheel size. Both main and secondary crossmembers are stamped for structural rigidity. Most LS engines are direct bolt in on DSE subframes. The DSE subframe comes as bare metal but it can be powder coated for an extra charge.

Optional equipment for the subframe is a Z-bar mounting bracket, stock parking brake cables, Baer brake packages, stock or half-height body mounts, custom rack-and-pinion hose kits, steering input coupler shafts, and stock-style transmission crossmembers.

Total Cost Involved Engineering

TCI's front subframe unit is billed as the only front subframe on the market that has dual camber curves so it can be effectively set up and performs well in a variety of competition situations. The subframe is a double-rail mandrel-bent design for exceptional strength and vastly improved performance over stock. Most mounts and necessary brackets are installed. Those include body mounts, engine mounts, suspension brackets, and core support.

Subframe equipment includes urethane-bushed tubular A-arms; coil-over spindles have TCI's custom 2-inch drop spindle or stock height spindle; billet rebound adjustable coil-overs with powder-coated springs; 1 x .156-inch-wide DOM steel upper tubular A-arms and 1⅛ x .156-inch-wide DOM steel lower tubular A-arms; Moog upper and lower ball joints; manual rack-and-pinion steering; 11-inch drilled, slotted, and zinc-plated rotors and big-bore calipers; 1-inch anti-roll bar; multi-position transmission crossmember; and mount.

Chris Alston's Chassisworks

While Chris Alston established a solid reputation for chassis parts in drag racing, he has produced high-quality subframes and suspension pieces for pro-touring F-Bodies. Chassisworks first started offering pro-touring subframes in 2001 and has kept pace with the sport since then.

The latest G-Machine bolt-on subframe kit features stainless-steel A-arms, coil-over shocks, 11.75-inch Wilwood rotors with four-piston calipers, and Chassisworks hubs, anti-roll bar, manual rack-and-pinion steering, and transmission crossmember. The frame tubes are laser cut and welded from 7-gauge steel. The subframe allows the use of 17 x 8-inch front wheels. All of the other suspension parts are installed on the factory-welded subframe and dropped crossmember. Presently, LS-series engine mounts are in development.

The optional equipment for this subframe include billet engine mounts, power rack-and-pinion steering, A-arms in polished, stainless, or powder-coated finish, inner fender splash guards, urethane or aluminum body bushings, 13-inch Wilwood rotors with four-piston calipers or 14-inch Wilwood rotors and six-piston calipers.

Heidts

Similar to others on the market, this complete subframe simply bolts in place of the stock subframe assembly. The Heidts unit lowers the ride height by 3 to 4 inches and has a track width of 58½ inches. The Pro-G subframe features tubular A-arms in painted or polished finish, 2-inch dropped spindles, 11-inch Wilwood brake rotors and calipers, rack-and-pinion steering, and 10-position rebound-adjustable coil-over shocks. With this subframe, you can install brake rotors as large as 13 inches with six-piston calipers, choice of two different Heidts anti-sway bars, a kit for installing a stock steering column,

CHASSIS AND SUSPENSION

reversible transmission crossmember, and the transmission mount.

Speed Tech

After reviewing all the relevant market offerings, I installed a Performance Pro Touring subframe. If you're building an F-Body car for ultimate handling, you need to select a leading high-performance subframe. When doing so, you are making an investment in your F-Body and expect to pay $5,000 on up for one. In the case of the project car for this book, I opted for the Track Time package of the Performance Pro Touring subframe, which simply bolts up to the factory mounts on the frame and firewall.

This fully adjustable suspension tips the scales at only 125 pounds, so it takes a lot of unsprung weight off the front end of the car. It has a rear-steer rack-and-pinion system. It also includes tubular upper and lower control arms; a tubular, heat-treated, powder-coated, and chrome-moly sway bar; solid aluminum body mounts; and AFX spindles. It comes with adjustable coil-overs, but it can also be ordered with an Air Ride Shock Wave 3.0. It also carries high-clearance control arms that

While your spring rate may be different for your application, Speed Tech recommended a spring rate of 500 pounds on this front and 250 pounds on this rear. You need to determine the spring rates before installing your suspension because the spring rates must match your engine selection. You want to obtain the best handling possible and best weight bias, and therefore your spring rates and suspension setup must produce a balanced chassis. Typically an LS engine weighs less than the standard small-block if you have an aluminum block.

You many need to upgrade the steering linkage. Often the stock linkage is working just fine, but you may need to use a stronger unit, especially if you are using a stock power steering box. This kit is part of a Speed Tech frame combination. Each shaft must be cut to length and requires a solid-geared rag-joint adapter that comes in the kit. I recommend going slowly, so you don't make a critical mistake because you will have to buy another one if you cut it too short. I used a chop saw to cut mine into shape going inch by inch until I got the desired length.

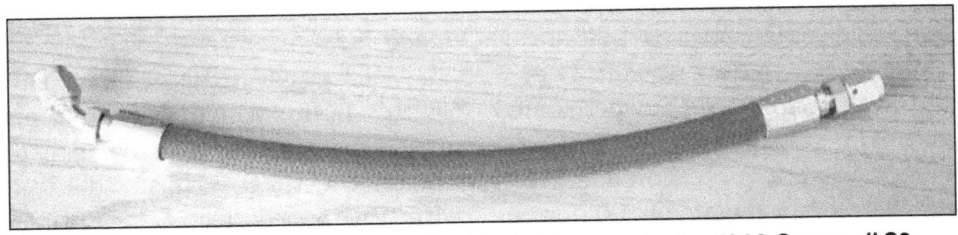

I assembled this complete power steering line to fit my particular 1968 Camaro/LS3 swap. You'll probably be making a couple of custom hoses throughout this process. To get comfortable, make a few practice hoses. You can always take them apart later to reuse the parts. Be aware that power steering hose is different from other types of hoses and is designed to withstand a lot more line pressure. It must also be noted that the line-side half of the hose end is reverse threaded, so make sure you take that into account. The return line on the power steering system can be any type of hose that can withstand hydraulic fluid, as it is not under great amounts of pressure.

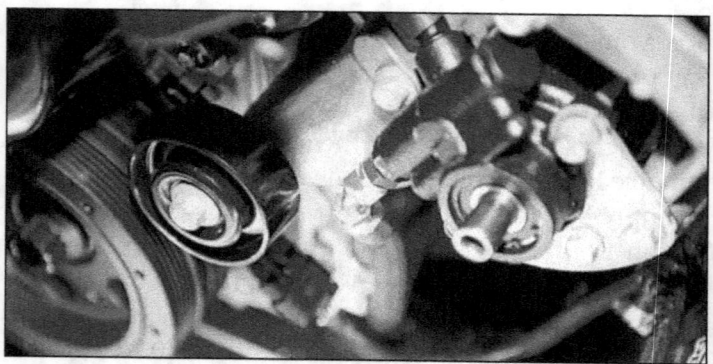
The Corvette-style front accessory drive kit hugs the block and heads very closely. I installed the power steering hose and had an interference issue with the pulley. I was able to lightly file down a leading edge of the fitting to get adequate clearance. As an alternative you can use slimmer fittings but they come with a cost.

I have fully installed the pulley with barely enough clearance for the fitting. Since the pulley should not have any deflection, this amount of clearance should be sufficient.

accommodate up to a 10-inch 295 wheel/tire with a 7-inch backspace. The crossmember is fully adjustable so it fits a variety of GM transmissions, including the Tremec T56 and 4L60E automatic transmission. This subframe readily accepts LSLSx engines.

With the Speed Tech subframe and others like it, it's simple and easy to install and I didn't have to cut, weld, grind, or fabricate the existing frame to install it. After all, it was a bolt-up procedure and that makes installing a subframe, such as this one, a less daunting affair. The subframe is designed to work with the rest of their suspension parts, engine mounts, and headers. It comes as a kit and is designed to work as one unit. I opted to have the subframe powder coated gunmetal gray and cleared over for a killer finish and professional feel.

A front spring rate of 500 pounds for the coil-over shocks was suggested to me. If you choose to keep the stock springs, the small-block front springs typically suffice. If you plan on having a more performance front spring, you have to check with your favorite suspension manufacturer for a custom spring rate.

Rear Suspension

You need a stiffness, damping control and the correct geometry for maximum road holding if your LS engine is going to effectively and efficiently transmit the torque and horsepower to the ground. Many aftermarket rear suspension systems are available today. These offer different approaches but all these suspensions are quantum leap beyond the stock rear suspension. These suspensions minimize if not eliminate all the those old handling traits of wheel hop, extreme body roll, and tire spin.

Speed Tech

As I looked at the original plan for this build, which was a performance car with enough balance to run on the streets, I decided to go with the Speed Tech rear torque-arm set up. When I purchased Speed Tech's Track Time package, the other half of this equation was their rear suspension kit. It differs from other three- and four-link aftermarket rear suspensions by being a rear torque-arm kit. It delivers exceptional road holding and vertical stability. The torque-arm setup has been around for years and the experience with the American Iron series in the NASA racing series has proven to me that the torque-arm setup is not only viable but established as a great performance suspension arrangement.

The spring rate in the back is set at 250 pounds for aggressive applications. The stock leaf springs do just fine, but again remember that if you want to step up the suspension, you have to check with your trusted suspension company to determine the correct rate for your application. I do recommend that if you have a stock mono-leaf setup, you want to look at upgrading them to something a bit stouter. Chances are that the engine you put in your car makes more power than whatever you just replaced. That said, the mono-leaves are notorious for wheel hop. If your plan is to only do parade laps, you should be fine, but I still recommend upgrading to multi-leaves or even a coil-over setup if the budget allows.

The kit includes the torque arm, a panhard bar, panhard mounting bar, coil-over shocks from QA1, the front mount for the torque-arm,

CHASSIS AND SUSPENSION

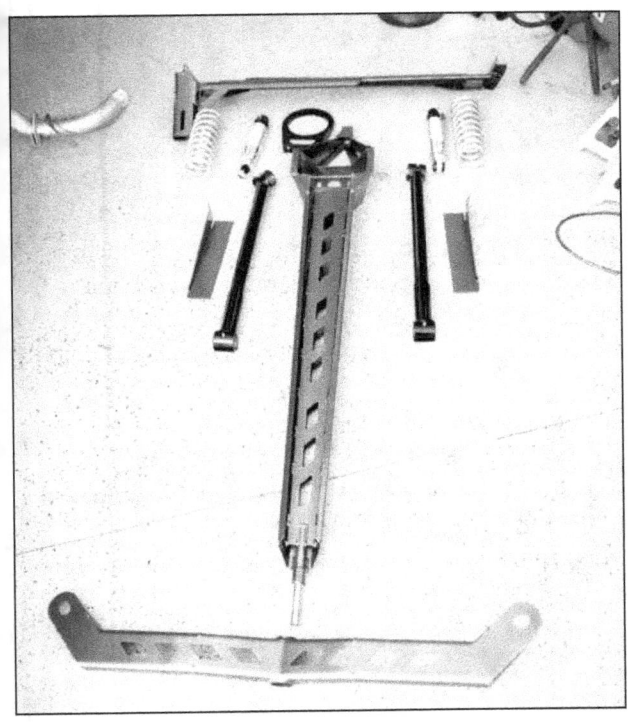

The Speed Tech rear suspension has a rear torque arm that is fairly easy to install, but exhaust pipe clearance may be an issue. Speed Tech made these stout parts. The kit comes with the complete rear torque arm and all the hardware you need to install it. This does require some welding.

lower Articulink lower arms, and all the hardware, which include the tabs that must be welded onto the rear-end if you choose to use your own rear end. The kit requires minimal welding compared to other similar rear suspension systems.

I purchased a 9-inch rear end with the mounting plates and tabs already welded into place from Bears Performance Products. They built me a custom length 9-inch housing to fit the wheel and tire package. They completed the rear-end package with a Strange center section and 3.89 gears.

The rear suspension setup is designed to work with the front subframe and ties into it using the rearward-most body mount with a special crossmember to hold the torque arm in place with a Delrin bushing. I chose the Speed Tech rear suspension because I wanted a balanced and integrated suspension system for the car. However, other creditable rear suspension options are on the market.

Chassisworks

The g-Link rear suspension package features VariShock coil-overs or air springs and tubular upper and rear control arms, control arm braces and spherical bushings, and an anti-sway bar. This full bolt-on system does not require a lot of fabrication for installation. The G-Bar air spring rear suspension comes with canted poly-bushing upper and lower control arms, suspension cradle and brackets, and VariShock adjustable-valve air spring shocks.

Art Morrison Enterprises

Art Morrison Enterprises offers two different rear suspension systems for the first-generation F-Body: three- and four-link. Both have 2 x 4-inch mandrel-formed frame rails that provide exceptional rigidity and maintain suspension geometry. Both suspensions are compatible with the stock gas tank. The frame rails and components offer a design that provides optimum ground clearance. These rear suspensions are built around the venerable Strange Engineering 9-inch differential, featuring Strange adjustable coil-over shocks and a special sway bar.

The three-link suspension uses a special Watt's linkage in which two links are connected to a shorter adjoining link for lateral stability; it's well suited for pro-touring applications. It has a lot of adjustability for particular operating conditions. This geometry provides excellent rear end articulation without any binding. It has an adjustable Watt's linkage track locator and it includes all the suspension links and rod ends, sway bar, adjustable shocks, and a 9-inch housing designed for your particular application. With this suspension, you retain the stock gas tank but sometimes it can encroach on the rear seat area and you need to make a floorpan modification. This suspension geometry is often preferred for a competition car.

The compact triangulated four-bar four-link rear GT Sport suspension is a popular choice for pro-touring applications. The four-link design with coil-over aluminum shocks capably handles forces placed on it and it fits below the stock F-Body floorpan. "Johnny Joints," are integrated into the suspension, which uses special spherical bushings that use a Delrin cushion inside the joint for a compliant ride with accurate linkage actuation for superior performance.

Detroit Speed and Engineering

Many consider the Quadra-Link the finest aftermarket solid-axle rear suspension on the market, and it certainly is a leader in the market and delivers impressive road holding and traction. Like several of the other rear suspensions, this offers a quantum leap in road holding, traction, and ride quality but the installation requires substantial cutting, fitting, and welding. This fabrication includes cutting and modifying the rear frame rails, which is not a job a novice installer can often tackle. If you're not skilled or comfortable using a pneumatic cutting tool, welding, and metal working, I recommend having a professional shop install this suspension for you.

The Quadra-Link features the Swivel-Link so the suspension is enabled to articulate. That allows it to adjust to suspension loads and road conditions. Keep this in mind: You may have to install wheel-well tubs so you can run large 12-inch-wide wheels with this rear suspension installed. Similar to installing the suspension, integrating wheel tubs into the body requires extensive, cutting, welding, and fabrication. A well-positioned adjustable panhard rod effectively controls roll center, ride height, suspension loads during aggressive cornering, and enhances handling and traction. This suspension uses high-durometer rubber bushings to control suspension movement. The extended upper arms provide an ideal pinion angle from the driveshaft to the differential for long life and effective transmission of torque. It also uses DSE/JRi aluminum body coil-over shocks that are specifically valved for it.

Heidts

The Pro-G complete bolt-in independent rear suspension (IRS) provides incredible performance and tremendous road holding, so it does not require extensive fabrication work to install it. It has a track width of 58½ inches, uses top-quality tubular upper and lower A-arms, 9-inch aluminum coil-over shocks, front pinion support, 10-inch Wilwood brake rotors and calipers, billet single-adjustable coil-over shocks, and steel outer uprights.

According to Heidts, the upper link has a -.5 degree of camber curve and delivers 3/4 inch of total travel during aggressive cornering. The subframe connectors attach to the forward struts and anchor the rear suspension during heavy acceleration.

This is an actual IRS complete with half-shafts, rather than an engineered and tuned solid-axle suspension. In a turn, the outside wheel in an IRS suspension is able to squat and transfer its torque load better to the pavement while the inside rear wheel remains in contact with the pavement and does not lift. With a solid-axle rear suspension, the outside wheel stays planted during hard cornering, but the inside wheel is placed under a reduced load and often lifts. When hitting road bumps, potholes, and so forth, the force or jolt is absorbed by that particular side of the suspension and does not upset the balance of the car as in a solid-axle setup.

Wheels

Wheels are your direct connection to the road, and as such, you need high-quality wheels to transfer the torque to the pavement. You also need strong, well-built wheels because you cannot compromise safety. When installing an LS engine into an F-Body car, the horsepower increase over the stock engine is significant and in many cases tremendous. A stock LS engine often produces more than 100 hp over a stock Gen I Chevy small-block from the 1960s and 1970s.

If you're installing a high-performance LS engine, you can easily double or triple stock horsepower levels. If that is the case, you need a much larger contact patch than the

---

Art Morrison Three-Piece GT Sport Chassis Package

The GT Sport Chassis is a complete chassis and suspension solution for the first-generation F-Body, and it operates as a fully integrated system. It readily accepts the LS engine as well as the big-block and small-block Chevy V-8s. This system accommodates the wide production variances or differences from the Van Nuys, California, and Norwood, Ohio, plants. This three-piece system allows you to install it according to the production differences and suitably position it to fit the floorpan of a particular car. The GT front subframe uses C6 Corvette geometry and parts while the triangulated four-bar rear delivers excellent road-holding characteristics for 1967–1969 Camaros.

This suspension does require some fabrication and fitment of the suspension links. In fact, you need to cut a couple of channels in the factory floorboard and the unibody rear frame rails need to be modified to accept the suspension. If you're running tires up to 335 in width, mini-tubs need to be installed to accept wheels and tires of this size. The system is compatible with a stock gas tank and rear bench seats. ■

CHASSIS AND SUSPENSION

stock 14- and 15-inch wheels offer to harness that power and effectively apply it to the ground. Otherwise, it's simply wasted and your engine's horsepower goes up in tire smoke when you get on the throttle.

Therefore you need to carefully consider whether your rear suspension and wheel package is adequate (or preferably, ideally suited), for your particular setup. Wheels are only one aspect of the complete high-performance transformation. Suspension, brakes, and wheels should be purchased as a complementary package because the operation of these components is interdependent. Therefore, you have to consider all the aspects involved in the total package, such as suspension, drivetrain, brakes, and wheels. Your wheels need to have the ideal combination of strength, light weight, and the correct size and backspacing.

Material Choices

You need strong wheels because you can't afford a wheel to collapse at high speed on an autocross track, road course, or on the street. The results will be disastrous. While cast and billet aluminum wheels are available, most pro-touring drivers select forged wheels for strength, lightweight, and affordability. My goal is maximum handling and minimal unsprung weight.

Two-piece forged wheels are now available but they are offered in limited varieties. The three-piece design is still the most prevalent forged wheel type. The center sections can be cast or forged, but I recommend forged because the molecular structure of the forged center delivers higher strength. The 18-inch or larger wheels that carry low-profile tires are subjected to substantial loads during high-performance use and bumps and pothole jolts can be transferred to the wheels. Weak off-brand wheels or cheaper cast wheels can easily bend.

Size Options

Also keep in mind, large wheels and tires are necessary to transfer more horsepower to the pavement, and are heavier and therefore have greater rotating mass. As a result, you need larger than stock brakes to provide adequate, if not excellent, stopping power. Therefore, if you're running 17-inch or larger wheels, you should use 11- to 14-inch high-performance aftermarket brakes.

Let's take a little trip back in time. In the 1960s, many muscle and passenger cars were fitted with 14-inch wheels from the factory, and special high-performance cars, such as the Z28, were fitted with 15-inch wheels with 60-series tires. In stock form many of the V-8 F-Bodies of the late 1960s and early 1970s cranked out 200 to 400 hp. Flash forward and today's popular LS engines often produce at least 400 hp. The LS3, which is one of the most popular engines for LS swaps, cranks out 436 hp in stock trim. To utilize the output of a modern LS engine, you need large wheels that give the tires a large contact patch on the pavement.

It's a balancing act to optimize handling and traction and therefore the selection of wheels is critical. Some of the suspension manufacturer may have recommendations for your setup. Commonly, for a pro-touring setup, the 17- and 18-inch wheels offer the best balance of traction and handling. Pro-touring owners avoid 19-inch or larger wheels because there is not enough clearance between the axle and steering components and stock sheet metal. Often large wheels require large fender flares and a custom body. That's added expense and on the aesthetic side, 20-inch or larger wheels are sizable and many owners feel they are proportionally too large for the F-Body. Most of the front subframes accept 8-inch-wide wheels up front and some accept as much as 9-inch-wide wheel.

You also need to take backspacing (see below) and fender clearance into account, and you should have a 1/2-inch clearance between the bodywork and tires. In addition, you need to take your brake system rotor and caliper size into account and make sure there is enough clearance between the wheel's edge. The stock front subframe accepts up to 18-inch-size wheel with back spacing of 4.5-inches, while the rear suspension accepts 18-inch-size wheel with backspacing of 4.75 inches.

Many top-quality forged wheels are available on the market and new ones are entering the market all the time. I would not buy more inexpensive aluminum cast or heavy steel wheels. These do not have the desired strength for high-performance use. HKE, Weld, M/T, Boze, iForged, Fikse, and many other top brands make premium forged two- and three-piece wheels. When it comes to buying wheels, buy the wheel with the correct dimensions and rely on a reputable brand. I could fill an entire book with all the different wheel constructions, types, and designs. I selected Forgeline, which is one of the most popular manufacturers of wheels on the market. My wheels measure in at 18 x 9 inches with 6.5 inches of backspacing up front and 18 x 12 inches with 7.5 inches of backspacing in the rear. The fronts and rears have the standard GM 5 x 4.75-inch bolt pattern. I opted for the titanium-color centers with a brushed outer lip. The center sections are left matte, and the lip has been clearcoated. These wheels bring an updated stylish look to the project car. Now, these wheels aren't by any means cheap. The old phrase "you get what you pay for" certainly rings true with wheels as well. These ultra-light wheels are as attractive as they are durable.

Fender Clearance and Backspacing

With any wheels, you need to get the backspacing correct for your particular suspension and brake setup. If the backspacing is excessive and there's negative offset, the suspension arms, tie rods, and other components may interfere with the wheel. If there's minimal or little backspacing and a positive offset, the wheel may extend too far and contact the fender or wheel-well lip.

To best allow for the correct fender clearance, measure the width of the wheel-well housing. Be sure to take into account that some lowered cars with a shallow wheel-well housing many limit the size of tire you can mount on the rear axle. Once the measurement has been taken, subtract 1 inch so you can have the necessary suspension clearance of 1/2 inch. Up front you may need more clearance so you may need to subtract 1½ inches.

You also need to determine the amount of wheel backspacing. Place a straight edge across the brake rotor. Then use a tape measure to determine the distance to the inner wheel well. You should factor in 1/2 inch of wheel-well clearance and then you have your backspacing measurement. Following these procedures helps you to determine maximum wheel/tire size for your particular car.

Tires

At this stage, you know the application of your F-Body, and that dictates the choice of tires. High-performance street, street/strip, drag race, autocross/road race, and pro-touring all operate under different demands and conditions. For example, road-racing tires operate at sustained high speeds, under high loads, and therefore the tire is subjected to a lot of friction and heat. On the other hand, a high-performance street tire typically operates at low to moderate speeds and may be placed under high loads and high speeds for short amounts of time.

Tires need to be at their operating temperature to provide maximum performance. If your tires are over or under the ideal operating temperature, you'll be slipping and spinning. As a rule, you can have a soft tire that provides exceptional grip and short life. Or you can opt for a hard tire and long life, but then it delivers reduced grip. Tires do not exist that provide ultimate grip and long life, so you have can't have it all when it comes to tires.

This means that selecting tires is a compromise and it takes some research and careful consideration to find the ideal tires for your car. The following are examples of leading high-performance tires. It isn't possible or practical to provide information on every single relevant tire model for a high-performance F-Body car. Therefore, I provide guidelines to help you select the ideal tires.

Let's assume you're building a high-performance or pro-touring F-Body car and are looking for high-speed, aggressive handling, and sticky tires. Most of these tires fall into ultra high-performance summer tire category and are suitable for a high-performance street car. These tires often have a relatively high tread wear rating of 300, traction grade is the highest at AA, temperature is the highest grade of A, and a speed rating of W, Y, or ZR. If you're going to use your F-Body car for road racing or autocrossing, it needs to have a tread wear rating of 200 or lower.

Many ultra-high-performance summer and extreme-performance summer tires are available, and new tires are introduced in rapid succession while established tires are often discontinued. In the lower R-rated performance category, many tires are suitable for high-performance street use.

Street-Oriented Tires

The Bridgestone Potenza S-04 Pole Position offers excellent traction and road-holding characteristics in a variety of conditions. The tire's asymmetric tread design features interlocking tread blocks and a large outboard shoulder. A central rib promotes exceptional steering response and road holding. The intermediate ribs have high-angle tread blocks, which help prevent tread squirm for improved braking performance. The tire's carcass uses two steel belts supported by and spirally wrapped with aramid/nylon cord reinforcement for high-speed driving and longevity. These R-rated tires have a 280-tread wear rating, AA traction rating, and A temperature rating. The 17- and 18-inch wheels weigh between 23 and 31 pounds.

Another R-rated offering is the Yokohama S Drive, which provides solid and predictable performance in most conditions and applications. These tires feature a nanotechnology-based micro-flexible tread compound, which produces a silica-based compound for excellent grip and response. This high-tech compound is molded into a directional tread pattern that also has independent shoulder blocks, notched intermediate ribs, and a continuous center rib. The tire's carcass features jointless nylon cap plies that reinforce twin steel belts and belt-edge strips for increased longevity.

These R-rated tires have a 300-tread wear rating, AA traction rating, and A temperature rating. The 17- and 18-inch tires range from 20 to 28 pounds.

The Nitto NT555 285/30–20 tire is another ultra high-performance summer street tire. It features Nitto's Extreme ZR compound that delivers exceptional grip and precise handling. An excellent choice for street applications, the tread pattern provides high-speed stability and superb cornering performance. The relatively stiff high-tread block maintains consistent road contact in a variety of conditions and offers a sizable contact patch. The high-traction tire also provides respectable tread life. Both the tread pattern and the compound were designed to deliver exceptional dry performance. This particular tire has a W speed rating, tread wear of 300, traction of A, and temperature of A.

Michelin recently released its top-line Super Sport that has been tested and developed into a leading ultra high-performance road tire. Michelin's Bi-Compound tread is in an asymmetric design that has an inboard wet design and an outside dry design. In other words, the outside shoulder is a very grippy compound for high-speed street and track duty while the notched center ribs and inboard shoulder feature a compound designed for superior performance at very high speeds and in wet conditions.

The tire's carcass contains two steel belts and a spirally wound Twaron cord. The high-density Twaron fiber in the carcass delivers structural reinforcement so the tire maintains its shape at all speeds. The tires deliver enormous grip at mid-corner allowing the driver to hold the chosen line even when the tire is under great strain. In road tests, you can actually turn in more when the tires start to push and it holds its lines.

The tires are offered in sizes from 18 to 22 inches in widths ranging from 225 to 345 and aspect ratios from 25 to 45. These ZR rated tires have a tread wear rating of 300, traction rating of AA, and temperature grade of A. The tire weight for 17- to 18-inch wheels ranges from 20 and 26 pounds.

Street and Track Tires

I chose the BFGoodrich KDW2 street tire for many reasons. The car will see some street time, which may include wet weather driving. These are well rated for grip in dry and wet weather. This tire has a speed rating of ZR, a tread wear rating of 200, a traction rating of AA, and a temperature rating of A. This tire fits another one of the categories for road racing regulations. Autocrosses and road races in which street-going cars compete are now mandating tires with a tread wear rating of 200. Thankfully these tires came in my size.

The events I plan on running are local autocrosses and big-time pro-touring events, such as the Optima Challenge in which I recently participated with a respectable showing for a brand-new car. The tires for my car measure 275/35/18 on the front and 335/30/18 on the back. The bigger contact patch should help plant the power I make from the upgraded LS3. You want to take this into consideration when planning your build. Often times, the theme of the build dictates what wheels and tires are used and what sizes are required.

BFGoodrich has recently released another extreme-performance tire: the g-Force Rival. It's one of the leading tires for pro-touring and track-day cars. The g-Force Rival combines the best qualities of the R1 street tire and g-Force Comp2 tire. In skid pad tests and on road courses, this tire has proven to have extraordinary grip for rear-wheel-drive cars. It supplies copious amounts of grip and provides road holding that's difficult to match. This tire has a ZR speed rating, 200 tread wear rating, AA traction rating, and A temperature rating.

Yokohama ADVAN Neova AD07 is another tire that is designed for the demands of racing and autocrossing. It features micro silica tread compound for excellent grip. The directional tread pattern has sizable tread blocks and rounded edges for precise steering. Five large circumferential and multiple directionally aligned lateral grooves resist hydroplaning and enhance wet traction. The AD07 has a 180 tread wear rating, traction rating of AA, and temperature rating of A.

The Dunlop Direzza Sport Z1 Star Spec is its Extreme Performance Summer tire and it has performed very well in independent tires tests. This particular tire is suitable for F-Body pro-touring, autocrossing, and road racing. The Direzza Sport Z1 Star Spec comes up to temperature quickly and delivers phenomenal grip. The tread compound features continuous shoulder ribs and big shoulder blocks. The carcass has two wide steel belts reinforced by JointLess Band (JLB) Technology. The structure of the tire also contains steel cord reinforced two-ply polyester sidewalls, and spiral-wound polyamide to maintain uniform roundness. This tire has a 200 tread wear rating, A traction rating, and A temperature rating.

Installing Mini-Tubs

If you're going to run 17-inch or larger wheels with 275 width or larger, they do not fit under the current bodywork, and as a result you need to install wheel tubs to fit the large tires required for maximum performance. Many wheel tub kits are available on the market for first- and second-generation F-Body cars. These include Chassisworks and DSE. These kits make completing these projects much easier than having to fabricate all the parts. However, you need to keep in mind that installing wheel tubs requires extensive cutting, fitting, welding, and often some fabrication.

Installing mini-tubs can be done over a period of weeks and roughly 40 to 60 hours, depending on your skill level. You're widening the wheel wells and this is reducing interior space in the back, so you often have to shorten or eliminate the back seat. In addition, you often need to run shorter axles. While it isn't the most difficult and complex project, it is not a project for beginners. Performing a mini-tub install requires a fair amount of welding and metal fitting skills as well as patience.

You need to be careful if your car has a fresh paint job because you don't want to damage it. It's also smart to take caution not to scratch your paint or get near it with heat, even if the paint is old. I needed to install mini-tubs so I could fit the 18 x 12-inch tires under the quarter panels. These wheels provide a huge contact patch that enables the engine to transmit its power to the ground.

Each kit contains extensive instructions, templates, and parts needed to complete the project. First, you need to strip the interior of the car: seats, carpet, plastic interior pieces, and all the other parts that cover the trunk wall and the wheel wells. In a nutshell, you need to remove the old inner tubs.

Drill out the spot welds, place the template over the wheel well, and mark the cut lines with a sharpie or scratch shawl. Then use a pneumatic rotary grinding tool with 3-inch cut-off wheel to cut out the old wheel tubs.

Some kits require notching the rear frame rails to fit the new and larger tubs. If this is the case, the frame needs to be reinforced. Fitting the new inner tubs requires a lot of trial fitment and minor cutting in the appropriate places. Most kits have some trim or reinforcement strips that require extra cutting of the rear wheel well and trimming, fitting, and welding. As each install is somewhat different, you need to make new plates out of a minimum of 1/8-inch plate steel.

After welding the plates into place you can put the new inner tubs in and weld them into place. This can be somewhat difficult as you weld two vastly different thicknesses of steel. I fill small holes with thin-gauge sheet metal and finish off the install with a thick layer of seam sealer all around inside and out of the new tubs.

Once the tubs have been installed, you need to paint them in the wheel well, the trunk, and the passenger compartment.

Brake Systems

For the first two years of production, F-Body brake performance was lackluster to say the least with four-wheel drum brakes on many cars. Chevy offered a heavy-duty brake service package and JL8 brake system; a four-wheel disc brake system, was a rare option in 1969. The JL8 was not a great brake system and the brakes that followed on the second-generation cars weren't great either.

To determine which brakes are best for your F-Body and application, you need to determine the relative size of the brake rotors and calipers because these parts must fit under the wheels. You need to consider styling price, overall production quality, and suitable strength for your application.

Brakes are your number-one safety feature so you need to invest in a top-quality brake system, such as from Wilwood, Baer, AP Lockheed, or another manufacturer. I strongly recommend against using off-brand brakes. You don't want to use suspect or substandard brakes because a loss or failure in braking power puts your life and others' lives at risk. Therefore, the braking power needs to be at least equal to if not greater than the power output of your car. The stock brakes on an F-Body car are not designed to handle the increased speed and performance of an LS engine. A stock LS engine produces about 400 hp, and most of the installs I've run across have well beyond that.

When upgrading the power, it's also important to take safety into consideration. The brakes are your defense against plowing into the car in front of you and help you avoid

CHASSIS AND SUSPENSION

hazardous conditions. Making sure you can stop in time is equally, if not more, important than getting your car up to speed. If you're using your F-Body for street cruising and have only a few hard-braking situations, you could use the stock brakes, but I still wouldn't recommend it. If you're increasing the horsepower and torque significantly over stock, you need a brake system to match it. Brakes turn kinetic (motion) energy into thermal (heat) energy, and a high-performance F-Body needs large discs, calipers, pads, and the right brake fluid to handle all this energy and heat created by high-speed and aggressive braking. Achieving top brake performance is part of getting maximum performance from your car.

If you're building a high-performance street car, street/strip car, autocross, road race, or pro-touring car (and that's what this book is for), aftermarket high-performance brakes suited for these applications are an absolute must. I implore you to always upgrade to the best braking package you can afford so that you can enjoy your F-Body for a lot longer. After all, you can never have brakes that are too powerful or responsive.

You need to be sure your wheels are large enough to accept large aftermarket brake rotors and calipers. Wilwood, Baer, and other top manufacturers typically require the use of 15-inch or larger wheels for many of their top brake kits. If you're building a genuine high-performance F-Body, you should be installing a 17-inch or larger wheel. Many owners are using 18-inch wheels so brake caliper clearance with the wheel is more than adequate.

The aftermarket offers a wondrous variety of brake system kits and brake parts for your F-Body car. While I can't possibly cover every single combination for wheel sizes and popular suspension setups, here are some popular brake manufacturers.

Wilwood

A top manufacturer of high-performance brakes for several decades, Wilwood offers several brake systems that are designed for the F-Body. All the major aftermarket brake companies, including Wilwood, offer disc brake conversions as well as drum to disc brake conversion kits that contain all the brackets and hardware.

If you're converting a disc-brake 1968–1969 Camaro, Wilwood offers the D52 calipers as one of the easiest brake upgrades for an F-Body because it's a direct bolt on to the existing brackets.

If you've chosen to stick with smaller or stock-type 15-inch wheels, they are a suitable choice because they clear most wheels of this size.

The dual-piston aluminum calipers replace the stock single-piston calipers but provide far superior braking performance. The dual-piston design applies pressure across a larger surface area of the backing plate so it provides greater braking power and more consistent pressure against the rotor.

The forged aluminum caliper body is far more rigid than the stock cast caliper body so it provides exceptional strength as well as cooling. The floating Wilwood caliper operates by sliding on two pins and pulling both pads into the rotor with about equal pressure. These substantially stronger calipers and the stainless-steel design provides improved performance over the long haul because the pistons don't rust or pit like the cast OEM calipers. In addition, the pistons maintain their seals better.

For the rear axle, Wilwood offers the aluminum dual-piston D154 caliper but these are smaller than D52 front caliper for accurate brake bias with the front end.

The Dynapro brake system calipers and rotors are the next step up from the D52 parts and deliver a substantial increase in brake performance. The Dynapro Big Brake Front Brake Kit (PN 140-10510) supplies massive stopping power and features 12.18-inch rotors with four-piston calipers. These brake kits are a cost-effective solution for high-performance street use and some track use.

For a significant step up in braking power from stock, you can opt for a Dynapro 6 Big Brake Front Brake Kit (PN 140-10738). This brake improvement kit features Dynapro six-piston calipers and 12.19-inch rotors in a standard or drilled-and-slotted style.

Many owners building track cars and pro-touring cars choose the Dynapro 6 Big Brake Front Brake Kit (PN 140-104485) because it features the large 12.88-inch rotors in slotted or drilled-and-slotted style and forged Superlite 6R six-piston calipers. With the 13-inch rotors, the minimum wheel size is 17 inches.

Further up the product list is the Forged Billet Superlite brakes that feature 13-inch rotors in slotted or cross-drilled style with six-piston calipers. The billet brake calipers offer increased strength and improved cooling over the cast-aluminum calipers.

For F-Body rear axles, Wilwood offers rear brake kits, including the Forged Dynalite Rear Parking Brake Kit (PN 140-7149) featuring Forged Dynalite four-piston calipers. These calipers fit the 12.19-inch rotors in a standard or drilled-and-slotted style that works with the internal drum parking brake system. Additional kits are available to fit your particular application.

During the 1970s, the steering spindle evolved and became larger, but the Wilwood brake kits are compatible with these spindle changes, including the larger 1979 spindle.

Baer

Baer is known for its killer brake components so it was an easy call to install top-shelf Baer brakes with a 14-inch rotor and six-piston caliper combination front and rear to complement my killer wheel and tire package. (I used Baer PN 4301352 for the front brakes and 4302351 for the rears.) These massive rotors and premium-quality calipers deliver top performance on a road course as well as the street.

When selecting Baer brakes for your car, you need to select the brake kit for a particular spindle whether it's stock, ATS, or SS4-Plus Deep Stage. In this particular Pro-Plus kit you get a six-piston billet caliper with stainless steel pistons, abutments, noise suppression springs, and dual seals. The calipers hold 1997–2004 Corvette C5 and the 2005–2012 C6 pads for high-performance and easy replacement. High-performance 14-inch rotors are a one-piece design. A hat brake uses a drum for the rear brake system. If you have a C-clip axle, the kit includes Baer's Verislide self-centering brackets.

The Pro kit is the same basic system as the Pro-Plus kit but with a one-piece rotor instead of a two-piece. Don't be told by competitors that a six-piston rear is too much brake. Due to the fact that Baer builds all its own calipers I can spec the rear piston sizes to function properly, but also allow the use of a standard two-port firewall mounted master. In C-clip applications Baer's Verislide self-centering brackets provide the only proper engineering solution to mounting opposed piston calipers on C-clip bearings in housing-style axles. I also stagger the rear piston size (as with the front) to correctly minimize pad taper issues. Due to different wheel builds, templates are always recommended to verify fitment of the brake. Templates can be found in the catalog section of the Baer site once you search by your make and model.

The Baer Claw Pro-Plus disc brake kit converts four-wheel drum F-Body cars to four-wheel disc brakes. These are built for rigorous use under competition use so they are also suitable for high-performance running. The Baer 6P compact six-piston calipers are machined from 2618 forgings so they provide minimal deflection and excellent cooling under high operating temperatures. The brake rotors come with zinc-coated surfaces and a matched set of brake pads. The two-piece rotors have an aluminum hat for lighter weight and to accommodate rotor expansion. These kits provide exceptional performance but they are not cheap at more than $2,000.

Baer also has a kit that is a similar replacement to the factory disc brake kit. The kit contains 11-inch front discs and 10-inch rear discs, single-piston brake calipers, organic brake pads, caliper mounting brackets, stock-style spindles, gold cadmium-plated brake backing plates, single-piston brake calipers, and all related parts. The rear brakes can be installed on 10- or 12-bolt rear ends and with straight-across or staggered shock mounting locations. Baer offers 7-, 9-, or 11-inch brake boosters. These are dual-diaphragm units that are similar to the original AC Delco booster. The 7- and 9-inch brake boosters are compatible with most LS swaps while the 11-inch booster works with engines that have compact valve covers.

Prodigy Customs Brake Kit

A number of companies offer brake kits for the F-Body car as a complete bolt-on solution, and that includes spindles and other related parts. Prodigy Customs offers Total Car G-Machine Brake Packages for F-Body cars among many other popular muscle car models that contain high-quality Wilwood disc brake components. Many rotor and caliper combinations are offered so you can assemble anything from an entry level high-performance kit to an ultra-high-performance kit. All the pieces in the kits are compatible with one another.

This kit features front and rear Wilwood brakes. Up front, you can choose front rotors from 10.75 to 14 inches while the rear brakes are available in 12.2- to 14-inch rotors. You can fit the rotors with either four- or six-piston Dynalite and Superlite calipers. All related hardware is included so you can convert your F-Body to the latest aftermarket four-wheel disc brake system. Compatible hubs are included in these kits as well as front and rear steel braided brake hoses, adjustable proportioning valve, a safety wire kit, and pliers are included for the two-piece rotor assembly. ■

CHAPTER 4

FRONT-DRIVE ACCESSORIES

Many front-drive pulleys and kits are available from the aftermarket to suit a particular LS engine setup and accessory arrangement. Obviously, the LS engine was not designed specifically for first- or second-generation F-Body engine swaps. However, this engine series delivers exceptional performance, and with the correct complement of parts and some chassis modifications to the F-Body, it has proven to be an excellent power plant to replace the stock engine. In addition, you need to make a few minor adjustments to your car so it can have every major modern luxury that even the new fifth-generation F-Body is allowed. Fitting power steering, alternator, and even A/C components have all been worked out through a variety of methods using stock modern brackets.

There seems to be a lot of confusion about which accessories are compatible with which engines. The typical items that are hung on the front of the engine are the water pump, power steering pump, alternator, and A/C unit.

There are a few choices when it comes to obtaining and putting together a front-drive accessories kit. One is to head off to the local junkyard and start pulling parts. You save some money and get everything you need. However, I've found that in junkyard crawls, most of the components have either sat too long and collected a fair amount of rust, have been damaged by someone else who was less careful than I am, or that major components are missing.

To me it's a compromise. You certainly save a lot of money if you go the junkyard route. Used accessories and pulleys don't look shiny and new, like a full billet aluminum set from March Performance. The drawback is that you don't know what works and what doesn't until

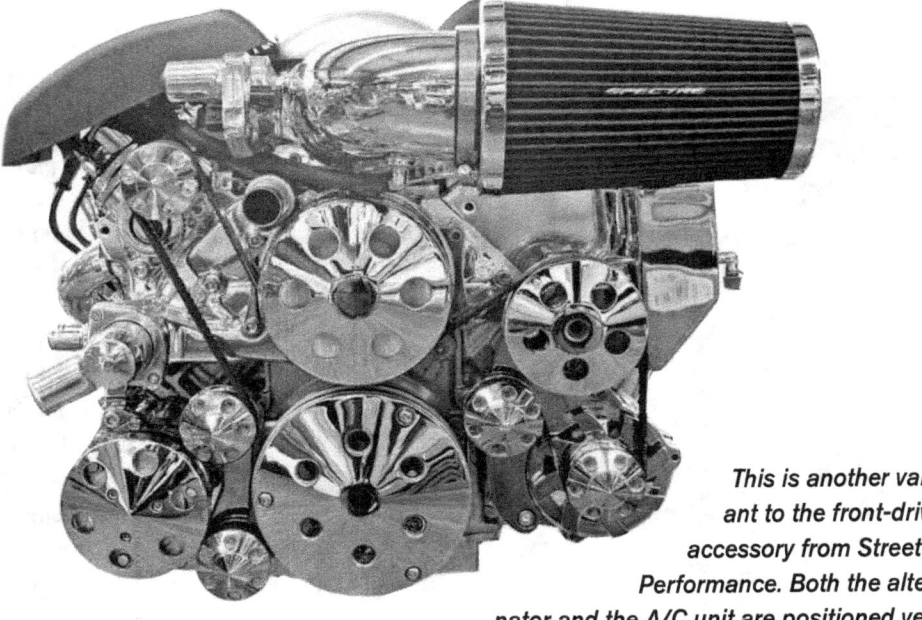

This is another variant to the front-drive accessory from Street & Performance. Both the alternator and the A/C unit are positioned very low, and this provides the "tight" look some people want. The LS platform allows for a variety of combinations to suit any need. (Photo Courtesy Street & Performance)

SWAP LS ENGINES INTO CAMAROS & FIREBIRDS 1967–1981   59

CHAPTER 4

the time comes to fire it up. You also don't get the prettiest of parts so you may have to spend some time cleaning up the accessories. If you do go this route, I strongly recommend pulling more than you need, such as the bolts and brackets. The LS drive system uses some specially sized bolts that might be difficult to find at a local hardware store. Also, take note that the three styles (Camaro, Corvette, and Truck) are not necessarily interchangeable, which means you might be limited in finding parts if your local yard doesn't have a lot of Corvettes in stock, for example.

The other side of the equation is buying new. Lots of options are out there to fit your needs. General Motors sells full kits with brackets, bolts, components, and belts for about $700 to $1,000. With these you typically get a warranty and the knowledge that the parts are brand new. You might not be able to save as much money, but you get a set of instructions, unlike pulling them off a wrecked car. Again, the compromise comes down to time versus money: How much of each are you willing to give up?

Camaro, Corvette, Truck and GM Kits

For the first- and second-generation F-Body, the Corvette accessory kit is most likely the best option as it moves the alternator and power steering pump into a location that does not interfere with the front K-member. This creates a new problem to resolve. The A/C pump that is located on the passenger's side in the low position must be relocated. You don't have to install or use an A/C system so that resolves the fitment problem, but for many, A/C is an absolute must. Using the Camaro, Corvette, or the truck kit, you shouldn't run into clearance issues with the radiator, assuming you've got the engine in the stock location.

A number of kits can be found at the junkyard or from a dealership, such as Scoggin-Dickey. Many owners use the Corvette-style drive kit because it gets the alternator out of the way. The various kits have major differences so once you decide on a kit, you are committed to that style. As a result, you're not able to interchange pieces and pulleys because the configurations are unique. Chevrolet Performance carries many of these kits.

The typical first-generation F-Body is most happy with the Corvette-style belt routing as it allows the alternator to be mounted high on the driver's side, well away from the frame and front steering components. In the second-generation F-Body, the alternator is low on the driver's side, which works provided you have clearance for the pitman arm. Due to tolerances you may have absolutely no interference and in other instances you may have to shave a little bit off the pitman arm bolts for full lock-to-lock steering.

Most owners don't run the truck accessories for several reasons, but chiefly it seems that they don't like the appearance of the accessories so far away from the engine. In some instances with various radiator and fan combinations, you may run into a lack of working space.

Chevrolet Performance LS2/LS3/LS7

The LS2/LS3/LS7 front kit is similar to the Corvette C5 kit. It moves the alternator up and away from the frame and it's great for LS swappers. This kit also puts the A/C compressor low and on the passenger's side, which does interfere with all first- and second-generation F-Body frames. You can, of course, forego the A/C compressor entirely and skip that problem. Be aware that is it not possible to reuse the VVT timing cover due to space constraints.

Front Accessory Drive Installation

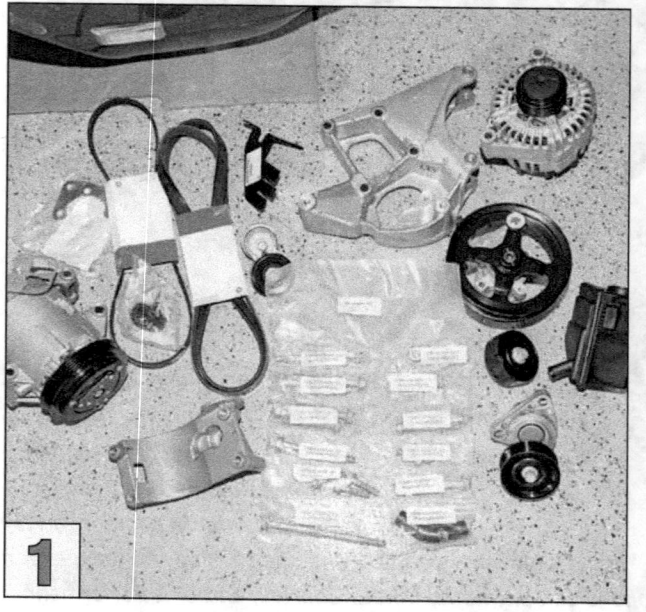

My accessory kit is from Scoggin-Dickey. It is the late-model Corvette style that calls for PN 1915506. I recommend the Corvette kit because it moves the alternator up and out of the way compared to the F-Body style. This is the kit that includes all the hardware and parts for the A/C compressor and bracket. This includes the nuts and bolts, clamps, PS pump, alternator, brackets, and belts. Beats sifting through a muday junk yard.

FRONT-DRIVE ACCESSORIES

2 The A/C bracket and unit are installed with a couple more bolts.

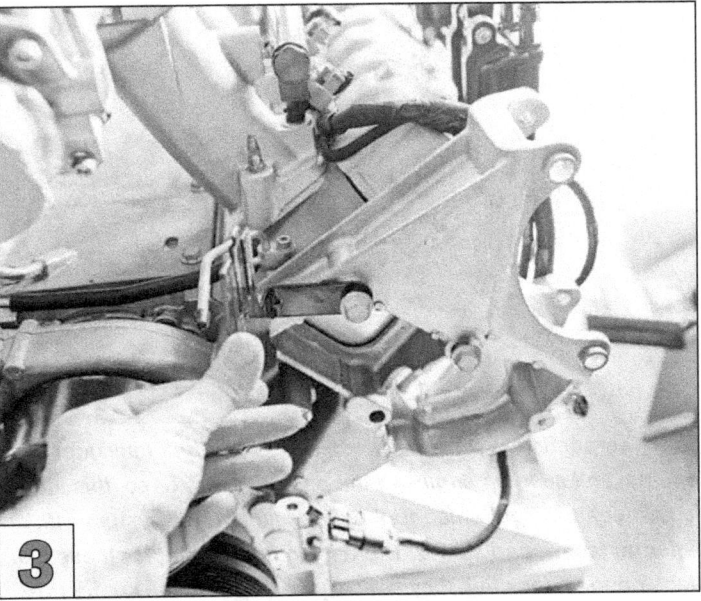

3 Near the massive alternator bracket is a series of bolts and an L-shaped bracket for the power steering assembly to clip onto. These have a specific order in which they are assembled, so be sure to keep the instruction book handy. With this setup, the brackets come first, then the power steering pump, followed by the alternator. The power steering pump has a bolt that goes through the pulley so make sure to install it.

4 The power steering reservoir and pump need to be installed as one unit; this allows you to make sure the reservoir tube is securely connected to the pump. The reservoir attaches to the pump through a small hose with small pressure clamps. They aren't delicate, but they also can't take a beating so care is needed when moving them. The pump came with the pulley already installed; this is a pressed-on piece and requires a special pulley remover if I want to replace it.

5 Seen through the spokes of the power steering pulley, a few extra bolts need to be installed with another L-shaped bracket (shown). This time, the bracket is aluminum.

Use a socket and ratchet to tighten the two bolts that fasten the alternator to the bracket.

6

SWAP LS ENGINES INTO CAMAROS & FIREBIRDS 1967–1981

7 Every serpentine system requires the use of a belt tensioner. If you haven't seen an engine in the past 20 years or so, this little guy keeps the right amount of belt tension on the system with an internal coil-wound spring. There is no adjustment for these belt tensioners. If they fail, they typically fail in the loose configuration, which is a telltale squealing from the belt during most of the operating RPM range.

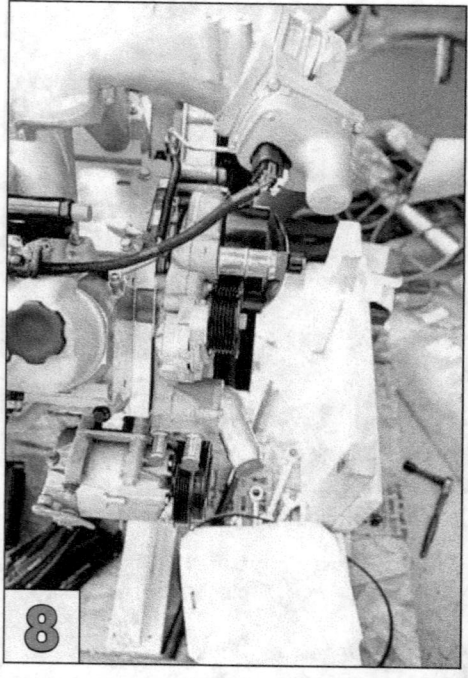

8 If you look closely, you can see that I made a major mistake. I incorrectly measured the crankshaft balancer and ordered the wrong kit. The balancer sticks out too far for the front-drive kit and would instantly throw the belt off if I could even get it on. Essentially, I have to replace the balancer to make it work.

9 Replacing the balancer bolt can be a difficult because it has a high torque spec. Use an impact wrench or a breaker bar to remove this bolt.

10 Once the balancer bolt has been removed, carefully install the balancer puller. Position the arms of the puller to engage the balancer and thread the puller bolt until it firmly snugs up against the crankshaft snout. Once it's snug, use a breaker bar to tighten the puller and drive the balancer off the crankshaft taper. Remove the balancer one turn at a time. You can damage the internal threads on the crank, so make sure you use the correct leverage method for your puller.

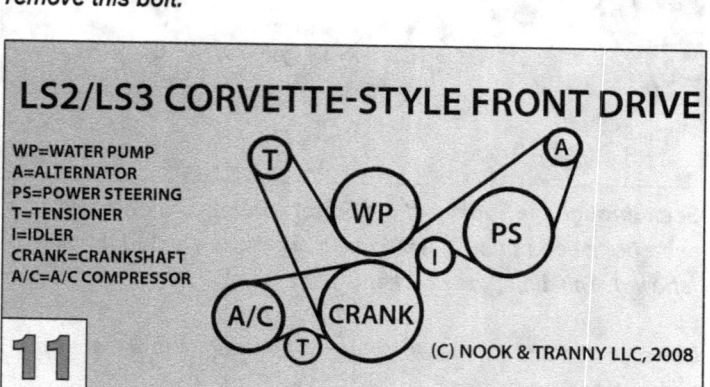

11 Probably the most useful stock kit on the market is the LS2/LS3 front-drive kit. It moves the alternator up and out of the way. The one drawback is that this kit uses the balancer that is closest to the block, making you come up with a creative way to route power steering lines. (Illustration Courtesy Nook & Tranny)

Chevrolet Performance CTS-V/GTO/G8/LS6/LS2

You can get these pulleys from junkyard engines and use them on most LS engines. This kit can be adapted to almost any block/head combination, but you need to pull the balancer and pulley off the particular engine so the entire group properly matches. This kit typically comes on LS2 engines as well in the Pontiac G8, F-Body, and GTO.

Again, frame clearance is a problem for the A/C compressor. Notch the frame, move it out of the way with an aftermarket kit, or skip it. It's your call.

LS9/LSA Front Kit

The LS9 front-drive kit is unique. Unfortunately, there are not a lot of alternative options out there for LS9 engines other than the GM kit (PN 19243524). The supercharger requires its own special belt and the routing of all the accessories. At the time of writing this, there are no alternatives for remounting the A/C compressor from its stock location. That means that you have to notch the frame on virtually all frame choices available, stock, or otherwise. Companies can and often notch it for you, but that typically involves a separate and extra cost. You can of course, notch it yourself as Mark Stielow has done on his 1969 Camaro "Red Devil," if you are brave enough and have the correct skill and tools to complete the job. Chances are that if you are looking at putting the LS9 in your F-Body, you won't mind the $1,800 price of the GM front-drive kit.

Balancers and Dampeners

To date there are three basic balancers that General Motors made at the factory: Corvette style, Camaro/F-Body style, and truck dampener. General Motors did this mainly for space constraints. The major difference is the distance the belts are from the block when everything is fully installed. All dampeners fit the crank of the LS engine; it's up to you to figure out the version you need.

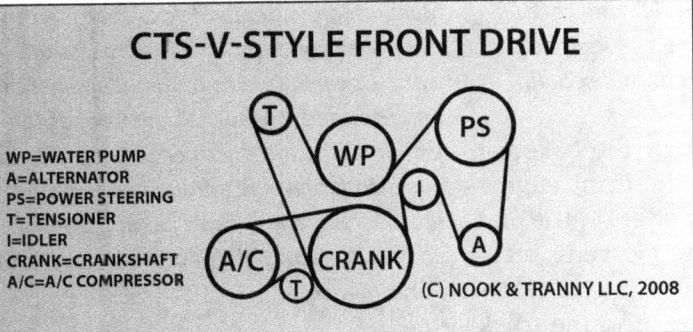

The A/C compressor runs off a separate belt that is behind the main longer belt. Even though the LS9 and CTS-V are similar in many ways, their front drive configurations are entirely different. (Illustration Courtesy Nook & Tranny)

The CTS-V front drive requires significant modification to work with just about any platform. You have to watch out for frame clearance issues as well as suspension clearance problems.

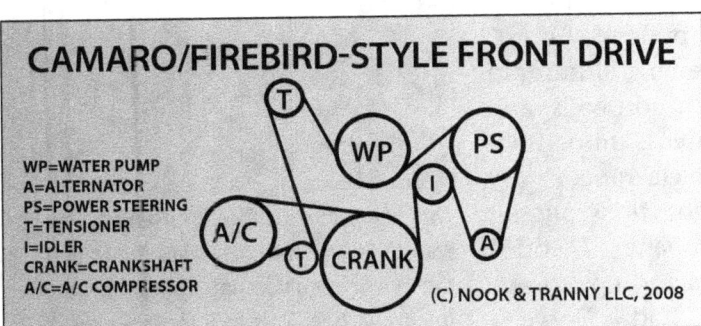

Unfortunately, the bad news is that front drives are not all that interchangeable. Once you go with a certain kit, you will always need to select compatible pulleys and parts. The truck version keeps accessories more vertical and might work for those trying to get the alternator off the frame. (Illustration Courtesy Nook & Tranny)

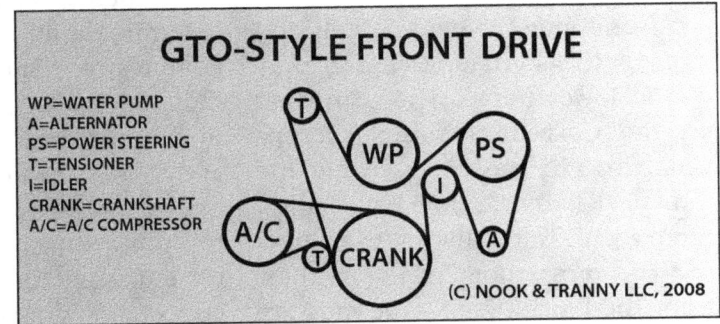

The Camaro/Firebird/GTO front-drive setup can be used if you have room for the low-mounted alternator but most first- and second-generation F-Body swaps do not have enough room to mount it low. (Illustration Courtesy Nook & Tranny)

CHAPTER 4

Here's a quick comparison of crankshaft balancers. The longer one (left) is the Camaro style and the shorter one (right) is the Corvette style.

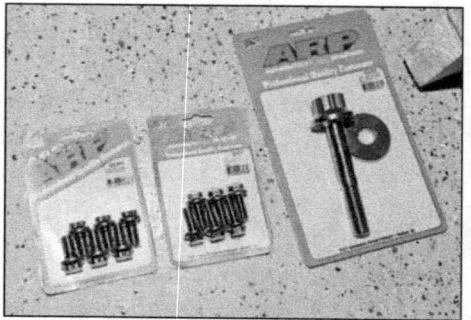

I bought the new ARP balancer bolt (PN 234-2503) on the right from Amazon. This should fit most, if not all, LS applications. The only difference is the 12-sided bolt head instead of the standard hex bolt.

Measuring the depth of your setup to see what style you have is fairly straightforward. Use a flat piece of metal against the balancer and measure to the front of the engine. Although the truck version may be easy to identify, the differences between the Corvette and F-Body version are not so readily apparent. (Photo Courtesy KWiK Performance)

Remember, you need to use the same type of accessories. In other words, you cannot use a Corvette balancer with a truck power-steering pulley because the offset differs too much. You must also match the water pump pulley with the similar offset of the balancer. The Corvette and Camaro/F-Body style accepts the same water pump, but do not play well with the truck water pump pulley.

Three different crankshaft dampeners fit the LS engine, which are the Corvette, Camaro/GTO/Firebird, and truck. All of these pulleys fit virtually any LS application. The determining factor is how close you want the accessories to hug the block. I chose to go with the Corvette kit to obtain adequate clearance and accessory packaging. With these pulleys, the accessories hug the block closely and it moves the alternator out of the way of the lower frame. The dampener on the Corvette typically mounts very close to the block, while the Camaro/F-body version has slightly more room. Naturally the truck having the most room is the farthest from the block. Use a tape measure and a straight edge to determine which dampener you have. Stick the tape measurer through the balancer to measure it from the front engine cover to the straight edge on the end of the balancer. The Corvette measures $2\tfrac{1}{8}$ inches, the Camaro/GTO/Firebird is $2\tfrac{15}{16}$ inches, and the truck is $3\tfrac{11}{16}$ inches.

Installing a New Balancer

A swapping project is not precise science because there are differences in the engine equipment and accessories, and as a result many variables come into play. As part of that, there are countless combinations and many manufacturing variances from one F-Body car to another. It's difficult to determine if all components for a particular build package are compatible with one another. Therefore, until you install all the components, you cannot definitely determine if all the pulleys, the A/C compressor, dampener, aluminum radiator, headers, ignition coils, and many other components properly fit and there's adequate clearance.

For example, I got the wrong kit for the wrong dampener. I ended up replacing the balancer with the correct version. (We had a Corvette accessory drive kit and an F-Body-style balancer.)

To remove the old dampener correctly, you need two very important tools: a big three-jaw-style puller and a flywheel lock-down tool. If you don't have one, you can use a pry bar, but I don't recommend it.

A breaker bar or impact gun with a 15/16-inch six-point socket is required to remove this bolt with traditional thread style. This factory

This is the correct tool for doing anything with the crankshaft. It holds the teeth of the flywheel so you can tighten or loosen the crank bolt. This tool replaces the starter and bolts in using the existing boltholes.

FRONT-DRIVE ACCESSORIES

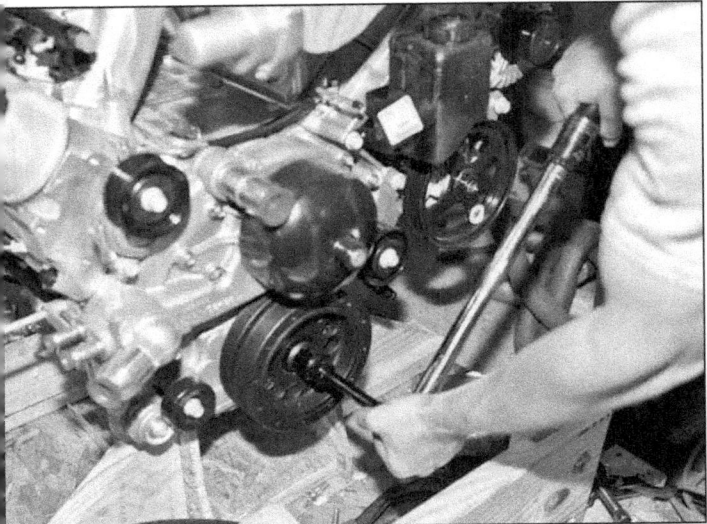

Use a torque wrench to install the new ARP crank bolt with 250 ft-lbs of force.

A three-jaw gear clamp helps remove the balancer in small increments. Some force here is necessary.

bolt stretches so it's recommended that you replace it with a new one on re-assembly.

Once the bolt has been removed, install the three-jaw puller over the dampener and tighten the puller end until the dampener pops off the crankshaft taper. You may have to use the old crank bolt as leverage. Once the balancer is out of the way is a good time to replace the seal if yours needs it.

Installing the new dampener isn't very complicated. You need the proper tool or an M16 x 2.0-mm threaded rod and some washers with a nut. This exemplifies (once again) the need for proper tools for the right job. Just don't use a block of wood and a hammer because you can damage the dampener and/or the crank snout.

You need to use the old crank bolt. Thread the old bolt to cinch the pulley into place by tightening it to 250 ft-lbs of torque. Now, remove it, install your new bolt, and follow the instructions. Mine is from ARP and uses a 12-point socket to torque to 250 ft-lbs.

Aftermarket Options

In another stroke of good luck for first- and second-generation F-Body owners, the aftermarket has many solutions for fitting front-drive accessories with a variety of equipment packages. While these may not be the most inexpensive options, they resolve many packaging and fitment issues. Most kits come with a power-steering delete or an A/C delete option, but not both. For many kits, you also need to determine the compatible headers, frame, and mounts because these components can interfere with some of the front drive components.

Vintage Air

The high-quality Vintage Air Front-Runner System features a Sanden SD7 compressor with O-ring adapter blocks, which works well with their under-dash retro-fit A/C units. A Vintage Air kit comes with everything needed to mount your LS engine with the proper accessories. It moves the A/C compressor up and out of the frame location and moves the power-steering reservoir to the rear behind the belt. This is different than the stock front-drive kit that places the reservoir next to the alternator up high. These systems also come with options to delete the A/C pump or the power-steering pump, but not both. Vintage Air is probably the only kit that is able to retrofit just about any F-Body with A/C if yours didn't come with one or you just really want to hide it under the dash.

Eddie Motorsports

Eddie Motorsports has several versions and options for LS front-drive kit, which includes A/C or no A/C and power steering or no power steering, or all of the above. Like most kits, you can get Eddie's S-Drive kit in polished or milled finished to fit your application. These kits use an ATI balancer so they can be used on all the LS variations, except the 4.8L version.

Complete kits contain an Edelbrock water pump, Sanden A/C compressor, Maval power-steering pump, and Powermaster 140-amp alternator. They are compatible with

SWAP LS ENGINES INTO CAMAROS & FIREBIRDS 1967–1981

The factory Camaro setup has a slight alteration on the lower A/C belt that has been converted to a single belt. It has been moved slightly to align with the rest of the accessories to run a single belt rather than two individual ones. You see how the older fourth-generation front-drive kit looks from this view. (Photo Courtesy Street & Performance)

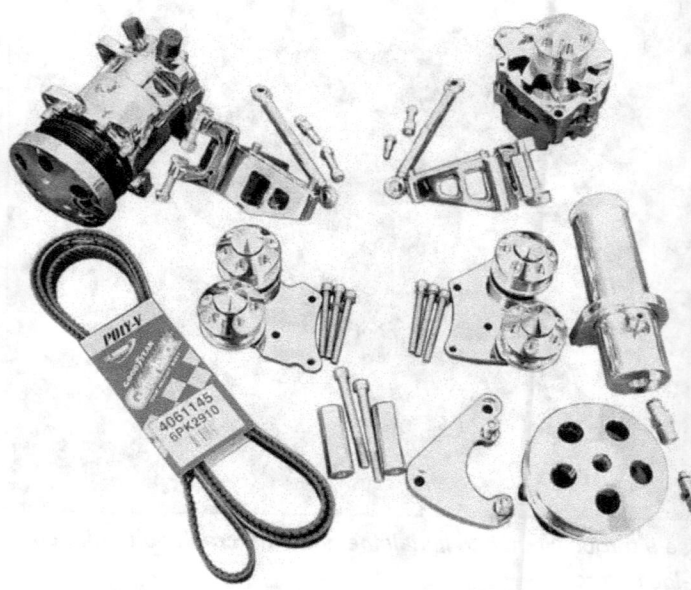

Aftermarket kits, such as these, are plentiful. This is a chrome version from Street & Performance: they can make a system that is as tight to the engine or as loose to the engine as you want with just about any configuration of the accessories. Therefore, you can order a custom exhaust to fit about any special requirement for an equipment package. If an off-the-shelf accessory package won't do, Street & Performance can build the correct system for you. (Photo Courtesy Street & Performance)

This version of the front-drive kit pushes the A/C and alternator out from under the engine and to the sides. Some like this look; others don't. (Photo Courtesy Street & Performance)

Another variant of the LS family is this LS6 setup with the alternator placed up high. This setup is much more friendly to hot rodders and Camaro swappers. (Photo Courtesy Street & Performance)

FRONT-DRIVE ACCESSORIES

rack-and-pinion as well as gearbox steering systems. Eddie Motorsports says that they include $800 worth of brand-new parts in the kit.

The kits include all the 6061-T6 billet aluminum pulleys and brackets for all of the components. This setup moves the alternator up and out of the way and also relocates the A/C compressor into a much more friendly area, which makes this kit very agreeable to almost any build. A complete kit costs $2,400 and has all the necessary front-drive accessories and pulleys. It's a very reasonable price, especially if you don't have any front-drive parts. Not only does it dress up the engine bay, it solves all of the front-drive problems at once.

Texas Speed & Performance

Texas Speed & Performance probably has the widest range of variations to the front-drive system. They custom-make systems to fit almost any need. Some of their full kits bring all the accessories close to the engine block and others spread them out. It's really up to you and what look you're going for. You can choose virtually any placement of the components and you can even get custom colors if you ask them nicely.

KWiK Performance

Air compressors for the LSX version from General Motors uses a variable-displacement compressor so it only works as hard as it needs to and is required by the A/C cooling load requirement. This was designed to improve fuel economy as the A/C compressor robs the engine of a significant amount of power, thus requiring more fuel to compensate for the loss.

KWiK Performance says some of people run into problems when installing A/C systems with modern compressors and try to use the old-style control units in old cars. They recommend that you replace the newer-style compressor with a conventional Sanden compressor, which is a constant running type of pump. These compressors are also smaller in size and may fit better with the engine package in your F-Body.

The Sanden SD5 part numbers for this conversion are 4514, 4522, 4665, and 9537. Sanden makes a variety of compressors, so you should call them to make sure the particular compressor is compatible with your engine setup. The KWiK Performance A/C compressor has a six-groove pulley as opposed to the five-groove belt that is used on the GM setup. You can simply slide the belt over and align it to the correct five grooves on the pulley. Apply the correct amount of tension and the belt stays in position and operates reliably.

Air-Conditioning Relocation Kit Installation

This version of the LS kit allows for everything to be out of the way without sacrificing any room. It replaces virtually every piece from the stock kit and uses its own brackets, pumps, and pulleys. The A/C unit from a stock Camaro or Corvette is not a good candidate because it uses pulse modulation, which many aftermarket kits don't use. A Sanden pump is a direct replacement.

KWiK Performance has this alternative setup for people with lots of hood clearance but a very narrow space.

CHAPTER 4

I felt that I only needed the A/C unit kit from KWiK Performance seeing that the rest of the system fit quite well in my 1968 Camaro test vehicle. The kit comes with all the hardware, brackets, and other stuff you need for the job. The Sanden pump was a bit extra but worth it knowing I was getting the right part.

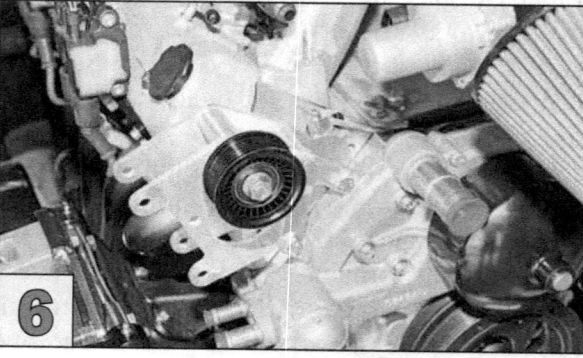

I pre-assembled the brackets for a smoother install.

I've installed the brackets on the engine. This process is a bit tricky and the parts are precisely machined so it might be worth having another pair of hands.

I replaced the tensioner pulley after unpacking the KWiK Performance A/C relocation kit. I simply threaded the tensioner pulley bolt onto the bracket and torqued it down.

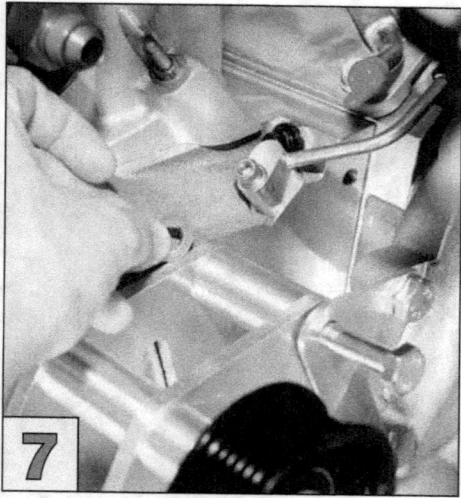

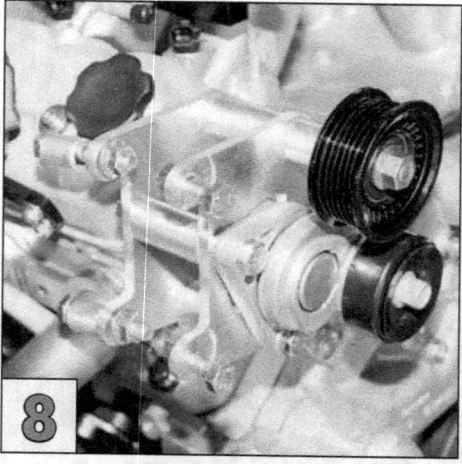

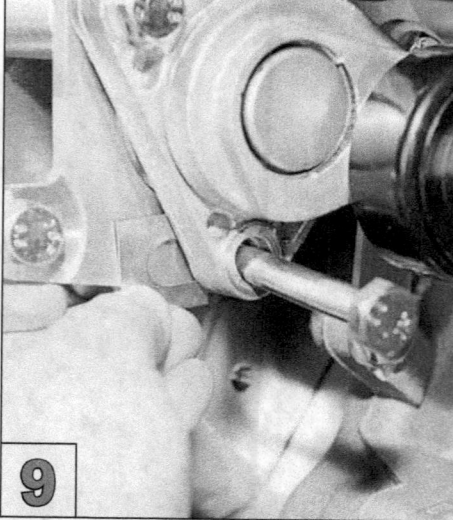

A small washer (provided in the kit) was needed to align the belt pulleys. The washer/spacer was placed between the bracket and the block to push the pulleys slightly forward for a more positive alignment.

Be very careful at this stage. The bolts need to go on in a specific way with the spacers in the back. Once again, you need a second or third pair of hands. The bolts must go through the bracket and the spacers (in that order) for everything to align properly.

The tensioner needed a small spacer for proper alignment. Yours might align just fine or it might be like mine and need a spacer in certain places. This is typical for any installation, so keep a few handy.

FRONT-DRIVE ACCESSORIES

This is the correct bolt pattern and spacer requirement for the pump. It helps to start with the lower bolts and then move to the upper ones.

Using a box-end wrench and a socket, I snugged everything down once I was happy with the location of the six-ribbed belt. The Sanden unit has a seven-ribbed pulley that works just fine with the belt.

I am ready to install a new belt on the new system. I like this setup as it uses one belt instead of two serpentine belts. I also had to tweak the pulley setup on the new A/C bracket. I had some clearance issues and had to change a few things. After only an hour, I was set.

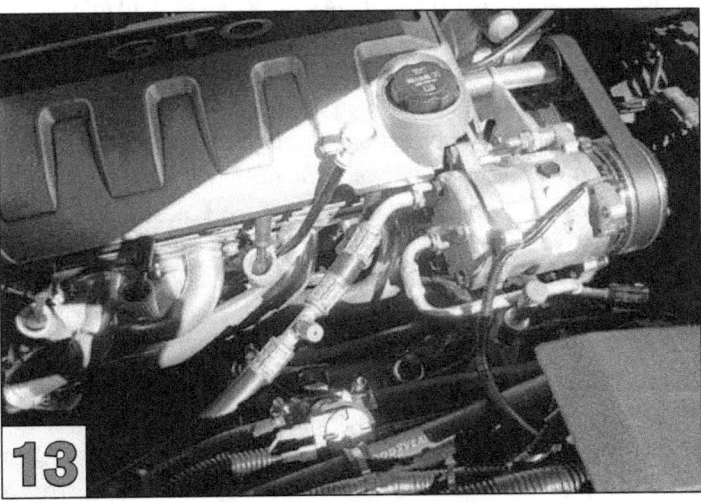

The KWiK setup and the original coil covers are compatible. This photo proves that it can work and provides ample clearance. (Photo Courtesy KWiK Performance)

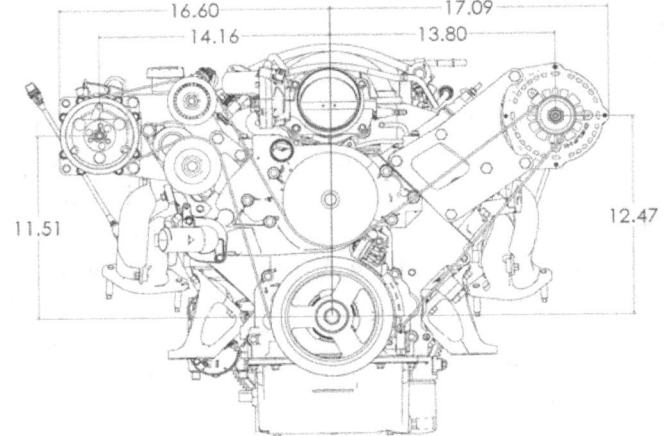
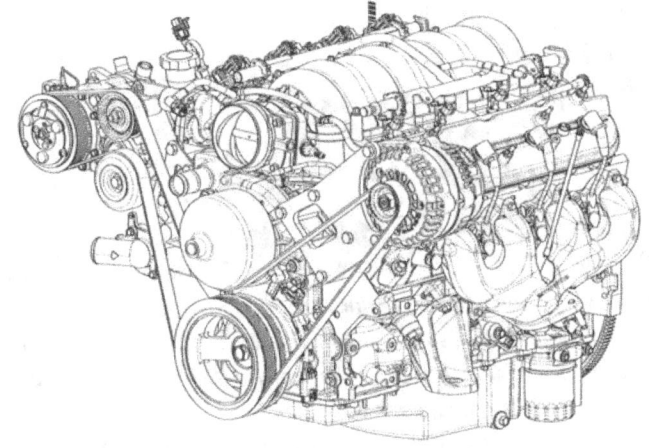

If you choose to forego the power steering on your vehicle (I highly discourage it) KWiK Performance has you covered. At left is a diagram of the dimensions and on the right is a good look at the final outcome. (Illustrations Courtesy KWiK Performance)

SWAP LS ENGINES INTO CAMAROS & FIREBIRDS 1967–1981

CHAPTER 4

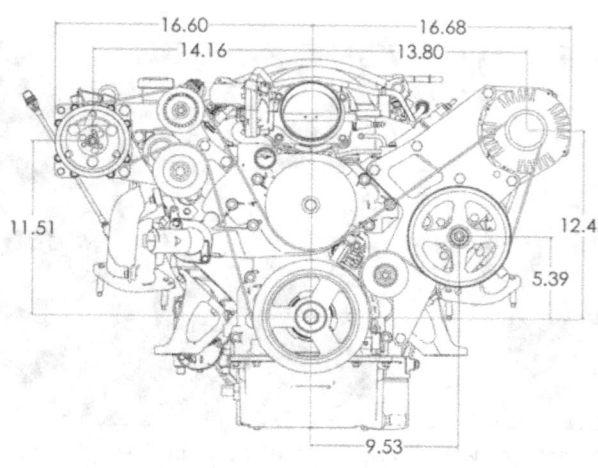

This accessory drive kit from KWiK Performance has the adjustability and the adaptability that's suitable for most LS engine swap projects. The KWiK system is a universal system that moves the major components away from the frame and suspension components. The drawback is that the accessories are moved upward, which can be slightly detrimental to performance. The system uses one long belt instead of two belts as with the factory setup. (Photo Courtesy KWiK Performance)

You have a lot of adjustability with this accessory drive setup. You relocate the A/C compressor and accessory pulleys to make space for various components.

Helpful Hints

It should go without saying, but it's usually best to install the accessories after the engine is firmly between the frame rails. You save weight, but also you reduce the amount of mistakes you can make by breaking something.

When installing a kit, it's fairly common to install the water pump and dampener before any other accessories. A few of the bolts in the power-steering assembly require the bolts to be installed through holes on the pulley; make sure you lay everything out and in order.

For example, I had to remove the power-steering pulley to access the high-pressure hose. Had I been smarter, I would have figured this part out before installing it. It would have been a lot easier than having to buy a pulley puller and learning how to use it.

The return hose on the power-steering reservoir is a 3/8-inch outbarbed fitting. You may need an adapter on the steering box or rack. Make sure that whatever adapter you get has a matching 3/8-inch barb fitting. The pressure side requires a custom-made hose with the correct pressure hose that can withstand the higher pressures. These are typically made from -6AN line and hose ends. There are also other options for making this work such as having a local machine shop make you custom hoses.

This almost goes without saying, but having the correct tools is a lifesaver. This belt tensioner bar makes life easier in really tight spaces. That said, your LS install should create plenty of room. These tools are readily available at any parts store for roughly $20.

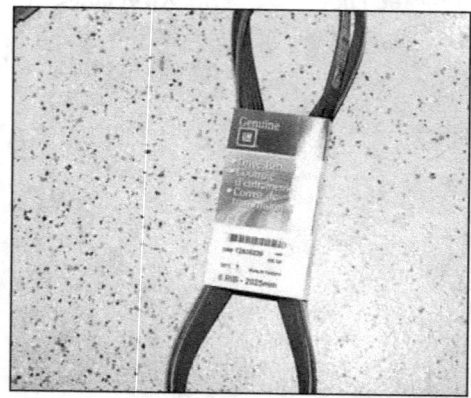

I had to try a number of belts to get it just right. I used a piece of string to came up with the correct measurement. You might have to find a belt between 1,000 and 1,020 mm to fit your pulleys. Of course, you can just use this belt (PN 12636226) if you plan to skip the A/C all together.

CHAPTER 5

FUEL SYSTEM

As has been mentioned before, the LS engines were not expressly designed to go between the frame rails of the first- or second-generation F-Body. Every modern LS engine is fuel injected while every early F-Body car carried a carbureted engine. Fuel injection has many different requirements than carbureted engines. To run the EFI system on an F-Body requires installation of more fuel system plumbing and either an internal or external electric fuel pump for the injection system. You also need to integrate the wiring into the main harness and install the drive-by-wire pedal. Even with these challenges, LS engines have been effectively installed in the 1967–1981 F-Body chassis and have delivered phenomenal performance.

The early Gen III engines from 1997 to 1998 and some 1999 engines used a return fuel line system while the 1999 and newer LS engines used a returnless fuel system. If you are installing a later-style Gen III or Gen IV engine, you don't have to route a fuel line back to the tank. If you're installing an LS with a return fuel line system, a regulator is installed between the fuel rail and tank to provide consistent fuel pressure. Then hoses must be run to a 3/8-inch supply fitting and 5/16-inch return fitting on the fuel rails.

Throughout this chapter, I show you various ways to build a fuel system for your LS-equipped F-Body car. I discuss the use of stock gas tank modifications all the way up to a custom-built stainless gas tank with a trick off-the-shelf pump. Of course there are many ways to complete the task and I can only show a few of them. This should help you decide the direction of your build.

By today's modern fuel injection standards, the first two iterations of

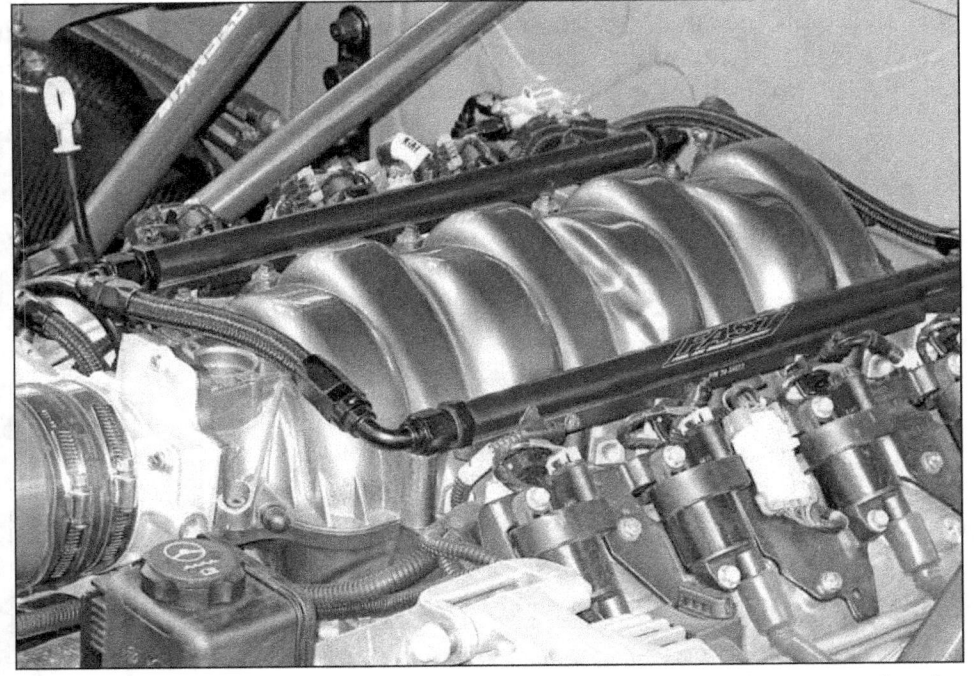
The FAST fuel injection system feeds the Chevy Fast Burn 385-ci engine in Mary Pozzi's 1973 Camaro. (Photo Courtesy Mary Pozzi)

SWAP LS ENGINES INTO CAMAROS & FIREBIRDS 1967–1981

the F-Body and its fuel system were crude and rudimentary. The stock F-Body used a mechanical fuel pump, which was driven off the camshaft, and it drew fuel from the gas tank to the engine. In addition, the LS engine has far greater fuel pressure requirements than the original carburetor-equipped F-Body. Carburetors were fairly reliable and easy to fix, but they featured a static setup and didn't change to accommodate varying conditions. They were prone to carbon build up and tended to blow out power valves if the car wasn't driven properly. Today, the fuel delivery system no longer requires engine power to drive the fuel pump and requires an electric pump to delivery fuel needs. The old system only needed a paltry 8 to 10 psi at the carburetor while an LS engine with an EFI needs a constant 58 psi at the fuel rail. This means that it's a necessity to upgrade your fuel system with an electric pump and a fuel pressure regulator. This means more forethought and some blueprinting of the new fuel system in your F-Body.

Proper Planning

A fuel system needs to be planned out prior to purchases being made and brackets formed. A solid fuel delivery system also requires a properly wired system. This means that you have to ask yourself what your plans are for your car so you can buy the correct combination of parts. One question that many folks face is, "Am I going to upgrade in the near future?" If the answer is yes, you might want to step up to a slightly better system to plan for the long haul.

A carbureted system needs roughly 8 psi to operate well under idle and under heavy loads. Unfortunately, the newer engines with EFI (and this includes the LS engines) require much greater fuel pressure and fuel system sophistication. The key number to remember here is 58 psi. If you are running a stock or mildly upgraded LS engine, this is all you need in terms of fuel delivery. If you are running an LSA or LS9, you might need to step up to a much better fuel delivery system that requires more than 58 psi. However, 58 psi is sufficient for most LS engines turning out 400 to 700 hp.

Fuel injectors require high pressure to deliver fuel into the combustion chamber in a microsecond. In order for the injectors to do their job, they need a constant supply of high-pressure fuel in sufficient quantities (flow rate) or the engine ceases running. In addition, the injectors need this much pressure to keep an even and consistent spray pattern. The system requires a constant high-pressure fuel to be available at all times. By comparison, a carburetor is vacuum operated and doesn't require high pressure to mix air and fuel together to feed the engine.

Fuel Pump

I went to Carl Casanova, the guru of fuel delivery, to gain insight and advice for planning and installing a fuel system. Carl has been known around the pro-touring and hot rodding fuel delivery arena for quite some time. You probably have seen his shiny red Gen I in multiple articles in various print and online publications. He teamed up with Hector Guerrero at Rick's Tanks to make a system that functions like factory equipment, with easy installation and the reliability of a rental car.

When it comes to fuel pumps, there are two basic kinds: in-tank and external. Both systems have advantages and disadvantages. The in-tank pumps tend to run quieter and cooler because they are immersed in fuel inside the tank. They also tend to perform at higher pressures. The trade-off is that they are often more complicated to install and relatively costly. To modify a stock system to work with an in-tank pump requires a greater investment of time and potentially more money.

To make your system an in-tank setup, you need the pump submerged in the tank as deep as possible but maintain a strong fuel feed. You don't want it choked off because of improper mounting. You need to mount the system carefully and properly for your particular setup and needs. This means you have

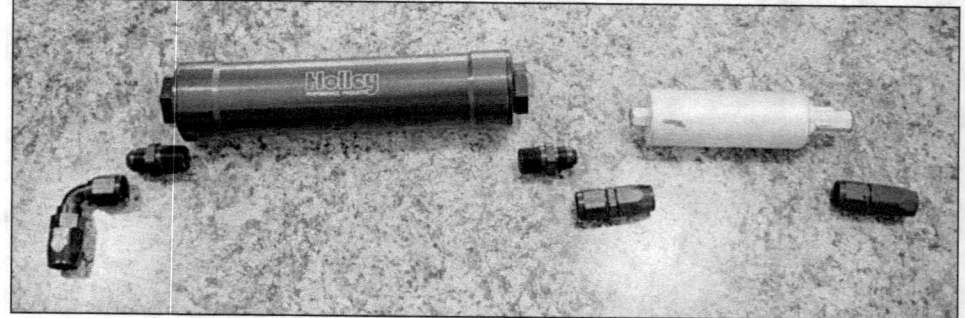

I've laid out a pre-filter (left) and the pump (right) to show you what it may take to make a system work. I left the post-filter out because you may not install one after-filter. The Corvette filter with the return line is a popular and practical choice.

FUEL SYSTEM

The regulator (if you chose to use one) also needs some planning as to how to route the fuel lines and a vacuum line. Most regulators on the market require it.

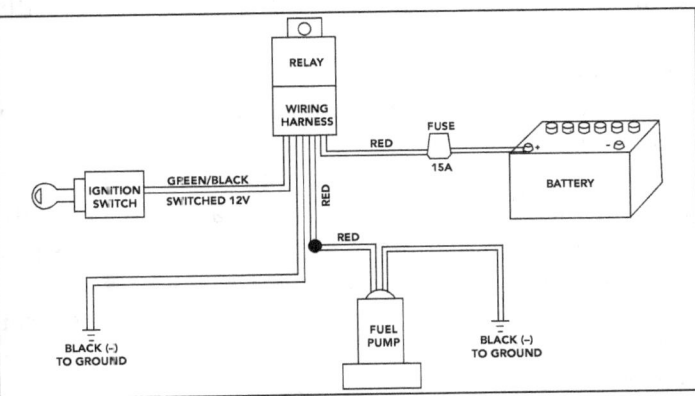

A relay is a fairly simple thing to wire. You need a constant 12-volt source such as a battery terminal or node, a ground, and an activator wire to the device you want to run. It clicks on when power is needed without overloading the system. It protects your vital electrical components as well as provides much needed power to things with heavy loads. (Illustration Courtesy Holley)

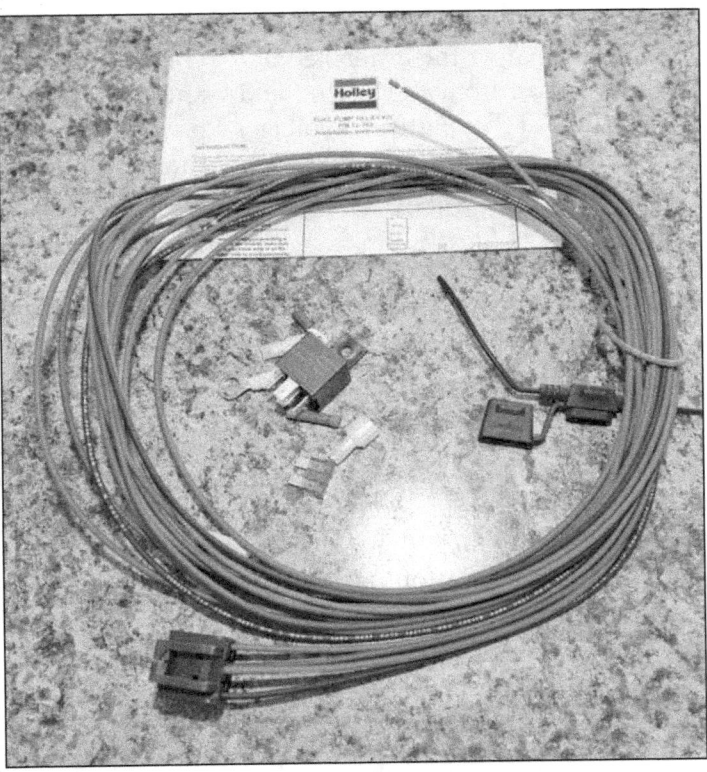

Holley's fuel pump relay kit is essential when installing a new pump. The relay provides power to the pump only when necessary. This prevents the pump from burning out prematurely and it shuts off when the key is in the off position.

to find a creative mounting system that is not only fuel resistant but also sturdy enough to handle a bit of abuse. Adequate tank pressure is necessary to keep the pressure up between the pump and the fuel line.

External pumps make the job a lot easier to install or replace in case of a failure because you can simply access the external pump where it's mounted to the chassis. With an in-tank system, the gas tank needs to be drained and dropped and then the pump has to be extracted from the tank. In-tank pumps are less expensive to purchase, but if you need to change a pump it costs a lot more in the long run. External pumps are typically noisier because they lack fuel to dampen the sound and they are exposed to the elements. In addition, the pump can transmit vibrations through the chassis to create noise.

The best and most logical place to put an external pump is as close to the gas tank as possible and at or below the fuel level. These pumps work best as "pushers" of fuel, rather than "pullers" of fuel. Pump life is extended because gravity is used to draw fuel to the pump and therefore a reduced load is placed on the pump to enhance longevity.

The other major problem with an external pump is that the fuel line is only pressurized *after* the pump. This means that the system relies on gravity to feed the pump. These pumps can provide some suction but should be gravity fed for optimal results. This means that your system can lose its siphon under hard cornering. If you plan to do any hardcore racing or severe lateral-g's, you should really look into an in-tank system.

Matching the fuel pump to the engine's fuel demands is vital. I recommend determining the amount of fuel needed for the engine, adding 10 percent for safety, then choosing the fuel pump that best matches the fueling need. A 255 lph fuel pump is usually a good starting point for comparison.

Determining which fuel pump is right for you requires a number of steps. First, you need to determine your engine's horsepower and torque target. It's typically safe to aim high here because it's better to have more fuel pump capacity rather than not enough. Second is finding the engine fuel efficiency and third is finding the maximum fuel pressure and flow volume you'll be running. Finally, you need to know the available voltage under load from the engine and flow volume at that particular voltage.

I spoke with an Aeromotive tech specialist about engine fuel efficiency, and he informed me that typically naturally-aspirated engines make roughly between .4 and .5 lb/hp/hr (pound per horsepower per hour). The tech strongly recommended engine dyno testing to determine your actual efficiency number, but these are good starting points. Engines with a nitrous addition often develop .5 to .6 lb/hp/hr and those with boosted applications are usually least efficient at ranges from .6 to .75 lb/hp/hr.

So, for example, if I used a 500-hp naturally-aspirated engine I would multiply 500 by .4 and get 200 pounds, which would be the expected fuel pump requirement. However, if I used a 500-hp engine that was boosted, I could potentially multiply that by .75 and get 375 pounds of fuel pump requirement. Aeromotive also informed me that this also plays a big factor in injector choice. Normally most engine builders like to use a duty cycle of .8, which gives them a window of 10 percent for unexpected occurrences.

Therefore, using our example of 500 hp and a naturally aspirated engine, I would get something like this:

500 hp x .4 = 200 lbs/hr
200 lbs/hr ÷ 8 injectors = 25 lbs/hr
25 lbs/hr ÷ .8 = 31.25 lbs/hr at
80-percent duty cycle

Next is finding the base fuel pressure for the engine, and of course, fuel system requirements change for boosted or nitrous applications. As pressure goes up, often pump volume goes down. It is important to check the fuel pump's specifications and read the flow charts for accurate pressure ranges. (If this is something that you find challenging, the Aeromotive tech line is a great place for asking questions about fuel pumps.) In the case of my build I knew going in that my LS3 as well as most LS applications require a constant 58 psi for the engine to run optimally throughout the power band.

Finally, you need to consider voltage. If the pump does not have the required power it under performs and does not run at peak efficiency. Higher voltage means that it increases power output so it is crucial to match your alternator's output with the fuel pump you are using to complement the entire system.

The following focuses primarily on fuel-injected setups, as those seem to have the most confusion. If you plan to run a carbureted LS engine, a lot of it doesn't apply.

External Fuel Pump Assembly

Several approaches can be used to install a fuel system. Often the most practical way to do this is with an external pump assembly. A few key features are critical when constructing a new delivery system. The best way to do this is to plan well ahead of your build so you don't end up having to redo it or buying the wrong parts. Remembering that an external pump works best as a pusher of fuel (not a puller) commands your next moves. You certainly want gravity to feed your pump, so it's best to place the pump as close to the tank sump as possible.

A typical setup consists of a pre-filter, pump, after-filter, fuel pressure regulator, return line, and feed line that is typically regulated by a vacuum source coming from the engine. The location of these components is dependent on available space. A lot of folks run the regulator on the firewall for easy access and that's typically a good idea. Keep in mind that you need to run a vacuum line and a return line back to the fuel tank. Some racing circuits do not allow this so you might have to get creative. For most street drives the firewall is the most useful, accessible, and logical place to put the regulator.

Because external pumps are "pushers," you want to mount the pump as close to the gas tank as possible. The most efficient way is to build a bracket that mounts between the front of the fuel tank and the rear axle assembly and rear suspension. Keep in mind that exhaust and suspension become major factors when you stray from stock components. For example, in this build adding an external pump assembly is impractical as the rear suspension is far too cumbersome to work around.

Fuel Level Sending Units

A lot of sending units are on the market right now. The key is to determine what gauge you'll be using. Almost all GM gauges and fuel level units use a 0- to 90-ohm reading. Virtually any company can supply you with a gauge that fits this criteria. The important factor here is that you correctly match the gauge to the fuel level unit in terms of ohms. Wiring is fairly straightforward; simple ground and positive wires usually do the trick.

Filter

I cannot emphasize this part enough: It is crucial that if you choose to run an external pump it is

FUEL SYSTEM

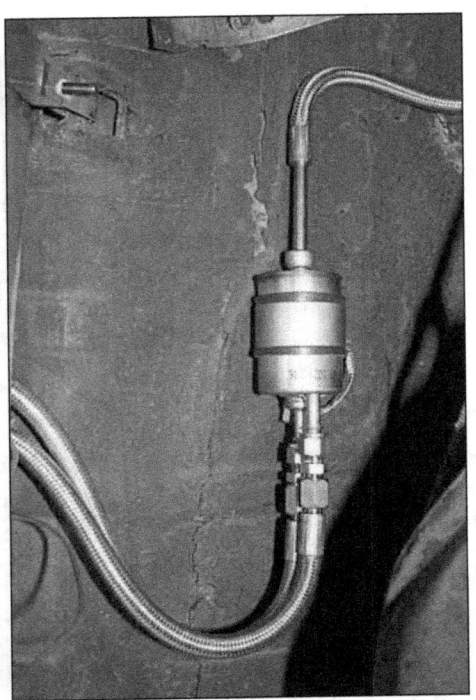

The Corvette fuel filter eliminates the need for two lines to be run to the engine. In this installation, the owner installed AN fittings over the hose ends to allow for braided hoses. (Photo Courtesy Street & Performance)

essential to use a pre-filter to catch debris before it gets to the pump. It's common knowledge to run a filter after the pump. It is also important to purchase the correct high-pressure filters as well; the old carburetor filters give out too easily for these kinds of pressures.

A neat trick for systems running a return line (which is most of them) is to run a C5 Corvette external fuel filter and regulator. If you have an LS engine that is 500 hp or less (which is probably stretching the limits of the C5 fuel pressure regulator), you might want to seriously consider GM PN 10299146. Not only does it act as a regulator designed specifically for LS engines, it does triple duty as a filter and provides a return line to keep the number of pressured lines to a minimum. Again, this has the standard 3/8-inch quick-connection for the inlet, and a 5/16-inch quick-connection on the return side. So make sure to plan on purchasing the correct number of adapters for your project.

Hose and Fittings

You need to use the correct hose for the correct component; otherwise you risk hose failure and a fire. Not all fuel lines are created equal. Fuel lines rated for carburetors are inadequate for the pressure of fuel-injection systems. Typically, an EFI system applies triple the pressure to the hoses as fuel hoses for carburetors. In fact, a carburetor fuel pressure is 8 to 11 psi while the fuel pressure for an LS3 is 60 psi and most LS engines have 40 to 60 psi. If you rupture a fuel line, it can easily create a fire and your car can potentially burn to the ground. You must use hoses that are rated to handle the pressure from your fuel system. You must use the correct fuel-injection rubber hose or, even better, braided fuel line.

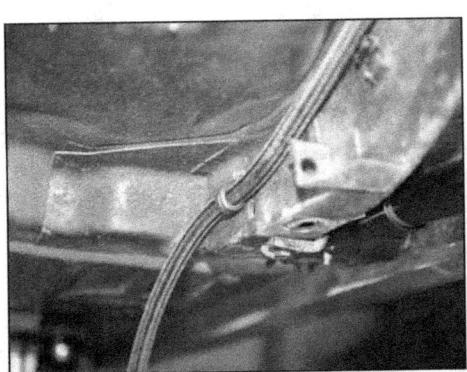

I used a series of these clamps to keep the fuel line away from heat and other hazards. You can use any method you want to hold them down. I prefer self-tapping sheet-metal screws because they can be reused. Pop-rivets also can work equally well; it's your choice.

I recommend using braided (PTFE) lines over rubber lines for a few simple reasons. They prevent premature wear by being much more durable and resist wear better than the rubber lines. In addition, they are less likely to kink compared to rubber lines. It might be advantageous to use hard lines for long runs under the car and add a few adapters. I prefer to keep the system as basic as possible (in this build I used one long piece of -8AN braided fuel line from the pump straight to the fuel rail). You can use either -6AN or -8AN fittings for mild to medium applications.

When I saw the quick-connect ends of the fuel pump and the fuel rails on the stock LS engine, I thought I had run into a big compatibility issue. Thankfully companies have come up with reliable adapters to help fit stock fuel lines to AN-sized fittings and hoses. Here, for example, I used Russell's (PN 644000) to connect the fuel pump to a -8AN fuel line (mine are black). A -6AN line is fine up to about 700-hp engines; bigger than that and you might want to step up to -8AN.

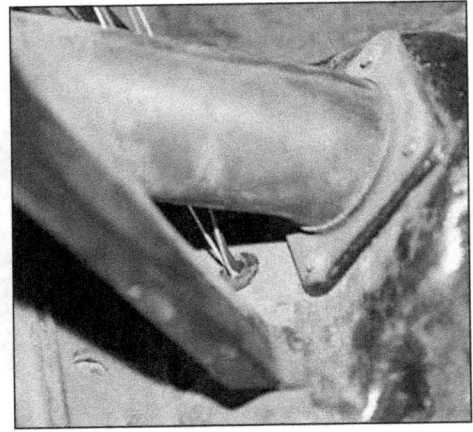

Using the stock hole in the floor for the fuel-level sending unit, I slipped a grommet over the wires and positioned it in the floor. I then replaced the access cover and it looks nearly factory.

Stock Fuel Tank Replacement

Removing a stock tank is not difficult and I've included a couple of quick tips to help you make the job a lot less messy. Depending on your vehicle, you might have a two-piece downspout, such as on my 1968 test car, or it could be like the 1969 version where the spout is built in. With either downspout, disconnecting the spout from the car is the first priority. The fuel line connections to the tank come next (these are located through the rear passenger-side wheel well on my car).

Make sure you remove all the old gas or run the risk of getting a lap full of nasty old gasoline. Siphoning the tank is fairly easy but can be a pain. Doing this lightens the load when you pull the tank out.

Two bolts hold the tank between the rear bumper and the trunk. A deep-well 9/16-inch socket does the trick. Make sure to remove the electrical connectors as you slowly lower the tank. I used a board and a jack to guide the tank out of its cocoon.

Fuel Tank Removal and Installation

To remove the old gas tank in a 1968 Camaro I first have to remove the fuel filler neck cover to reveal the rubber housing protecting the filler neck. On the 1969, the filler neck is attached to the tank. On the 1968, I used a socket to unbolt the necessary pieces and slid them out of the way.

Use a 5/16-inch socket and ratchet to remove the four outer bolts that anchor the fuel filler neck.

Once the bolts have been removed, the old filler neck is easily lifted from the car.

Remove the screws or fasteners that secure the license plate. Once removed, you have access to the two clamps that hold the gas tank and filler neck together. This is also a good place to access the tan fuel gauge wire.

FUEL SYSTEM

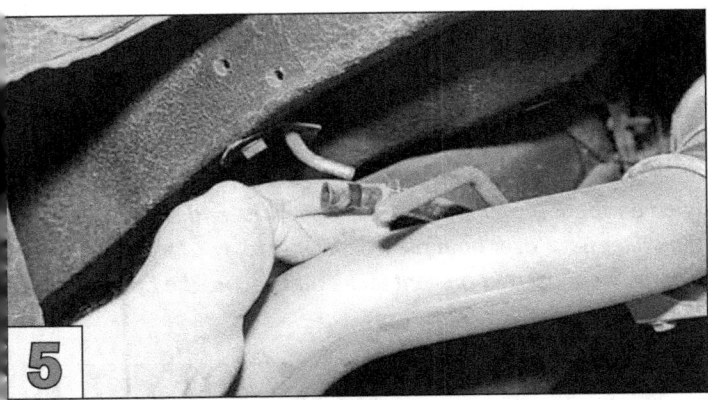

5 Before lowering the tank, remove any attachments, such as the ground wire, gauge lead wire, and fuel feed line, which is located right behind the passenger-side rear tire. Typically, a small worm-gear clamp is all that holds the fuel tube in place. Be prepared to cut it off if it's cracked or the rubber has gone bad.

6 Use a deep-well 9/16-inch socket to remove the two nuts that hold the tank straps in place. Even though the tank had been replaced in the past five years, it was still a difficult job to remove the large and unwieldy gas tank. The nuts and bolts are exposed to the elements so these fasteners typically rust and therefore it's much more difficult to remove them. Using a thread lubricant to spray the nuts makes the job much easier.

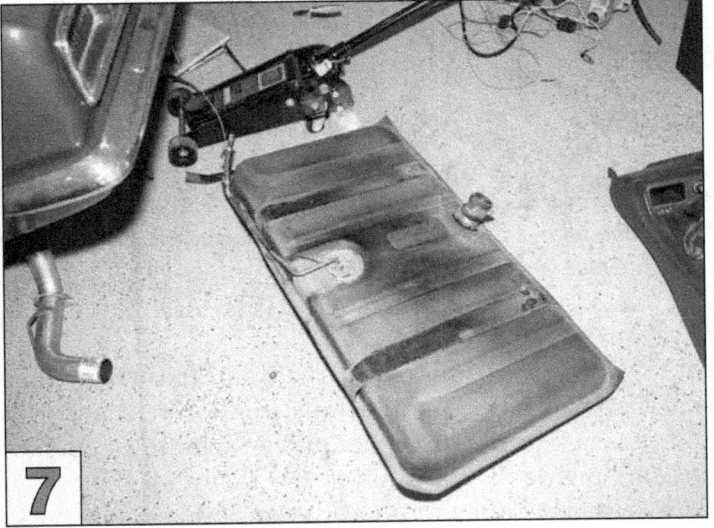

8 Using a flathead screwdriver and a hammer, gently drive the ring off in a counterclockwise direction. The ring holds the sending unit in place and usually takes a few taps for removal.

7 I recommend using a jack and a flat board to support, lower, and remove the tank from the chassis. Raise the jack high enough so the board makes even contact with the bottom of the tank. Remove the nuts from the tank straps and balance the tank on the jack. Slowly lower the jack until the gas tank is close to the floor and can be properly moved. Turns out I had about 3 to 4 gallons of fuel I couldn't siphon out. It got recycled to lawn mower duty.

Carefully place the fuel tank on the floor jack for installation. The tank is a fragile box fabricated of sheet metal so handle it and install it with care. Move the tank into the proper position for installation. Gradually raise the jack and make sure the tank doesn't bottom out against the trunk. Don't dent the tank. Essentially everything goes back in the order in which it came out. Don't worry about the space between the gas tank and the trunk floor; it has a good 1/2 inch of clearance.

SWAP LS ENGINES INTO CAMAROS & FIREBIRDS 1967–1981

CHAPTER 5

Everything is ready for hook up. The downpipe for the fuel filler neck comes next and the wiring harness quick-disconnect. I used a rubber grommet to protect the wires and slipped the gas tank filler hose over both pieces. Afterward, two large worm-gear clamps were used to prevent leaks and secure the bond between the filler and the gas tank.

Cinching the two 9/16-inch nuts slowly secures the tank to the car and forms the correct bends for the straps (they begin as straight pieces).

Route the rubber shroud over the filler neck and secure it in place with the four machine screws.

Tank Replacement Sources

The following are a few companies that sell stock replacement fuel tanks.

Robb McPerformance

Contrary to some popular hot rod lore, a stock F-Body gas tank can be converted to fuel the LS engine to supply its fuel injection system. You need to install an aftermarket fuel-sending unit in the tank, and this process requires a significant amount of work. If you are up for the task, it is a good way to a save a few bucks along the way.

You need to install a fuel-sending unit that is entirely different from the

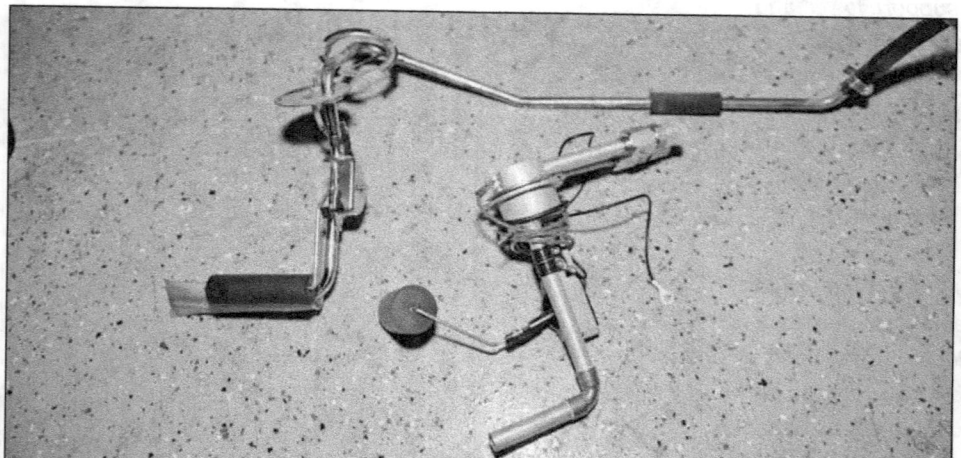

This is a comparison between the stock sending unit and the RobbMc sending unit that is designed for fuel-injected applications. Beefier is a good adjective.

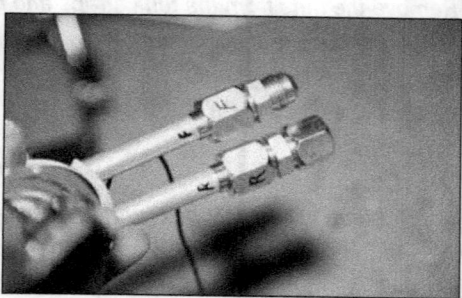

The RobbMc sending unit has been labeled with R for return and F for feed lines. The -8AN male ends allow for a quick assembly.

FUEL SYSTEM

The RobbMc sending unit is a direct fit for a stock tank. You need to install a new rubber O-ring gasket so the sending unit is sealed well. The red and black wires connect to your fuel level gauge with the red going to the positive and black to the negative side of the gauge.

stock unit. Many in-tank fuel pumps are compatible with the stock F-Body tank and the LS engine series. Aeromotive offers the in-tank 340 Stealth Fuel Pump and Racetronix offers a kit for LS engines that has a drop-in wiring harness and a Walbro GSS340 fuel pump. For my particular build, I selected a kit from Robb McPerformance (RobbMc) that does the trick.

I spent a few extra bucks and had them add an -8AN option that allowed me to run the -8 line to and from the fuel tank. This is a direct drop-in replacement for the factory unit and gives me an option to run a return line via this sending unit or just cap it and not use it. RobbMc told me that it would be best to run an external surge tank with their system to aid in fuel delivery and stop unwanted fuel starvation under lateral forces. They recommend a 1-gallon upright tank between the fuel tank and the fuel filters.

As far as I know, no one makes a tank for this specific purpose, so you might have to make one to fit your custom application. I have found a few surge tanks on eBay going for roughly $250; the route you wish to take is up to you.

Tanks Inc.

You can also install an internal pump and sending unit in the stock gas tank to complete the task of plumbing a fuel system in your F-Body. The system comes from Tanks Inc. and requires a fair amount of fabrication and fitment, but if you are looking for a low-buck way to go, this might be the ticket.

The system uses an internal pump assembly that needs a large hole cut in the fuel tank to allow the pump to rest inside, as the stock hole isn't big enough. As of this writing, Tanks Inc. has changed their design from this version; so current units may look slightly different.

At the same time, you reuse the stock sending unit opening. You have to remove the collar that's welded on from the factory to make this work, but it allows you to run a fuel level sending unit without interfering with the new pump. The important factor to remember is the ohm reading from your gauge, which typically is 0 to 90 ohms for a standard GM gauge.

Electric Fuel Pump Installation in Stock Tank

1 *I purchased a stock second-generation fuel tank from Tanks Inc., and I will install an electric fuel pump and related parts in this tank for an LS engine setup. You need to start out with a new tank when installing an electric fuel pump. You risk creating an explosion by drilling into a used tank. (Photo Courtesy Dennis Warhurst)*

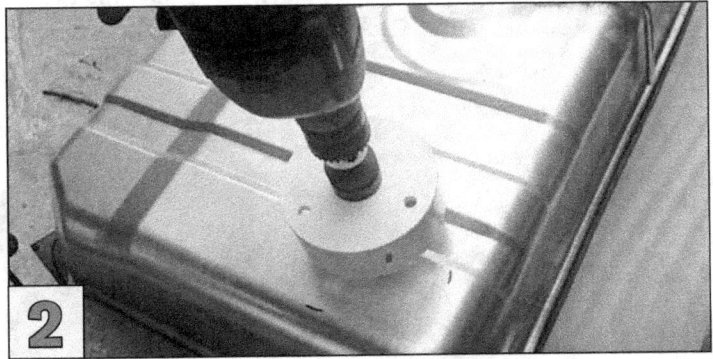

2 *Use a hole saw to drill a 4½-inch hole in the tank to accept the fuel pump unit. Using a sheet-metal hole saw from the local hardware store I made the cut at the most obvious location to get the most fuel to the assembly. Do not drill holes in the firewall any larger than necessary. You want to be able to adequately seal the passenger compartment and keep moisture and the elements out. (Photo Courtesy Dennis Warhurst)*

SWAP LS ENGINES INTO CAMAROS & FIREBIRDS 1967–1981

CHAPTER 5

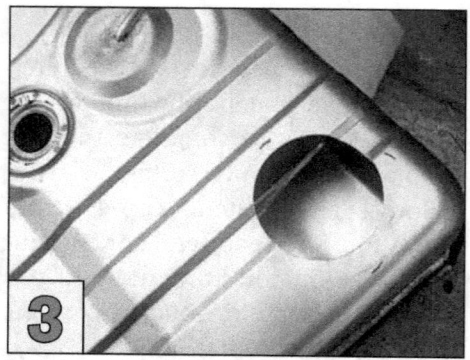

3 This is a perfect spot for a new pump assembly. Use a file or a sander to clean up the edges and take the burrs off. (Photo Courtesy Dennis Warhurst)

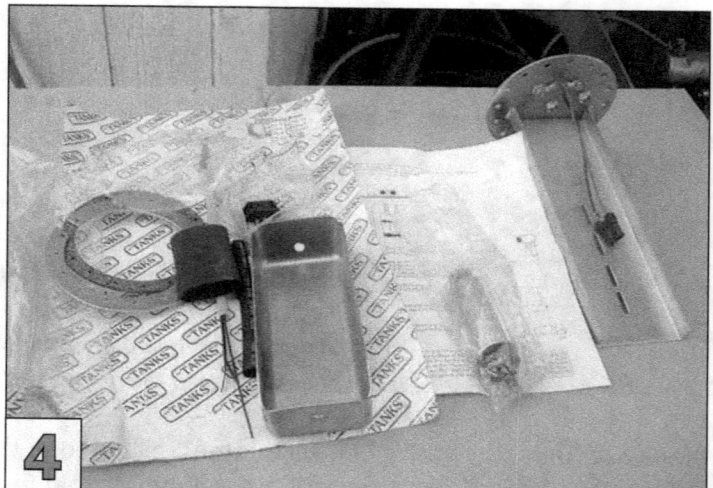

4 The kit includes a fuel pump, mounting hardware, and the correct wiring to complete half of the job. A Walbro 255-lb/hr pump is usually sufficient for most stock LS engines. (Photo Courtesy Dennis Warhurst)

5 Cut a significant chunk out of the assembly as these are designed to be universal. Take a quality measurement before cutting. Ideal clearance is roughly 1/2 inch from the bottom of the tank when measuring from the top of the tank. You want the fuel pump filter sock to be close to the bottom of the tank, but not so close that it cuts off fuel supply. (Photo Courtesy Dennis Warhurst)

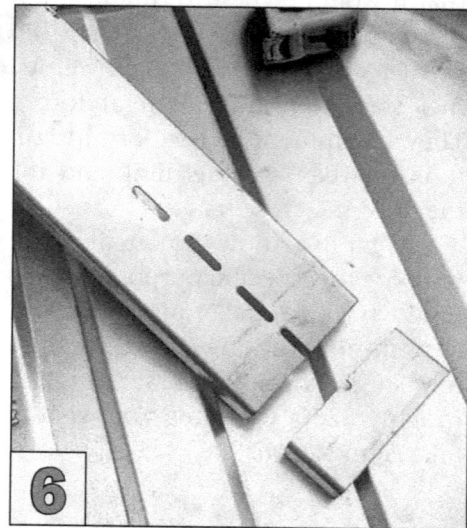

6 Remove the excess length by using a hacksaw or reciprocating saw. (Photo Courtesy Dennis Warhurst)

7 A series of holes needs to be drilled to properly match the unit to your fuel tank. Using the unit as a template is the easiest method. Install the support ring that comes in the kit. Some rings snap into place and others bolt. My version bolts into place from the top and bottom. Pop rivets were used to firmly attach the lower ring. (Photo Courtesy Dennis Warhurst)

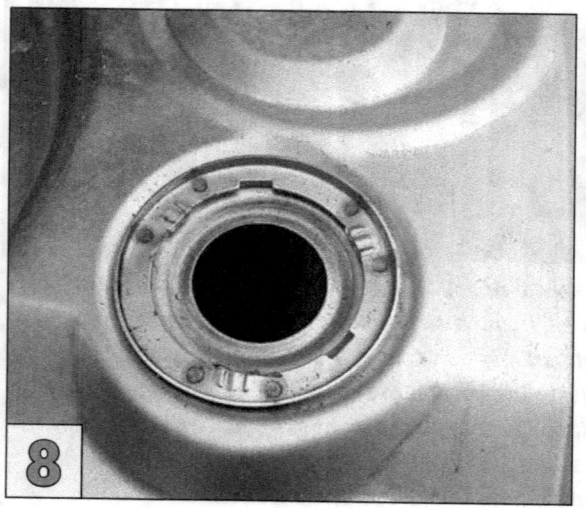

8 9 The stock sending unit hole needs to be covered. You can use a variety of methods to do this such as welding it closed or fabricating a cover with a rubber gasket, but it needs to be watertight to prevent fuel from sloshing out. The top ring needs to be removed carefully. (Photo Courtesy Dennis Warhurst)

80 SWAP LS ENGINES INTO CAMAROS & FIREBIRDS 1967–1981

FUEL SYSTEM

10 I bought a fuel level sending unit from Auto Meter. Although Auto Meter doesn't make a GM version, Ford makes one that uses an incorrect 240-33-ohm reading. Instead, a VDO version (PN 226008) can be had for $40 and works equally well. (Photo Courtesy Dennis Warhurst)

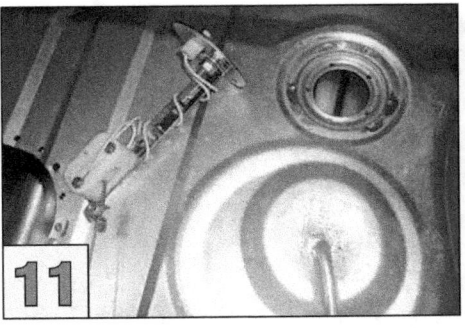

11 You have to shorten the level sending unit to match the depth of the tank. Measuring the tank depth gives you an idea of how much you need to remove from the universal sending unit. Using your favorite method of metal removal, you can then reattach the fuel bucket for a custom-sized unit. In addition, drilling a couple of holes to accept the new sending unit is required (shown). (Photo Courtesy Dennis Warhurst)

12 A fully installed sending unit complete with cleaned-up welds. Depending on your welding skill you may have to use an aggressive grinding pad. The point of this exercise is to make as clean a connection as possible. (Photo Courtesy Dennis Warhurst)

13 This is the bottom of the tank. In order to have your gauge read correctly, you need to carefully measure your level sending unit so it accurately functions. (Photo Courtesy Dennis Warhurst)

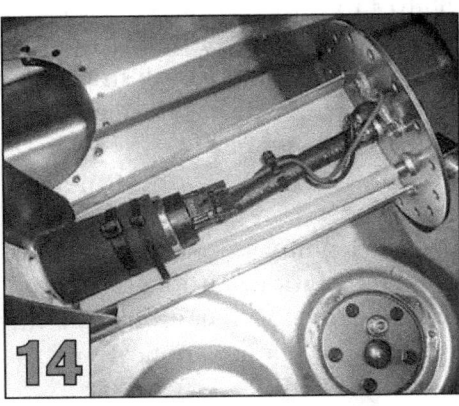

14 This is the pre-assembled pump unit with the sump. The return line is neatly secured and not dangling. (Photo Courtesy Dennis Warhurst)

15 A completed gas tank fully assembled and ready for install and no welding was required. (Photo Courtesy Dennis Warhurst)

16 The kit from Tanks Inc. comes with a cork gasket to close up any nasty air. So far this tank with this setup has not given me any problems. (Photo Courtesy Dennis Warhurst)

Aeromotive

You can also buy complete, ready-to-install fuel tanks with the electronic fuel pumps fitted inside them so you don't have to fabricate the fittings and install the fuel pump in the tank yourself. Aeromotive Stealth Style is a reproduction tank that simply replaces the stock one and neatly fits in the tank straps. This tank fits the 1967–1969 F-Body cars and contains the 340 Stealth Fuel Pump with integral in-tank performance baffling. The in-tank 340 provides enough fuel flow for up to 700 hp EFI and up to 1,000 hp carbureted, but it must be used in conjunction with the correct Aeromotive bypass regulator. You need to install the tank itself, hook up the electrical wires to the wiring harness, route a fuel supply and return line, and the job is complete.

The tank features a stamped steel fuel tank, silver powder coat finish, EFI-style internal baffling, 0- to 90-ohm universal fuel level sending unit, black anodized pump hanger assembly, 340 Stealth Fuel Pump (PN 11140), pre-pump filter sock assembly, and three ORB-06 ports (outlet, return, and vent).

This stainless steel tank functions like a stock tank and is quite possibly the best product on the market for fuel delivery of an LS engine, especially if the car is going to be raced in any capacity.

Rick's Tanks

My tank is a killer product from Rick's Tanks that is perfect for this application. It's a stainless steel direct replacement for the factory tank, and it's compatible with mini-tubbed cars. The 18-gallon tank is 38 3/8 x 20 7/8 x 7 3/4 inches, and has a 0- to 105-ohm fuel sending unit. This drop-in fuel tank is stamped similar to the OEM tank and the stock fifth-generation pump electric fuel pump supplies 50 to 60 gallons per hour at 85 to 115 psi.

To install it, you lift it into position, slip the factory tank straps over it, and secure the tank straps. Then you run supply and return lines to your injectors and connect the electrical wires to your 12-volt system. The fuel pump needs to be primed before operation. Although this tank far from cheap, I have to run this type of tank for my application.

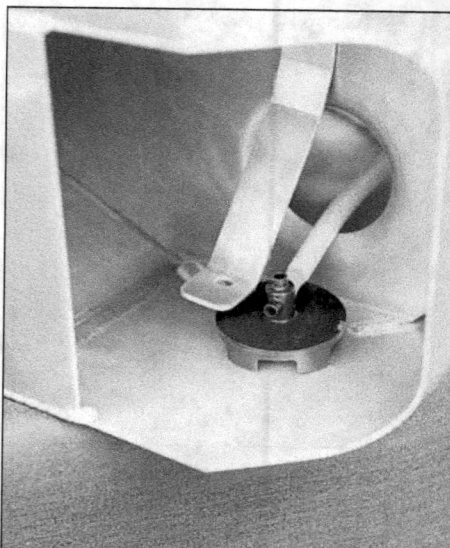

This is a good look inside the tank from Rick's Tanks that demonstrates the fuel pickup and internal bafiling. I can run this tank close to empty and still make it back home.

VaporWorx

The VaporWorx fuel setup has a great design, which uses two pickup points on either side of the fuel tank and one at the pump to pick up every last drop of fuel even in hard-cornering situations. These pickup points eliminate the need to run a surge tank and also allows you to really throw the car around without worrying about fuel starvation. This system is an add-on for the stainless Rick's tank and in my opinion is money well spent.

The system uses an off-the-shelf GM fuel pump that you can get at your local parts store (probably special order, but you get the idea), which is a major bonus if something ever goes wrong and you need a part fast. I have heard that the stock GM pump is extremely reliable so I'm not too concerned. The fuel pump comes out of a fifth-generation F-Body with a typical LS3 installed.

Don't forget that the LS engine needs additional fuel pressure. I used a Rick's stainless tank with the VaporWorx fuel pump and pickup system as this prevents fuel starvation on turns. The Rick's tank fits perfectly and is a direct swap from the OEM tank. VaporWorx is sold separately and the tank must be modified to accept the fuel pump and bucket assembly. (Photo Courtesy Mary Pozzi)

FUEL SYSTEM

Fuel Pump Installation in Fuel Tank

1

The fuel pump for the VaporWorx fuel setup is installed in the Rick's stainless steel tank. I dropped in the fuel pump, connected the side pickups, and locked it all in place with a lock ring. Then a custom-made harness by Carl Casanova at VaporWorx makes sure all the electrical connections are secure. The opposing fuel port and electrical port tell you that this is the stock pump and not the upgraded version for LS9 or LSA requirements.

2

Russell's makes the fuel line adapter, which is essentially two halves squeezed together. It installs and tightens in a jiffy. The part has a small collar on one end that sandwiches the plastic nipple on the fuel pump. Be very careful as these plastic nipples can break easily; I went through two pumps having to learn the hard way. I went with the -8AN (P/N 644003 black), which is the push-on style and requires the standard GM 3/8-inch SAE disconnect.

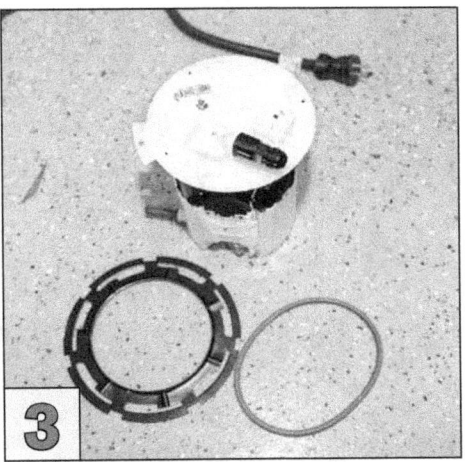

3

To complete the install, an F-Body fifth-generation fuel pump, O-ring, and sprocket to tie everything down are needed (G5FM for the fuel pump), all from VaporWorx.

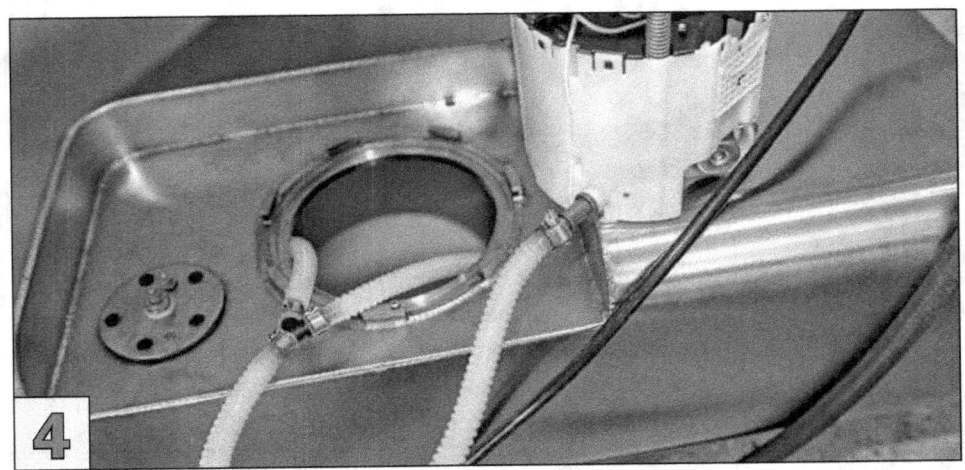

4

Make sure to connect the two-sided feed lines to the lower inlet tube for the pump. Slip the fuel lines over the nipple and then tighten the pipe strap fittings.

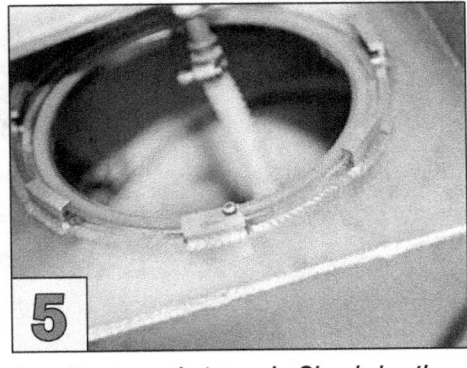

5

Install your gasket snugly. Simply lay the gasket into the channel, making sure it stays in place. Press it into the channel of the sending unit hole. Also notice the setscrew for the locking ring.

6

Use a pair of pliers to firmly seat the ring into the grooves and pull tight. You must rotate the ring until it locks into position.

SWAP LS ENGINES INTO CAMAROS & FIREBIRDS 1967–1981

CHAPTER 5

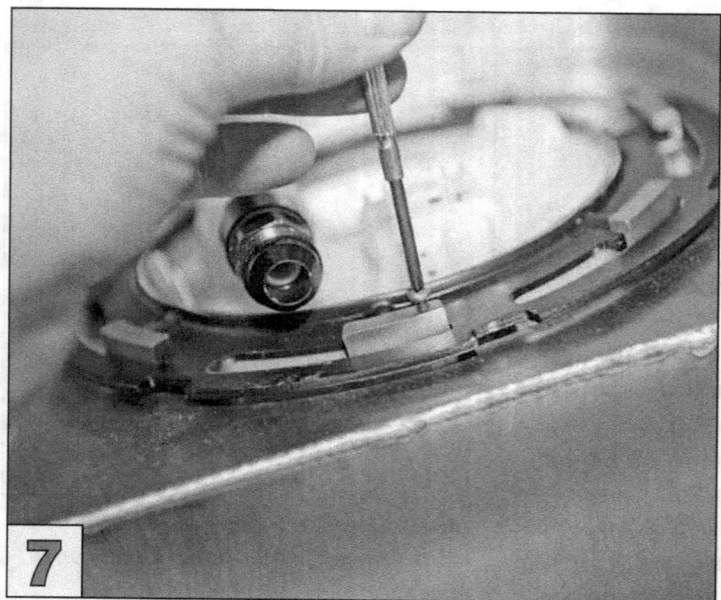

Use a small No. 1 Phillips screwdriver to tighten the setscrew.

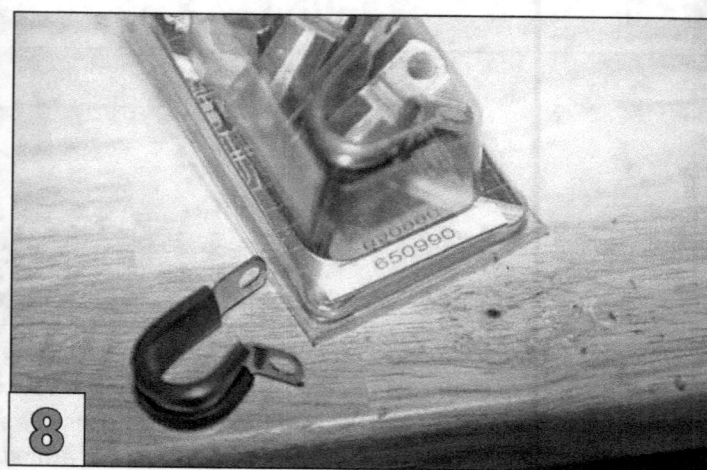

I ended up using about ten of these hose clamps throughout the car. These clamps are available in packages of six from Russell (PN 650990). I put these at regularly spaced intervals to keep the cable routed out of the way of potential hazards, such as road debris and heat from the exhaust.

Simply attach the end of the hose making sure you have the correct radius bends.

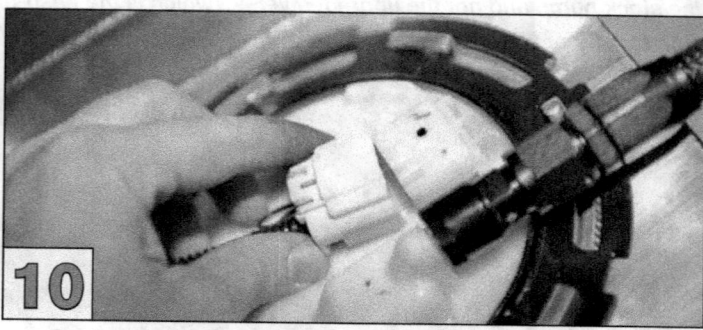

The weather pack snaps right in place. A weather pack connector is a plastic connector that protects the electrical components from the weather and elements. The wiring harness has a provisional weather pack that is the perfect reciprocal for the pump and harness.

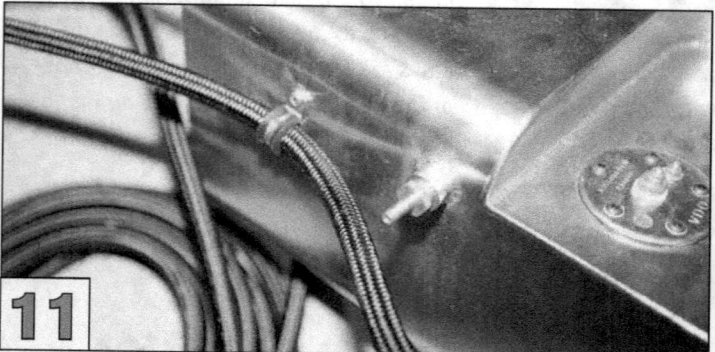

On the Rick's Tanks tank, a provision is made for a 10-mm bolt to be screwed in to hold a fuel line clamp. A standard 10-mm bolt will work. I took quick advantage of that and installed the fuel tank breather tube right next to it. When installed, the breather tube has a small tube running above the tank to allow excess gases to escape.

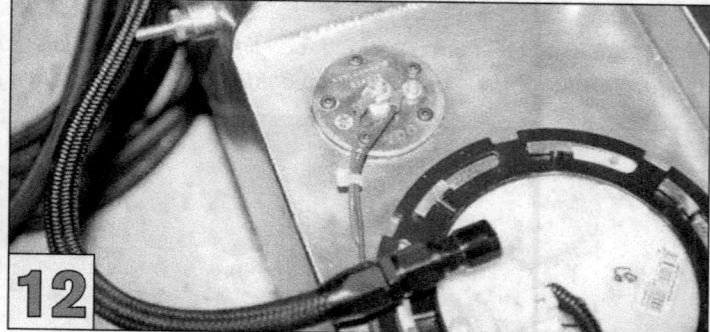

With the GM wiring harness matched up, I ran a positive and a negative wire to the fuel level gauge. I spliced the wires from the Mast unit and the gauge cluster, and then fastened them to the pump and sending unit. Now I can put the tank back into place.

FUEL SYSTEM

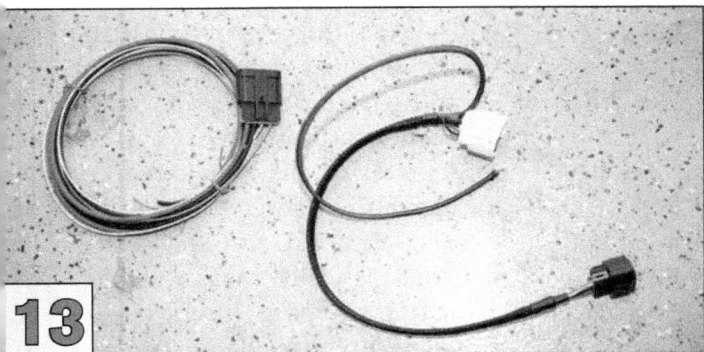

Carl at VaporWorx has reworked the stock wiring harness and created his own. He removed the unnecessary wires and only kept the important bits such as the fuel level sending unit and the pump wiring. The setup comes with the two halves and some extra clips if you need them. The two halves connect in the middle and allow you to run the wires from the main harness to the gas tank while allowing you to remove it without binding the way the original harness did.

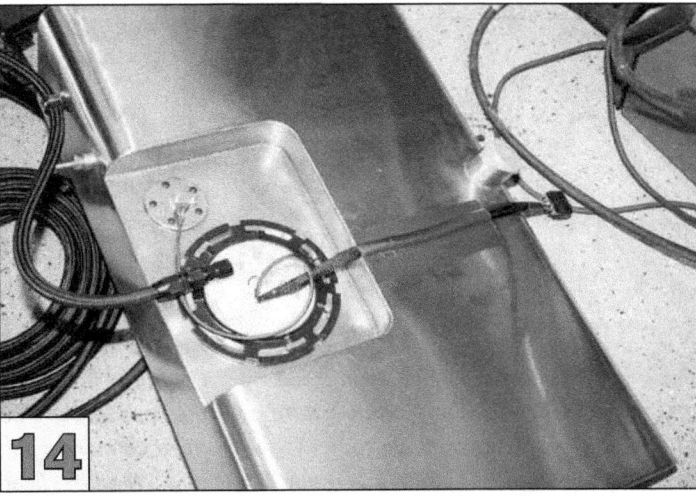

The new wiring harness has been installed and it looks very clean and fits well. I'll feed the other half through a grommet in the trunk where the fuel level wire would go and make the weather pack connection through the license plate access hole.

This tank-and-pump combination is an entire assembly in one unit. It may be a bit pricey for a fuel pump but you need to consider the value of this system because it saves time and is convenient. The returnless system is not vacuum regulated so that means you only have to plumb one fuel line. It has an internal regulator attached to it so that part of the equation is taken care of. It also includes its own filter built right into the fuel pickup of the unit. In addition, pump depth, the choice of correct pump, welding, and pressure testing of the tank (that's all the components) are set so you don't have do a lot of trial and error to figure out the setup. It's a foolproof system.

This pump is not correctly calibrated for the LS engine. The internal regulator of the pump comes with the fifth-gen pump that's not at the correct setting and has to be replaced with a fourth-generation fuel pressure regulator and adapter. Replacing the regulator with a VaporWorx adapter is fairly straightforward.

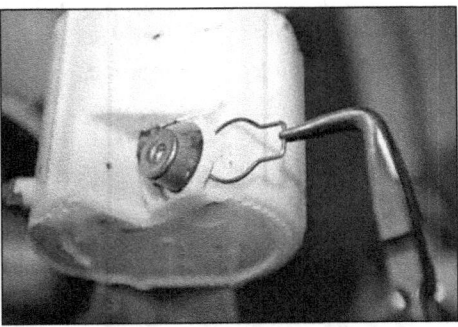

Carl Casanova recommended that I replace the internal regulator (relieves pressure in the fifth-generation only) with a fourth-generation regulator that is set for 58 psi. I can run this pump without it, but I'd be pumping out 95 to 100 psi at all times, which is far too much. First remove the retainer pin from the old regulator and keep it handy; you reuse it later.

I bought the fourth-generation fuel regulator (PN FP10021) for about $50; it's in stock at most dealerships.

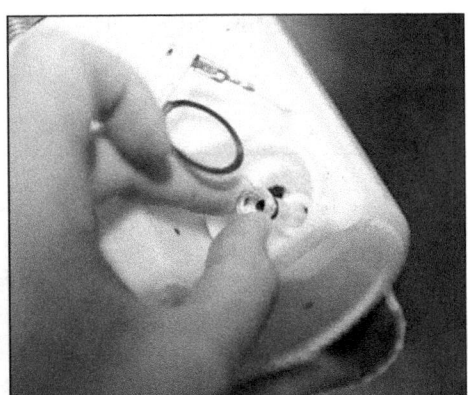

The regulator restricts flow and you cannot install it without restricting the flow, otherwise you blow out the regulator. VaporWorx sells you an adapter that corrects this and must be installed first in the back of the pump. The adapter slides into place where the regulator sits. Make sure the orientation is correct; otherwise it won't go back together properly.

SWAP LS ENGINES INTO CAMAROS & FIREBIRDS 1967–1981

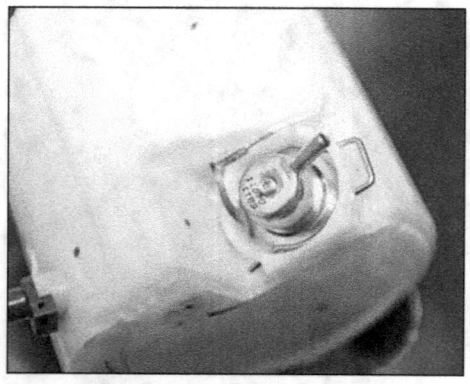

Install the new regulator and make sure to keep the retainer ring snug to hold the round wire in place. You are now ready to install the pump.

I plugged in the quick connection through the license plate hole, which was the supplied connector with the VaporWorx system. When the license plate is installed, all of this is hidden.

Adapting the wiring is the most complicated part of the setup. The fifth-generation pump has a four-wire weather connector that needs its own special male connector. You can always forgo the weather connector to cut and splice the wires. That typically means using a wire cutter, stripping the ends (using your favorite butt-style connector), and a strip of marine-grade shrink tubing. Some aftermarket companies have worked out solutions. VaporWorx has reworked the wiring to fit the older style (and simpler) wiring systems. They have specialty wiring harnesses for first and second-generation F-Body applications.

For my particular build, when I installed an LS3, I discovered that the LS3 pump for the fifth-generation F-Body and the CTS-V are different.

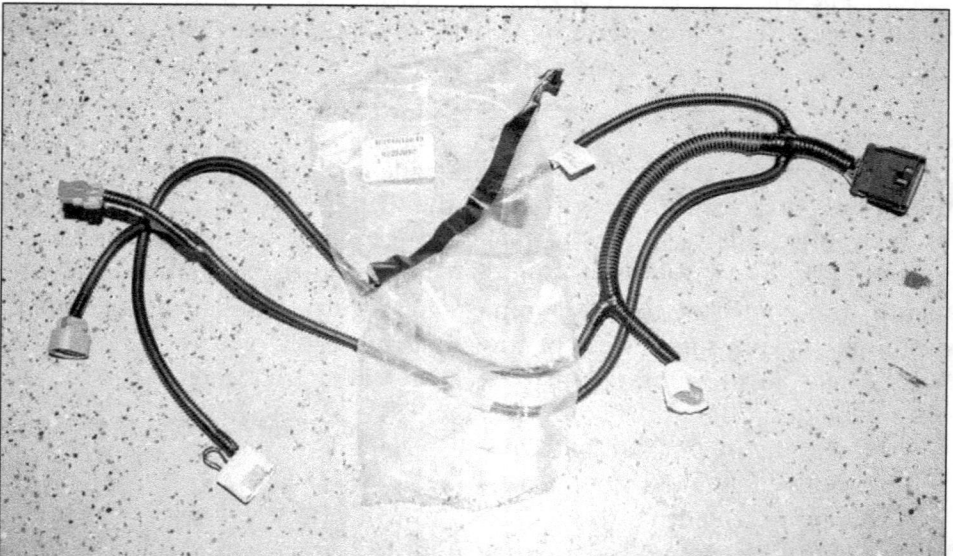

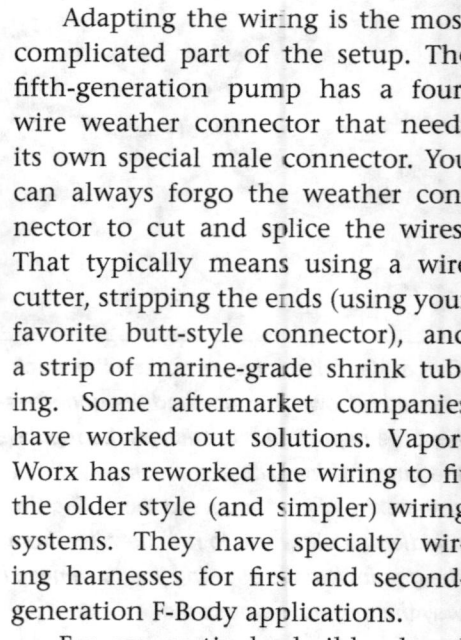

Using the stock GM wiring harness is one way to easily hook up everything. This one is for the LSA and LS9 (PN 92202097). You can get it to work with the regular fifth-generation pump, but it takes a bit more finagling. You must remove and disable a few of the wires, such as the second pump adapter and the fuel level sending unit wiring, to match to your pump.

It's a shame that such an amazing-looking unit has to be hidden away where no one can see it but it will faithfully serve the fuel requirements of the engine and keep the car in top-performing shape.

Here's a rear view of the tank installed with the rest of the rear suspension. The car has gone through a dramatic aesthetic makeover and performance transformation that will be proven on the track.

FUEL SYSTEM

In fact, the CTS-V delivers a much greater fuel volume because it has to feed a supercharged beast of an LS engine.

The easiest way to tell what pump you have is to look at the upper feed line. If it is parallel to the weather pack connector (like mine), you have an LS3 pump. If it is at a 45-degree angle, you have a CTS-V pump. The CTS-V is basically two 190 lph pumps in one unit with the similar proportions as the fifth-generation pump. If you have a high-horsepower setup, the CTS-V system might be your ticket. But it must be said that running this pump requires a lot more effort and is not the same setup as the fifth-generation pump. The CTS-V pump has two feed lines and it requires a different wiring harness than the fifth-gen version.

VaporWorx stocks the correct fuel pump harness for custom applications if you don't want to wrestle with making one yourself. It is possible to buy a stock wiring harness and modify it to fit, but from my experience, the VaporWorx is the best on the market at the current time.

AN Line Fabrication

You typically need to install a high-pressure line at some point in the build. A high-performance or pro-touring F-Body car must flow a lot of fluid through its systems, whether it's an oil cooler line, transmission cooler lines, power steering, or fuel. They all need to be correct to work best.

Most fittings have two parts with matching threads: a sleeve and an insert. These fittings are extremely durable and can be reused many times.

Custom AN Hose Fabrication

When first making a braided line, start with the correct-style end that you want to use and hold it in with a tabletop vise.

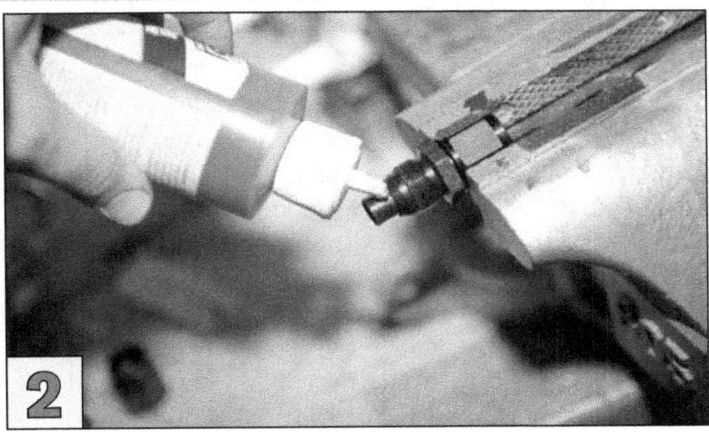

Use a dab of Earl's assembly lube to make the braided line installation easier.

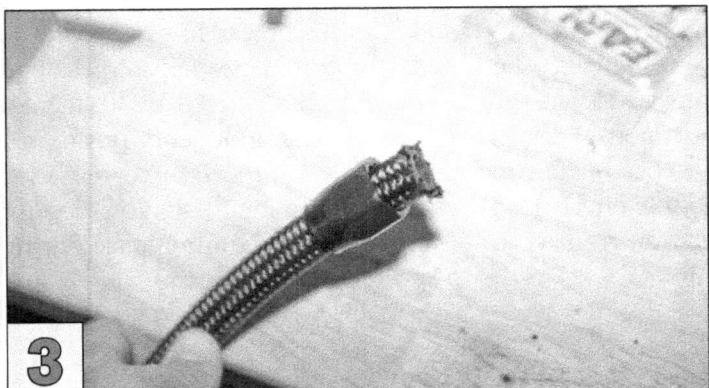

Make a clean cut on the hose. Use a cutoff wheel, hacksaw, or a sharp stonecutter and a mallet. Be sure the cuts are clean. Once it's cut to the desired length, you then slip the other half of the fitting onto the hose for mating.

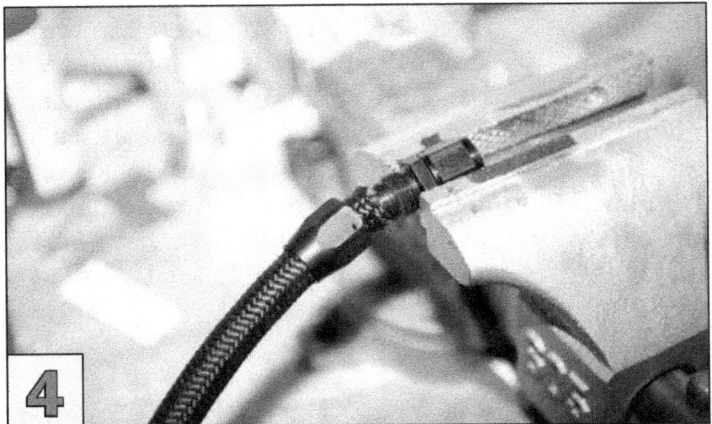

Push the hose onto the male end while screwing the female end into the fitting. This may take some force, so don't be afraid to really push.

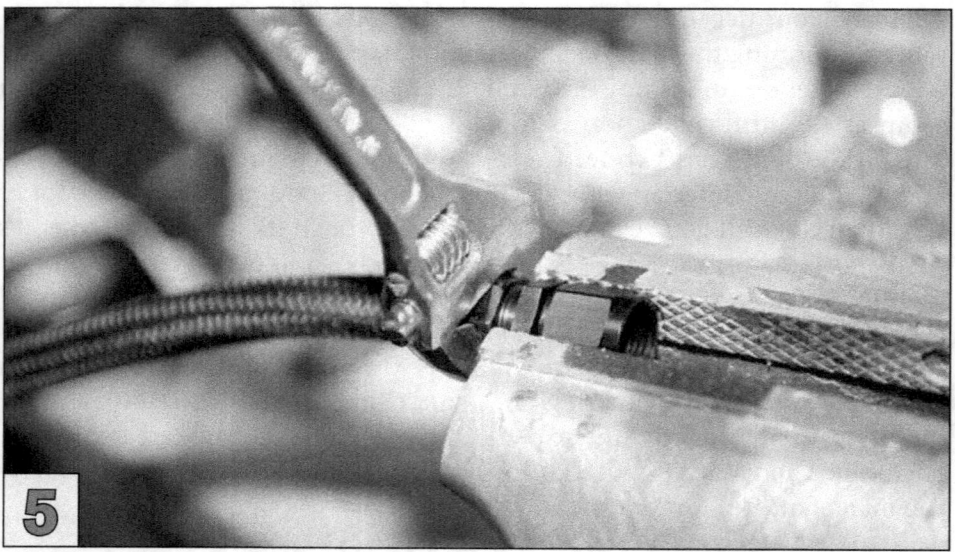
Finally, use the correct-size AN wrench to tighten the nut until it seats almost all the way. You have made one half of your new custom-made braided hose.

The procedure begins by taping the length of hose you need so when you cut it, it doesn't fray. Cutting the hose can be done with a hacksaw or cutoff wheel. Earl's recommends using a sharp stone chisel that creates a perfectly clean cut each time without tape.

Next, place the collar over the line using a vise to hold the collar in place. Sometimes a bit of force is needed to get it in place. Now you can place the threaded hose end in the vise and start threading the collar and hose into place. Continue to work it into place until the threads grab and turn by hand until you cannot turn it anymore.

At this point use a wrench to continue threading the hose onto the end. A little piece of mind goes a long way, especially at 7,000 rpm! This may take a few tries to get it right, but once you get the hang of it, making your own hose ends is the only way to go.

Gas Pedal

If you have a cable-driven throttle body, you can most likely skip this section and use your existing setup with a modified cable. Modifying your existing cable is simply a matter of determining the length you need to articulate the throttle body. If you've been running a carburetor to this point, you may have to replace your cable with a longer one and make the necessary length adjustment. Keep in mind that you have to be able to run it wide open, so double-check that you have full articulation from your pedal closed to open.

If you don't have a cable-driven system, you have a drive-by-wire (DBW) system. This means you need to mount the gas pedal. In all likelihood, this is the only bit of fabrication you will have to do. I have only seen two styles of DBW pedals: those that mount with bolts going through the pedal sideways and those with two bolts going through a bracket (such as the one I have in my car).

You need to have the correct pedal with the correct wiring harness for it to work properly. If not, you have to reflash the computer with a different gas pedal and this is extra hassle and expense. In some instances you can get away with it, but just to be on the safe side, you should have the gas pedal that came with the engine whenever possible.

Either way, you have to fabricate a way of mounting your gas pedal. In this case I chose to make a box that located the pedal in a desirable location. It is best to have the pedal closer to the floor than the brake pedal by about 2 to 3 inches and offset to the side an equal distance.

The floorboard/firewall of the F-Body has a lot of complex shapes and requires a bit of finesse to get the pedal mounted properly. Mine had to be cocked about 20 to 30 degrees to match the look and position I desired. It is important to reinforce whatever you build as you do not want this thing coming loose during a spirited driving session.

CHAPTER 6

COOLING SYSTEM

A high-performance LS engine generates much more heat than a Chevy Gen I small-block engine or a Pontiac V-8 that originally came in many of the F-Body cars, so you need a cooling system that effectively and efficiently dissipates and manages the heat. Therefore, you need the correct components, adequate capacity, and proper calibration for the high-performance engine you have installed in your F-Body. A proper cooling system helps produce horsepower and protects your sizable investment in your LS engine. Don't cut corners; invest in an aftermarket aluminum radiator, water pump, and related equipment that's well suited to your engine.

Interestingly, the coolant system on the LS engine lineup is not entirely different from a Gen I Chevy small-block that was installed in most of these first- and second-generation F-Bodies. The LS has two major ports: One comes into the engine while the other moves hot coolant out of the engine and into the radiator. Thankfully General Motors did away with the reverse cooling LT engine that seemed more of an experiment than a well-thought-out system.

Early F-Body cars run an open-bottle cooling system. However, a closed pressurized cooling system with a closed overflow bottle provides higher pressure and much better cooling than a standard open system. In addition, the extra capacity of the bottle in a closed system offers more cooling. While you can use the stock system with an open overflow bottle, it doesn't provide nearly the same cooling capacity as the modern closed system.

If you're scrounging the junkyard, you can pluck this system from many late-model GM cars, including the Cadillac CTS-V.

These are three typical water pumps. The one with the larger bells is the most versatile as it can be made to fit the F-Body and the Corvette-style balancers. (Photo Courtesy Street & Performance)

SWAP LS ENGINES INTO CAMAROS & FIREBIRDS 1967–1981

When installing a closed pressurized system, the lower line should be integrated into the return heater hose. For an LS engine this is the most forward 3/4-inch nipple on the water pump housing. The vent hose from the cylinder head should be hooked to the small upper nipple on the bottle.

Radiator

Although you may be tempted to use the original radiator from your F-Body with your new LS engine, this is not the right move and does not meet your high-performance goals.

While it could work, it won't provide enough cooling capacity, particularly if you're using your F-Body in competition. Therefore, I don't know of anyone who has tried reusing an original radiator from the 1960s or 1970s. It's simply not worth using an old-style radiator and risk damaging your engine. The cooling efficiency of the old-style radiators just isn't what they are today with aluminum radiators being the norm. I highly recommend upgrading your radiator as cheap insurance to protect against heat in your engine. Newer radiators are vastly more efficient, lighter, and use more reliable components such as electric fans and have larger cooling capacity.

Small-Block Radiator

While you can use a small-block radiator on an LS swap, there is one major difference. The upper radiator hose needs to be routed to the driver's side, which requires a custom application of the hose. The standard small-block radiator works exactly the same way as the LS specific radiators do, the difference is, you guessed it, the placement of the upper radiator hose.

Keeping in mind that the upper radiator hose is the "hot" side, pushing the hot engine coolant from the engine to the radiator to be cooled, the same approach must be taken regardless of which radiator you choose.

I've seen it done on a few cars that wanted to retain the stock small-block appearance and not give away the deadly secret underneath. This option might be for you, but remember it takes a bit of work to make it work properly and not look like a hack job.

LS Radiators

A myriad of aluminum cross-flow radiators are available for LS swaps into first- and second-generation F-Body chassis. The stock LS radiators have both inlet and outlet passages on the passenger's side of the engine. While you can route hoses to the driver's side of the engine, it's difficult to package all the components when running non-stock hose routes. Thankfully, several companies, such as AutoRad, Flex-a-lite, AFCO, and Be Cool, offer high-capacity aluminum radiators for early F-Body swaps.

The stock LS radiator out of a fourth-generation F-Body car installs because the first-generation's direct mounting to the core support, but it is different than the fourth-generation F-Body setup. You have to be a bit creative when mounting the radiator

This is the lower hose on Mary Pozzi's LS engine swap. Because LS swaps don't have specific hoses for the various water pump outlets to the radiator, I had to take a few home from my local parts house for some trial fits. The original hose was about a foot longer but the center section fit perfectly and now it clears the idler arm mount. (Photo Courtesy Mary Pozzi)

Mary and her crew had to trial fit the upper hose in the same manner as the lower hose. As the fitting for the water pump was a smaller diameter than that for the radiator neck, I used a reducer (available at parts stores) to get this hose working with the LS swap. (Photo Courtesy Mary Pozzi)

COOLING SYSTEM

The old direct-fit aluminum radiator and SPAL fan combination was used to cool the old small-block. It worked just fine and would probably work with the new Mast LS3. However, I upgraded the entire car and I needed to ensure the engine had excellent cooling so the engine could run at its best and not overheat. Besides, I wanted to run the A/C and I didn't think the old system could handle the cooling requirements.

This comparison of the new aluminum core support from AutoRad and a stock core support shows that the AutoRad is significantly bigger and lighter. All the factory holes are there so it's a direct bolt in. Of course, this is a lot more work, but the results speak for themselves when I can blast the A/C and hit some very high RPM, all while the engine stays cool.

Here is a close-up of the thermostat housing and heater core passages. The large port is the lower radiator hose and the two smaller ones are for the heater core.

You might run into this problem as well, which kind of threw me for a loop. The articulation of the heater wasn't enough to clear the control arm so I had to find a better solution to the problem. I ended up using a plastic elbow that reroutes the hoses.

Using an old coat hanger, I mocked up the basic shape of the radiator hose and this provided a sense for the required length of the hose. Obviously, it was a custom application.

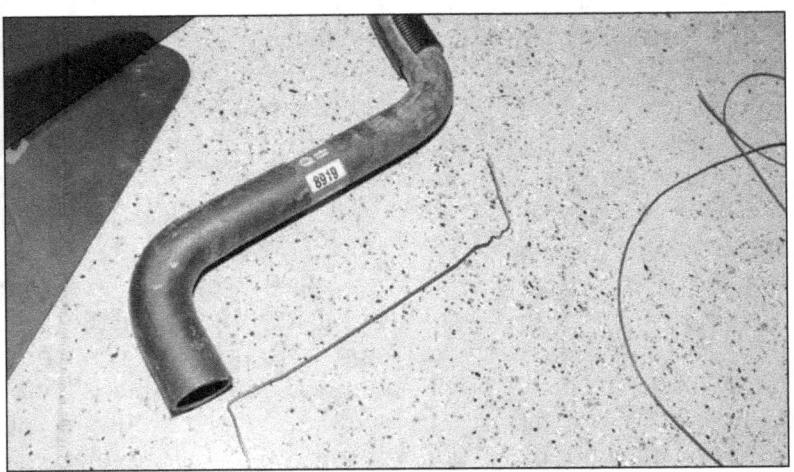

After searching my local Napa Auto Parts store, I finally found the correct hose for this application. The bends on this hose matched fairly well and the inside diameter (ID) of the hose was close enough for my comfort. The AutoRad radiator puts the opening farther away on the passenger's side than the stock LS location, so I had to do some research. I dug around the cooling hose bin for quite some time before I found the right hose. I performed the same basic procedure for the lower hose as well.

SWAP LS ENGINES INTO CAMAROS & FIREBIRDS 1967–1981

CHAPTER 6

My 1½-inch ID hose worked out quite well. Looks like a factory part after I trimmed it to fit better. For those with this configuration, the upper hose was PN 8919 from Napa Auto Parts.

Here's a side shot of the hose. Notice the clearance with the LS engine and no need for a clutch and fan blade assembly.

and fan combo. Most people choose to make a bracket to mount to the bottom and top of the radiator to support it. This method is likely the most effective and easiest.

The upper and lower radiator hoses now need to be run. This typically isn't an off-the-shelf part so I have to come up with a better idea.

If you plan on running an LS-specific cross-flow radiator (and why wouldn't you?), Goodyear makes a number of upper and lower radiator hoses that are compatible with an LS radiator, but you're going to have to cut and fit to install them. Those part numbers are: Goodyear MH585 for the upper radiator hose and MH1235 for the lower hose. These part numbers may have been different in previous years and are not direct-fit hoses. In addition, they may be somewhat difficult to install and may take some muscle and trimming to get them in place.

While you are at the parts store rummaging through the radiator hoses for the right one, it is helpful to know that the inside diameter (ID) of the hose you're looking for is 1½ inches. This is for both upper and lower sizes. You might have to cut and adjust a bit on each hose to make it fit just right but if done correctly, it looks factory.

AutoRad

This radiator and fan combo boasts a 40-percent surface area gain over a stock radiator and a 20-percent surface area gain for even the best radiators on the market, which is impressive. I want the capability of blasting the A/C while hitting the corners hard at the track. A radiator that can keep it all under control is a big bonus to us. In addition, if I choose to upgrade to even more power in the future, this unit is up to the task and one less thing for me to worry about.

To install this radiator, the core support needs to be replaced. If yours looked as butchered as mine did, replacing it is probably a wise thing to do. Another reason I went this route is that the stock LS radiators typically have a sandwiched design; the two side-headers are made of plastic and are joined to aluminum cores. This is typically the weak spot in a modern radiator and after repeated heating and cooling cycles those joints wear down and eventually leak and need replacing.

With all the options available from AutoRad, I opted for the dual fan setup and the A/C condenser already mocked up into place. AutoRad throws in all the hardware you need so this really was a no-brainer.

COOLING SYSTEM

The AutoRad radiator has in and out ports for the radiator hoses on the same side of the radiator; this is different than a typical GM setup. The radiator also came with two electric fans each requiring 18 amps of power. The Mast wiring system is a bit different, so it works with one fan. However, I was able to connect both fans as the Mast harness has a 40-amp relay and can handle the power of both fans at once. A typical LS system has a relay for each fan. You may have to modify yours to fit your application.

The radiator and fan combo has been installed just like the stock one would have been (with two on each side of the radiator). The supplied catch can for the radiator mounts on the cap side with the same two bolts that hold it in place. The fans came with a premade wiring harness. Because the Mast harness comes with wires for electric fans (much like the stock ECM), hook up was a breeze by simply splicing the ECM wires into the fan harness.

Radiator Hose Location

On an LS engine, both radiator hoses route from the passenger's side of the engine. The accessories can interfere with connecting the upper radiator for certain engines and set-ups for folks who want to run a stock first- or second-generation F-Body radiator or in applications where a turbo or supercharger has been added. Dropping in a dual-pass cross-flow radiator resolves this problem by connecting both hoses on the passenger's side of the engine.

An additional benefit to dual-pass radiators is that they keep the coolant in the radiator longer. This allows the fan to remove more heat, and it increases the ability of the radiator to cool more efficiently. Every LS engine is equipped with a 195-degree thermostat. The major difference is that the outlet for the thermostat is not in its typical position directly on top of the intake as with the small-block. The engine must retain the thermostat because it's a direct flow-through design, so you don't want to remove it and damage the engine.

The LS engine doesn't run its coolant through the intake manifold like previous Chevrolet engines did so there are some subtle differences in operation. Many swappers simply drill and tap the water pump and direct the flow straight into the water pump and back into cooling system. This works well and I have seen no problems from many different installs.

Another way to do it is to put an inline adapter from the upper radiator hose or possibly the heater hose. Either way works equally well. The real question becomes, "How much work am I willing to put in?"

CHAPTER 6

The new core support differs in size and the way it mounts to the front grille and latch support. A slot is on the inside of the core support; these two bolts need to thread through before you can attach the radiator. The new core support replaces the stock support and mounts in the exact same way using the stock bolt locations.

The steam tube comes off the head and needs to be correctly routed. This owner tapped the water pump and took the steam tube directly to it. You can do something similar or just go to the radiator with standard coolant tubing as I did.

The steam line is behind the power steering pump and reservoir on the driver's side of the engine. It needs to be routed back into the cooling system. It can be done in many ways, but I routed mine to the steam vent tube on the AutoRad radiator with standard coolant hose and hose clamps.

The correct 3/4-inch elbow made it bend out of the way. I found this piece at the local hardware store for less than $3. I have since learned that you can find pre-bent coolant tubing at the local parts store. This is a much better alternative because it removes many of the clamps required with a plastic elbow. I don't prefer this method as it creates more areas for problems and leaks, but sometimes it's a necessary evil to finish a job.

COOLING SYSTEM

A number of radiators have a steam vent bung that comes already attached to the radiator if you choose to use it; otherwise put a plug in it. This is by far the easiest conversion method, but also the least clean-looking way to install it.

Coolant Steam Line

Another unique feature of the LS cooling system and the LS system itself is that it uses a coolant steam line. The coolant steam line is designed to vent excess air pockets from the coolant system. Air is the enemy of any proper cooling system and this system does a nice job of removing unwanted air pockets without a lot of mess. When performing a swap, you need to route and connect the tube to the upper radiator hose. This line must be hooked up or the engine could overheat.

Heater Outlets

The heater hose outlets are pretty consistent from car to car. Even the new-style C6 Corvette and the first-gen F-Body share the same heater hose size and routing plan. The LS engine locates the heater hose outlets directly behind the thermostat housing.

When looking direct at the two plugs from the passenger's side, the rear-most port accepts a 5/8-inch heater hose and has a matching port on the heater core, this is the "in" port as hot coolant passes from the engine to the heater core. The forward-most facing port is a 3/4-inch heater hose and is the "out," or return, side of the system. The heater core returns the cooled coolant from the heater core back into the engine.

You may have to purchase a truck-style thermostat cover. It allows for a better angle of attack on the lower radiator hose. (Photo Courtesy Street & Performance)

Coolant Temperature Sensor

For some reason my PCM and gauge cluster did not like to play well together so I had come up with another solution to gauge the coolant temperature rather than the typical places. I found a coolant adapter from Auto Meter that taps into the feed line of the heater hose and uses a 1/8 NPT fitting for the coolant temperature sensor.

Remember to ground this piece or your gauge reads zero.

Electric Fan

Electric fans come in numerous shapes and sizes. The stock Corvette and F-Body LS engine typically comes with two fans: the main low-speed fan and one that comes on at high speed when the engine requires the extra cooling. You might want the dual-fan setup if you're on a budget because it's a proven system that works well. The dual fan setup can be had from junkyards fairly cheaply.

If your wiring harness doesn't have any relays, you have to add a couple to precisely match the situation. Relays are a great way to power something off the battery without causing any serious drain and provides safety by allowing power to be turned on only when truly needed.

If you choose to use a Gen IV style ECM, you have some extra wiring to complete the pulse-width modulation system. This is the same technology used in the fuel pump, essentially only going as fast as it needs to on short electrical pulses. Since this is the aberrant situation rather than the norm, I stick with the on-off style of fans.

A lot of aftermarket kits are available today. AFCO, BECOOL, and Ron Davis are just a few names in the market now. I'm sure others complete the

CHAPTER 6

job adequately. All of them have a variety of setups available that include bare radiators all the way up to full kits with fans, shrouds, and wiring harnesses. It's really up to you how far you want to go with it. If you're planning on running some big power, you might want to look toward Ron Davis or AutoRad for your cooling needs.

The fans I had on the AutoRad system use a dual 18-amp fan system. Because my Mast ECM is only programmed to work with one fan, I simply hooked up the fan wires to both fans at once. The Mast ECM is designed with a 40-amp breaker, so I had plenty of power to spare.

PCV System

The LS PCV (positive crankcase ventilation) system is a little different than the standard system that is on a typical small-block. The system on the LS engine has three ports that need to be routed correctly. The LS engine, like most other engines, makes positive pressure when in operation. These pressures need to be dealt with or the engine starts leaking profusely through the weakest part of the engine, typically the gaskets. The PCV system allows the engine to expel those gases (known as "blow-by") through three ports: one on each valve cover, and one on the front port coming off the intake valley. Do not block these ports or modify them as they provide crucial venting for your shiny new engine. The last thing you want is a sick, weeping, and puking pile of aluminum.

If you choose to order a crate engine from Chevrolet Performance or a GM dealership, be aware that their instructions are slightly different but that both work.

Installation

The strict Chevrolet Performance instructions say that you should connect the two foul side ports to the intake manifold and be exposed to vacuum at idle. These two ports are the valley port and the driver-side valve cover port. The passenger-side port should be connected to a clean air source such as the air cleaner. If you chose to use a MAF sensor on your car, the passenger-side port should be mounted between the MAF and the throttle body, typically on the intake tube. If the port is connected before the MAF, it confuses the sensor and possibly throws an erroneous code.

I set up this system as simply as you would want to. I routed both valve cover ports to a T-fitting with 3/8-inch vacuum line and then a single line to a small and unobtrusive catch can to catch any excess blow-by. The can is topped with an air cleaner so that any return air or oil isn't contaminated. The valley port is connected to a vacuum source, this can be virtually any vacuum source, such as a brake booster, but I chose the shortest and easiest route, which is directly to the intake pipe right before the throttle body.

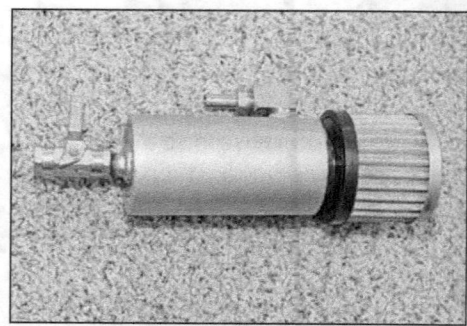
Chad Vancura made my oil catch can. You can purchase one from an outlet catalog, such as Jegs, Summit, and others, but I wanted mine to be a very specific size to match my application. I had a small area to work with so the only real option I had was to fabricate one to meet specific needs.

This port on the oil valley needs to be hooked up to a vacuum source. I ended up looping this up to the intake. One note of caution: It's wise to use a catch can with this look primarily because any oil that gets puked out of the engine just gets sucked right into the intake, and that's never a good thing.

CHAPTER 7

TRANSMISSION

You have a universe of transmission options for swapping an LS into an early F-Body, and like other components of your equipment package, the transmission you select should be based on application. Most owners stick to a transmission that has a compatible bolt pattern for the LS because it's convenient and many superb transmissions simply bolt up to the LS bellhousing. You can opt for a classic GM automatic or manual transmission, but for a pro-touring or track car, most owners choose a late-model 5- or 6-speed transmission.

General Motors designed the LS platform with much platform commonality. Similar to the common engine mount bosses on all LS engines, every LS engine uses the same transmission bolt pattern. The bolt pattern layout allows for a direct bolt up of all LS-compatible transmissions, so 4L60E, 4L80E automatics bolt up and so does the Tremec T56 and other similar manual transmissions. However, you don't need to use a current transmission. You can use a classic transmission, such as the Muncie M20, M21, and M22, or Turbo-Hydramatic 350 and 400. These were industry-leading transmissions for their time and while you may be able to find a more efficient modern transmission with an overdrive gear or ones with the particular ratios you are looking for, these still remain capable transmissions. Mating a classic transmission originally made for the Gen I Chevy small-block is not difficult. The classic Chevy transmission bolt pattern has one less bolt than the modern LS transmissions. So when installing the transmission on the LS, you leave out the passenger-side center bolt, which would enter the water jacket of the LS block.

Many new transmissions are available to harness the power of the LS-series engines and direct this power to the rear axle. A myriad of automatic and transmission options are available for LS engines and F-Body swaps. After all, transmissions play just as much of a vital role in a build as the engine does. Also, in defense of the mostly unseen transmission, it is probably one of the major factors in how much fun a car is to drive. It's amazing how easily a manual transmission suddenly turns

You need to find the pinion angle of your drivetrain to match it to the rear end. A $10 angle finder like mine makes it fairly simple. A general rule is that 3 degrees is sufficient for street use.

CHAPTER 7

You will most likely have to modify your driveshaft to fit your new engine and transmission combo. I don't have the capability to do this myself so I measured for a new driveshaft to be built. It may not look like much here, but a couple of inches does make a difference in proper fit. The new shaft (top) is made by Bear's Performance. The original shaft (bottom) was shortened for my small-block Chevy and Tremec T56 Transmission. A machinist needs to do any shortening.

Because of the new power demands, I asked Bear's Performance to beef up the components. I upgraded the driveshaft as well as new 1350-style U-joints. I went from 450 hp to 600 hp. I also swapped the old 10-bolt for a Ford 9-inch rear end.

You will most likely have to cut a new access hole for the transmission shifter. So you measure it, mark it, and use a cut-off wheel to shorten it to the correct length. I tried to use the old hole, but as you can see, it's a bit off. Installing a fireproof shifter boot is a top priority. It's typically easier to remove the carpet before modifying the floor panel. I used a cutoff wheel on a grinder and a tin snip to make the final cuts.

a pretty average driving car into a race car.

In this chapter I cover the basics and some subtle nuances for putting just about any transmission in the GM lineup behind an LS engine into a first- or second-generation F-Body. In all the transmissions I've seen swapped behind LS engines in these cars, I have yet to see a stock location engine/transmission combo that needed the transmission tunnel cut. There are those who have had to cut and modify the transmission tunnel, but typically these are for very specific reasons, such as having the engine raised higher than the stock location, lowered, or broken body mounts.

In the following case, Mary Pozzi's car needed a new tunnel because she wanted to shove the engine farther back for better weight distribution. In such a situation, you certainly have to cut the floor and tunnel; otherwise feel confident that the stock tunnel can remain intact.

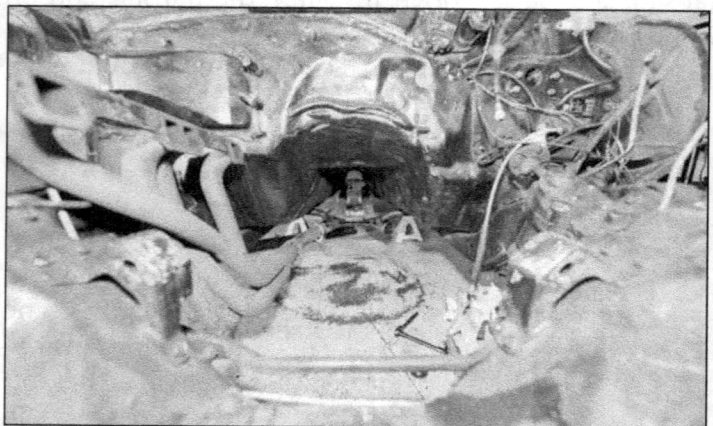

Thankfully I started out with a fairly solid Camaro body. The transmission tunnel doesn't need to be cut up. Contrary to popular belief, you don't have to cut the transmission tunnel to get a T56 to fit well. If you have a modified frame mount or lower than usual mounts, this may change.

The back of the LS engine is different in two major ways. First, it doesn't have the familiar 1 o'clock position bolt, and second, it's .400 inch from the back of the engine to the flange that mates the transmission to the engine.

TRANSMISSION

The obvious difference between the blocks is shown here. The upper right bellhousing bolt has been eliminated but it does not affect performance of the bellhousing or its strength.

T56 Install

I suspect that this transmission is the most likely candidate for hot rodders building an F-Body, and for good reason! Most variants of the T56 can withstand at least 450 hp and 450 ft-lbs of torque, which can usually fit most builds. The T56 is also a killer road-race transmission. With a choice of close and wide ranges of the first four gears, you have a great selection of how aggressive you want to be.

In addition, the T56 is an excellent cruising transmission that has two overdrive gears. Not one, but two! With fourth gear being a 1:1 ratio, the two extra gears are just a bonus. Chances are that you probably won't ever need sixth gear as most people running this setup have to be running 75 to 85 mph to ever see the benefit of it, but it's nice to know that you can run 75 mph down the highway at close to idle speeds.

The only downside that I see with the transmission, and my only gripe, is that this bugger is big and heavy. The T56 weighs around 125 pounds where a typical T5 runs a mere 85 to 90 pounds. Still, the extra weight is worth it.

Tremec T56 Transmission Installation

1. *I like Tranzilla transmission fluid because major race teams use it. If it's good enough for them, it's good enough for me. It's a fully synthetic oil that protects greater than stock OEM fluid.*

2. *The ATS T56 crossmember fits as well in a stock frame as it does in a modified one. It has lots of adjustability and cutouts to fit the exhaust snugly to the floorboard. Use Grade-8 hardware to bolt it into the same location as the stock crossmember.*

3. *The clutch slave cylinder has been installed; two bolts on either side that go into the transmission. The top port is used for bleeding the system while the lower port is used as the quick connect for the master cylinder.*

CHAPTER 7

4. This crossmember came with the Speed Tech frame. It's fully adjustable forward and backward to accept virtually any transmission I can throw at it. Grade-8 hardware fastens it to the frame.

5. The correct bolts were not included with the slave cylinder so I had to source them from the local hardware store. They are M6 x 1 x 16 mm. Torque them to 25 inch-pounds.

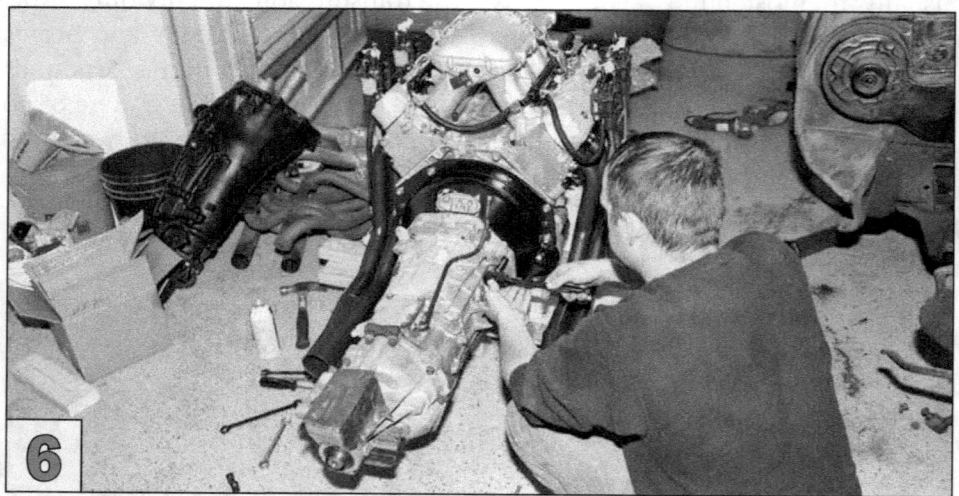

6. Use a dab of red or blue Loctite. Slowly guide the transmission into place, being careful to seat the input shaft snugly into the pilot bearing. You should have a buddy help in the process because the transmission is heavy and difficult to move into position. You could use a floor jack to slide the transmission into the proper position in the transmission tunnel.

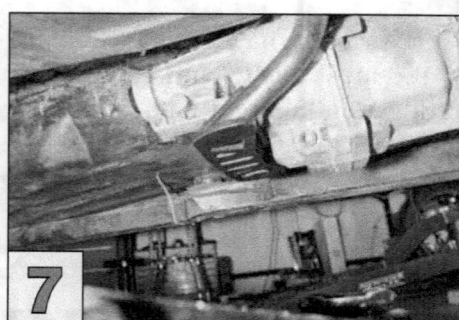

7. Whether it's behind a small-block Chevy or an LS engine, the ATS crossmember works well. The ATS piece reuses a stock TH400 transmission mount to secure it to the transmission and crossmember. It mounts and bolts in just as the stock transmission does. Tolerances on these pieces are tight so be prepared to do a fair amount of maneuvering.

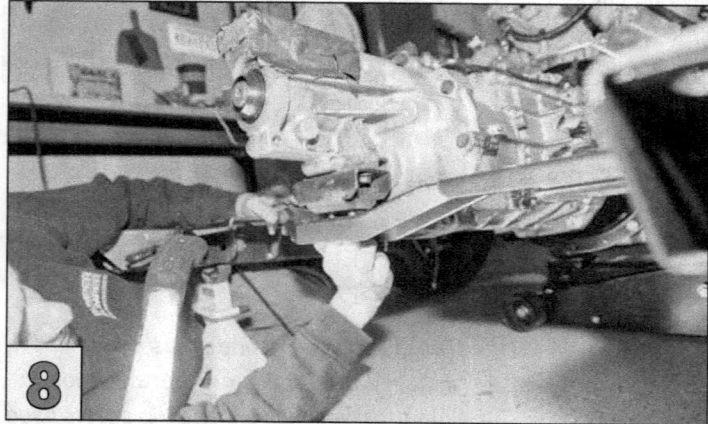

8. The Speed Tech frame uses the same transmission mount as the ATS piece. It's secured with two bolts. I left the bracket bolts loose to make up for any slack the transmission needed to take up.

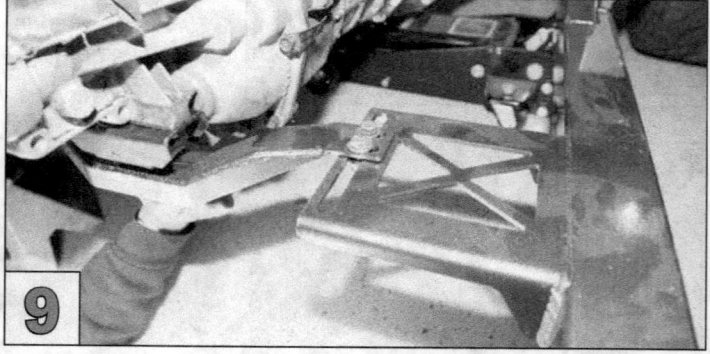

9. This is a good close-up of the transmission crossmember that comes with the Speed Tech front subframe. It has a lot of front-to-back movement that allows me to place the engine and transmission virtually anywhere I choose. Using Grade-8 bolts, the crossmember just sits in place on top of the frame and is bolted in.

TRANSMISSION

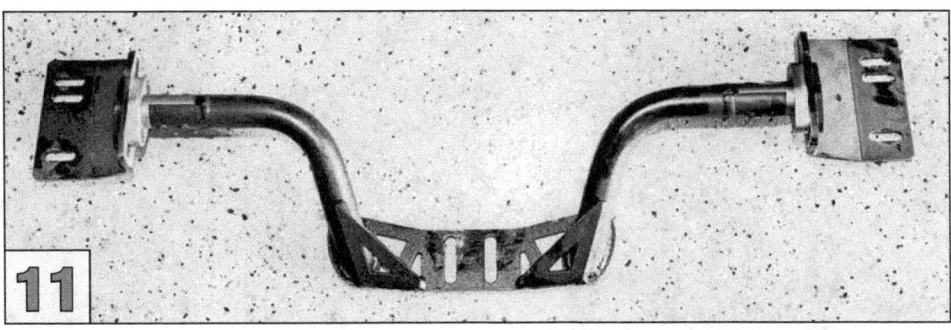

11 I pulled out the ATS T56 crossmember for a good look at this three-piece unit.

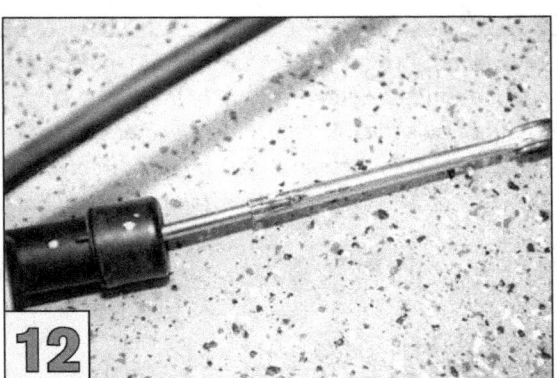

10 The T56 is fully mounted. The two openings in the front transmission plate are for the hydraulic clutch. The top one is the bleeder screw and the bottom one is the quick-disconnect port.

12 The clutch master cylinder from General Motors (PN 12570277) has an input shaft that needs to be shortened. I purchased a Speed Tech conversion kit and went to work cutting off the old sleeve. I used a cut-off wheel and pliers to remove the old arm. Be careful not to go too deep when cutting it off the sleeve or you could ruin a very pricey item.

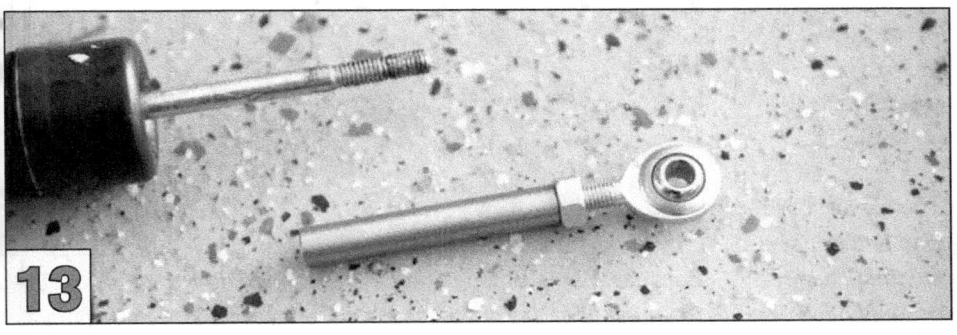

13 After removing the old sleeved shaft, you are ready to install the new joint. You use a vise to compress these two together and a chisel to dimple the shaft. The threaded piece is for the pivot arm. The tube must be pressed on; it's not threaded on the inside.

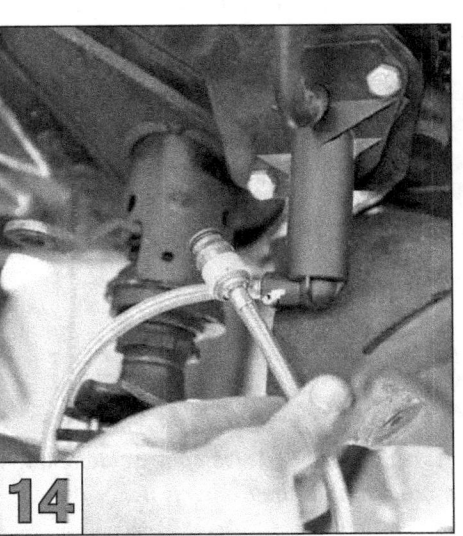

14 After your master cylinder is mounted, you have to find a safe passage to the transmission so that the braided line isn't kinked and is far away from any heat from the headers.

15 Mount the master cylinder reservoir close to the pedal and make sure it's at the highest point possible to prevent any air from entering the system. This helps in gravity-bleeding the system. I used sheet-metal screws to secure it to the firewall.

SWAP LS ENGINES INTO CAMAROS & FIREBIRDS 1967–1981

Here's how it should look when you are finished. Two bolts hold the master cylinder onto the booster and four bolts hold the booster to the brackets. Using sheet-metal screws the reservoir should be mounted high so that it is the highest point of the system and out of the way.

I had to make a significant modification at the arm coming out of the firewall to the clutch pedal. I removed the clutch pedal and drilled and tapped a hole for the clutch. The original holes are not in the correct location nor are they the correct size. You have to take the pedal out of the car.

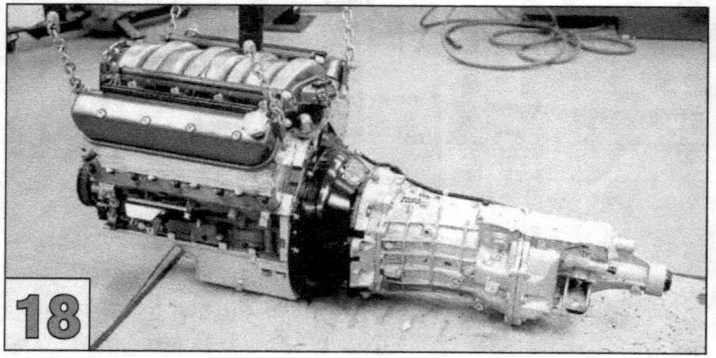

The engine and transmission are mated up and ready for the initial install. You usually have to install the engine and transmission assembly several times to ensure the steering linkage doesn't interfere with engine parts. Moving the engine back also presents issues; the headers may not clear the upper control arms and cross-shaft bolts. (Photo Courtesy Mary Pozzi)

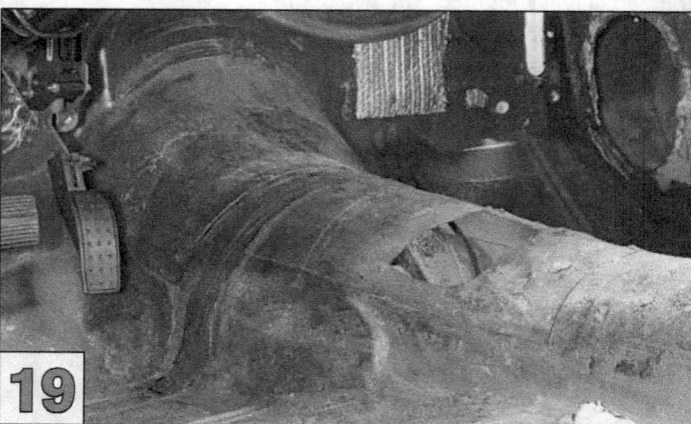

Because Mary wanted to move the engine and transmission farther back than the stock location, the transmission tunnel most likely required modification to allow proper fit for the transmission. (Photo Courtesy Mary Pozzi)

Here's the position of the tunnel after the initial trial fit. Additional metal is cut and welded to strengthen and reposition the original sheet metal so the transmission fits. (Photo Courtesy Mary Pozzi)

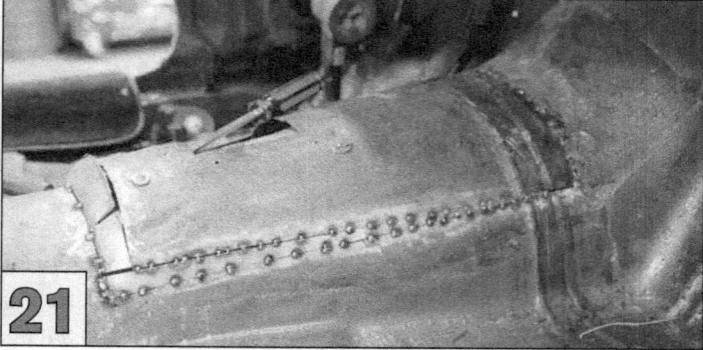

The transmission tunnel was enlarged. It was spot-welded and fabricated with a little more room for the transmission. (Photo Courtesy Mary Pozzi)

TRANSMISSION

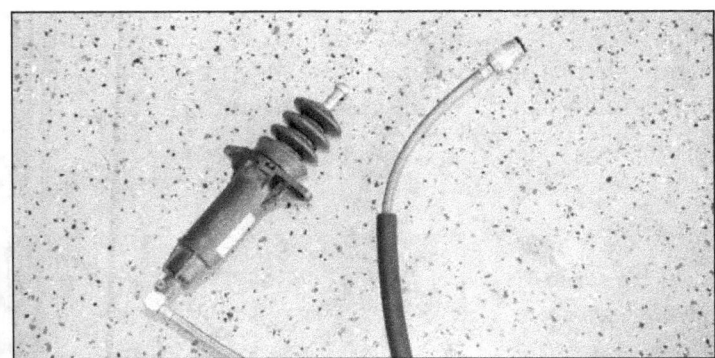

The differences between the LT T56 and the LS T56 hydraulics are shown. The LT version (left) has a plunger that actuates a fork that pivots inside the bellhousing while the LS version (right) uses hydraulic fluid (DOT 3 brake fluid) to actuate a slave cylinder attached to the transmission.

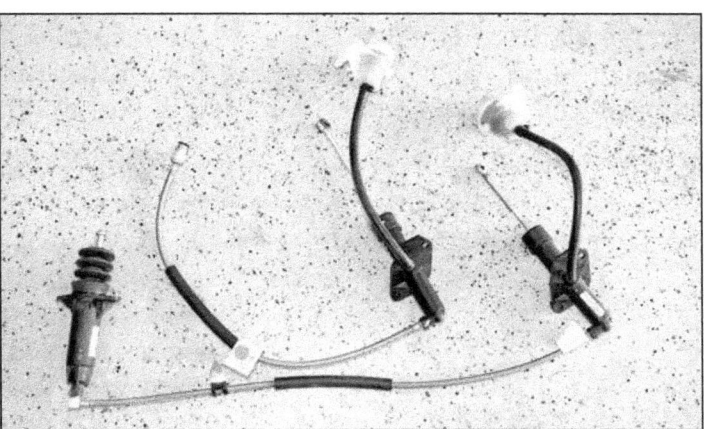

This is a good comparison of two master cylinders: a fully hydraulic LS version (top) and a hydraulic master and mechanical fork version for LT-style transmissions (bottom).

Bleeding the Clutch

One of the jobs that people seem to complain the most about is bleeding the clutch. There's no secret here that General Motors didn't necessarily make this the easiest job in the world, but it also isn't impossible.

Note that all T56s use a 7/16-inch wrench to open the bleeder. Do not let the reservoir become dry and always keep it topped off with DOT 3 fluid.

Here are three easy ways to bleed the clutch slave cylinder:

Gravity Bleed: This method is straightforward. Just open the reservoir cap, crack the bleeder with your wrench, and crack open a beer. It helps with the mess if you choose to use a catch can and to put a clear hose on the end of the bleeder to view the fluid. Wait for the fluid to start leaking out and you are good to go. This method is the slowest and often time doesn't always work. You can jump start the gravity bleed by lightly pushing the clutch pedal, but don't go crazy with it.

Hand Pump Bleed: This method is for the one-person show. The best way to complete this task is to use a hand pump just like the one you use for bleeding brakes. Open the reservoir and twist-open the bleeder. Use the vacuum pump just like you would a typical brake system. Make sure to keep an eye on the reservoir, letting that go dry makes your job much, much worse.

Traditional Bleed: The traditional way to bleed the clutch is just like a two-person brake bleeding operation. One person is in charge of the pedal and the other is in charge of the bleeder. The idea is exactly the same as a brake bleed, one person pushes the pedal down and barks out, "ON!" and the other person opens the bleeder to allow fluid to travel through the system. After the pressure is moved along, the bleeder operator informs the pedal person, and the process is repeated until all the air is out of the system.

T56 Connections

The T56 has a number of connections on each side of the transmission. The three that you'll be using are the vehicle speed sensor (VSS), backup lights, and reverse lockout solenoid. Depending on which speedometer you have, the VSS does or does not directly plug into the transmission. Most electronic speedometers are compatible with the transmission but need to be calibrated to it. Some may require an additional converter if your speedo is mechanical. ShiftWorks has a comprehensive kit that allows you to run a mechanical speedometer, but this requires replacing the tailshaft and slightly modifying the existing shaft. This is a really good option if you want a clean install.

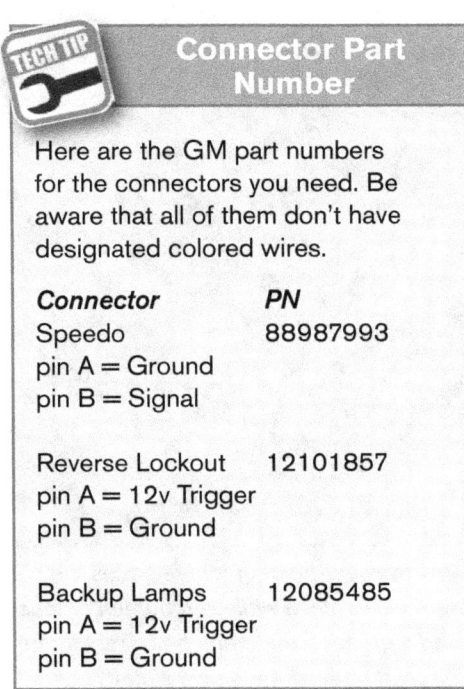

TECH TIP — Connector Part Number

Here are the GM part numbers for the connectors you need. Be aware that all of them don't have designated colored wires.

Connector	PN
Speedo pin A = Ground pin B = Signal	88987993
Reverse Lockout pin A = 12v Trigger pin B = Ground	12101857
Backup Lamps pin A = 12v Trigger pin B = Ground	12085485

CHAPTER 7

The other option that is fairly popular is the Cable-X system. It's a small electric box that converts the pulse signal from the VSS into a mechanical feed. They claim that this box works with virtually any speedometer on the market, and for the amount of work it takes, it's a good price at around $300.

Flywheel and Clutch Installation

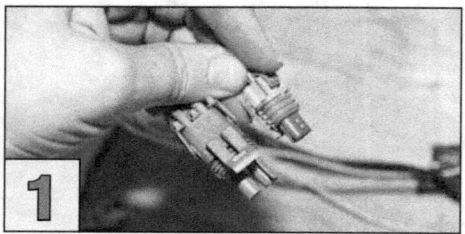

You need these two plugs for the T56. One (purple connector) supplies the speedometer while the other (brown connector) provides the switch for the reverse lights. The thicker of the two wires is for the reverse lights and the thinner provides the signal for the electric speedo.

The LS3 crankshaft has the standard six-bolt pattern for the flywheel. Use new bolts when installing the flywheel. You don't want to risk a bolt failure by using old bolts.

To convert your vehicle to a fully hydraulic system, a firewall clutch master cylinder adapter is necessary. This one is from ATS (PN 080002) and is a simple bolt-on.

This flywheel-holding tool replaces the starter and holds the flywheel in place while you tighten or loosen the bolts. It also works great on the crank bolt. It's a lot better than a screwdriver jammed against the block, isn't it?

The RAM Clutches flywheel (PN 98931HD) is aluminum and allows higher horsepower levels on the street without exploding on you. The guys at RAM didn't give exact power capability numbers but they did say it would help with throttle response. It's bolted on the back of the crankshaft with a dab of Loctite.

TRANSMISSION

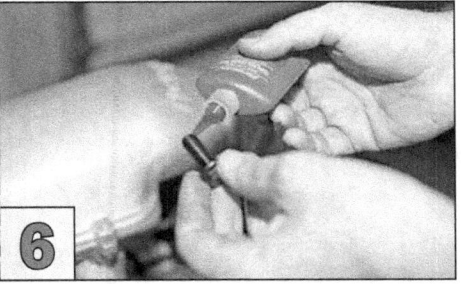

6 When installing any clutch bolt it helps to use a dab of Loctite on the threads. Again, insurance is cheap.

7 My QuickTime bellhousing (PN 8020) is SFI approved for almost every racing series and is a serious piece if you have a lot of horsepower. If a transmission fails, it can literally explode and send shrapnel at high velocity through the transmission tunnel. If your LS produces more than 500 hp, a heavy-duty bellhousing is a wise investment in safety equipment. You get the bellhousing, adapter plate, and all the hardware needed.

8 Install the adapter plate before the flywheel so that the bellhousing has a place to bolt onto on the bottom. The adapter has two alignment holes on either side that slide over the transmission bellhousing dowels. This is a good time to clean off the surface of your flywheel; most are shipped with a protective coating. Tighten these bolts to 75 ft-lbs with a torque wrench.

9 A cheap plastic clutch alignment tool is handy for aligning the clutch plate without it. Make sure this doesn't wiggle around when installing the rest of the system. Once the pressure plate is in place the alignment tool can be removed and put back into the toolbox.

10 Don't forget the pilot bearing. It's essential that you install it. The GM PN 12557583 is the pilot bearing. I was able to get one at the local NAPA auto parts store for $20 (PN BRG B657). Pound this in until it is flush with the rear of the crankshaft.

CHAPTER 7

11 At this stage, you need to install the pressure plate. Again, use some Loctite on each bolt and tighten to 75 ft-lbs.

12 The bottom bolts for the QuickTime bellhousing need to be installed in reverse with the bolt facing backward, otherwise you run into interference with the oil pan.

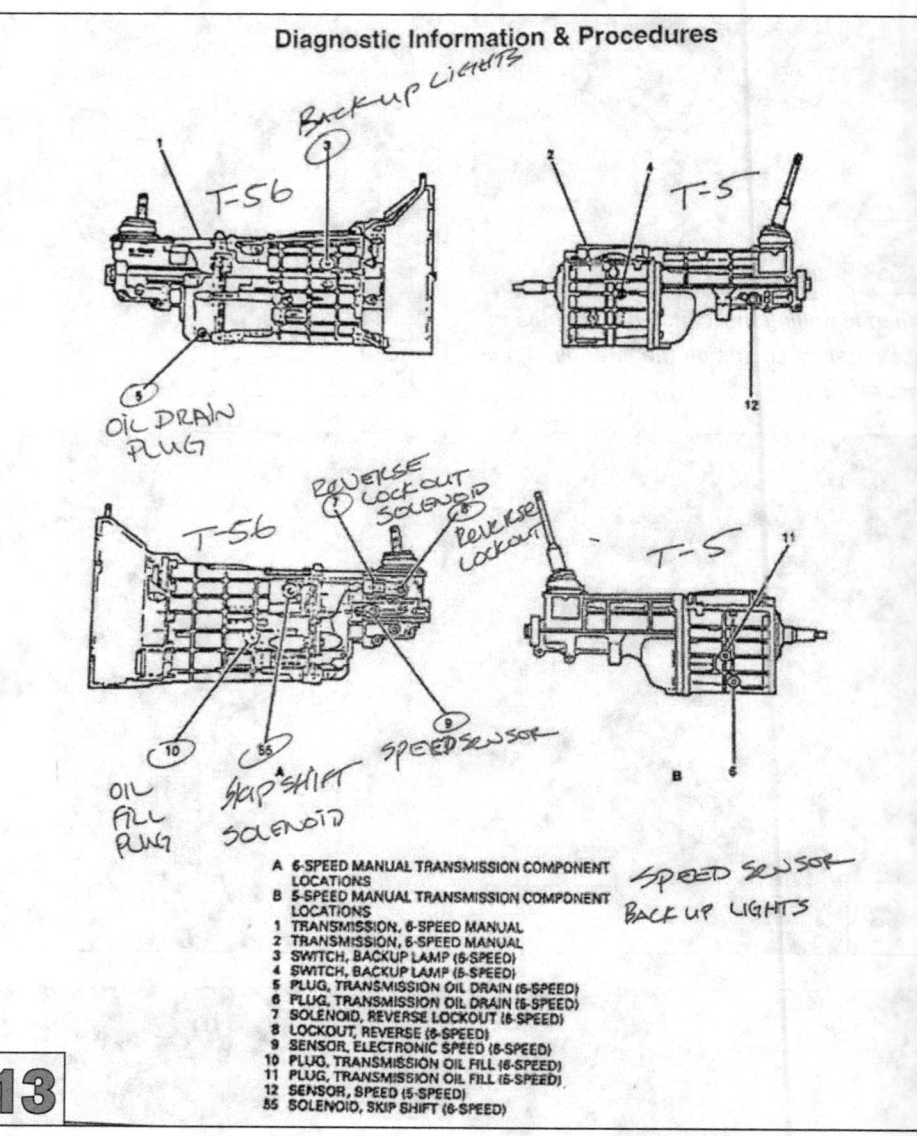

13 Here are all the locations for the plug-ins and ports for the T56. The transmission works just fine without anything plugged into it; you just may not have a working speedo. (Illustration Courtesy Alldata Illustration)

Reverse Lockout Solenoid

A quick word about the reverse lockout solenoid: You can wire this up, but I frankly feel it is almost not worth the effort. With the reverse lockout solenoid hooked up, you have to shift hard into fifth gear and slam the shifter into reverse. It's virtually impossible. The T56 shifts into reverse in conditions under 5 mph or basically stand-still. All that you need to do is just give it a little tap and the transmission shifts into reverse. For this very reason, most people I've seen just leave this alone and don't plug it in. It's your call.

Speedometer Output

Adding a speedometer to a T56 is fairly easy to do if you have the correct speedo. Options are available for those who want to use the stock speedo or one that is mechanically driven, which just takes a bit more work.

Right off the bat, almost any electric speedo works with the T56 output in the tail shaft. One wire is the exciter wire and the other is the ground. More times than not, getting the wires right doesn't really matter as long as you have both hooked up. However, you have to make sure that you calibrate the speedo. This usually involves driving a certain distance and hitting a couple of buttons. This is a requirement of most mainstream gauges, such as Auto Meter speedos.

My Stack unit is a bit on the odd side and requires a pulse amplifier and a little math. I had to push the car forward one full revolution of the tires and measure the number of pulses. Then using the length of one tire rotation I was able to calculate the number of pulses per mile and enter that into the Stack unit; a bit more lengthy, but equally effective.

Now, for you interior purists who just can't live without your factory speedometer, you are in luck. You have two options. The first is to replace the tail shaft with one that allows for a mechanical input such as the ones from Shift-Works. The other option is to run a Cable-X system. This converts the pulses from the transmission into mechanical movement. It's a simple three-wire setup that can be hidden under the dash.

Throwout Bearing Spacing

I had difficulty setting the correct throwout bearing clearance when mating the T56 to my LS3 combo. The clutch and the bearing must have 0.200 inch of clearance between them. If the clearance is too great, the throwout bearing extends too far and causes premature wear. On the other hand, if the clearance is less than this spec, the clutch disengages. This causes slippage in the clutch and effectively makes it seem as if you're riding the clutch, even when your foot is off the pedal.

Aftermarket spacers can be used to attain the correct clearance. Most speed catalogs, such as Jegs and Summit Racing, sell spacers and shims in various packs starting around $20. This is typically a bigger deal when purchasing an aftermarket bearing or a rebuilt one, as the tolerances are most likely not the same as factory stock.

To verify clearance, you need to install the clutch, pressure plate, and bellhousing on the engine. Use a dial indicator and a ruler or a flat edge to measure the distance from the bellhousing face to the clutch fingers, then write this number down. Go to your transmission and slip on the bearing. With the bearing flush to the transmission, measure the distance from the bearing face to the front of the transmission; write this down as well. Take your first number and subtract that from the second and you have the difference in fractions of inches. Use as many shims as you need to get within the parameters of .125 to .225 inch. The ideal is .200 inch but if you are within this range you are just fine.

Tremec Magnum

The Tremec T56 Magnum variant of the standard T56 is able to handle upward of 700 ft-lbs of torque while the stock T56 is typically rated at 450 hp and 450 ft-lbs of torque. The Magnum has a very short shifter throw with a very sharp engagement in the syncros when the shifter is maneuvered. The Magnum is roughly the same size as the T56 and looks very similar; it is a bit longer, almost 2 inches in overall length, so you have to shorten your driveshaft. The Magnum has two different gear sets: 2.66 or 2.97 first gear. I decided that the 2.97 first gear was more optimal for this application and for auto-crossing where the courses seem to be tighter and it allows me to dig out of the hole just that much more quickly. The two overdrives are another bonus (just as the stock T56 provides), so in my world it's the best of both.

The Magnum is a versatile transmission and it has three important design features to note. First is the reversible shifter. It allows for more varied placement of the shifter, which may allow you to reuse the stock shifter location with minimal cutting and prodding. Due to loose tolerances in the manufacturing of F-Bodies in the 1960s and 1970s, you may have to dimple the floorpan with a ballpeen hammer in a couple of places to make sure it fits properly. With my T56 I didn't have to do this, which is the norm; others may not be so lucky.

Second, the Magnum can use either a mechanical or electric speedo attachment, and this is great news for anyone who wants to run stock-style mechanical gauges.

Third, the Magnum has provisions for a Ford-style mount or the traditional TH400 GM mount.

If it's good enough for the ZR1 Corvette and the Dodge ACR Viper, it is suitable for the LS3 in my car. The shifting actuation, or shifting feel, is quite different than the typical clutch-bang-gas type of driving; rather, the Magnum is shifted with a light touch for optimal performance. The transmission I chose is the Tranzilla from Rockland Standard Gear (RSG). RSG first takes a Tremec Magnum T56 transmission, then adds a Viper tail shaft, and reworks some of the rings to make them handle roughly 1,000 ft-lbs of torque and abuse. With this transmission, you cannot reverse the shifter and it does not have a mechanical speedometer output. Instead, it only has an electrical speedometer output. But it has so many advantages. Regardless, I know that the RSG Tranzilla is able to keep up with me even if I upgrade engines or decide to add a power adder such as a supercharger.

New-Style Transmissions

One option for your transmission is to buy an engine and tranny combo all in one. You should also buy the main ECU and transmission controller as a single unit. If you have a manual transmission you can skip this section because you don't need it. If you don't, I cover the basics of installing a modern transmission with the LS beast.

4L60E/4L80E

The newer and more modern upgrades of timeless classics such as the 700 R4 and TH400 are great ways to get out on the road quickly and reliably. These bolt directly to your LS engine with no worries about modifications. The only catch is that these transmissions require a computer-assisted controller to make sure everything works properly. The 4L80E is a bit more robust and can be built for high-horsepower applications. The 4L80E case is larger than the 4L60E but neither should require transmission tunnel modifications. The only decision left is really what shifter you want to use!

GM Controller

If you choose to go with a modern automatic transmission, you have to find some way to control it. If you have created your own harness, you probably already have the proper connector and a built-in transmission controller. You can also specify to the maker of wiring harness that they include the proper wiring for your specific transmission; it just helps keep things clean and less complicated.

Of course there are aftermarket options for almost everyone. The obvious one is the standalone computer and harness from General Motors (PN 12497316). They come as a kit and can be used to control the 4L60E, 4L65E, 4L80E, and 4L85E line of transmissions. The kit comes with the computer connector and the ability to program virtually any parameter. A lot of other controllers may be on the market that do a swell job just like the GM controller, but for the vast majority of people, this controller does the trick quite well.

OptiShift Controller

For those of you who need a more programmable option, OptiShift has a slick controller unit that costs around $600 depending on application. This option can be fully programmed with a laptop and even has a cool-looking readout for temperature, sensor values, and fault codes. I've seen them in action and I am fairly impressed with how this unit functions. This might be a good option if you have a high-horsepower application and want a bit more control over your transmission functionality.

Classic Transmissions

When it comes to the installation of older-style transmissions into first- and second-generation F-Body vehicles, there's good news and bad news. The bad news is that things become a little more complex than the standard bolt-it-up way I am used to doing things.

First, you have to make sure that your wiring harness is correct. Whether you order one or make your own, you want to be sure the harness matches your transmission style. Most companies make sure it's the

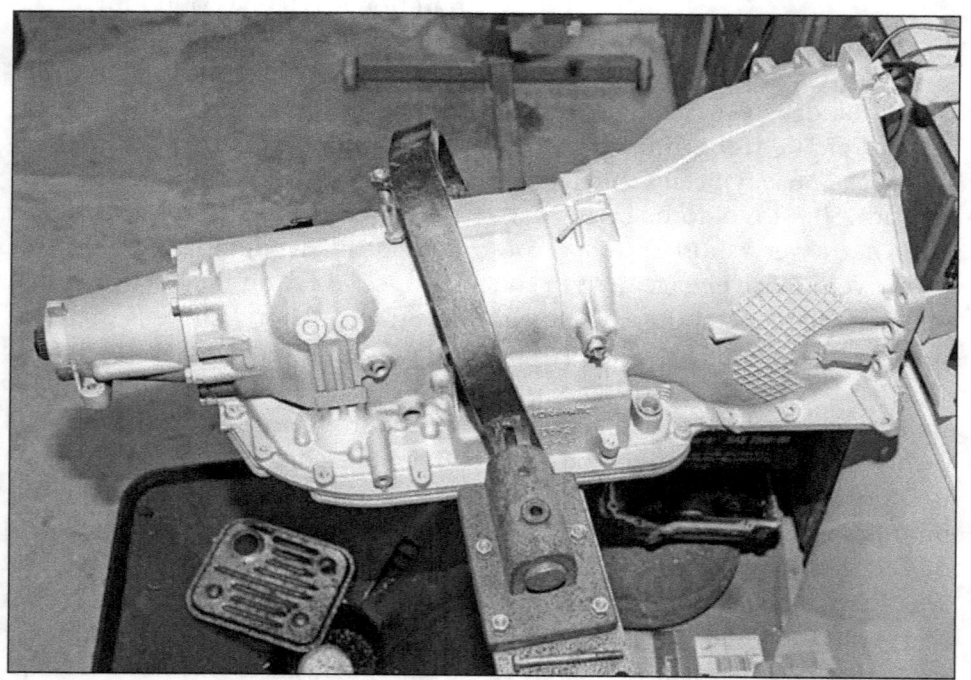
The 4L80E is a great automatic transmission. It can be built to almost any power level and still provides a smooth ride.

correct harness, but it never hurts to triple-check. For example, in the case of the T56 or other manual transmissions, you don't need an external controller like the newer-style automatics require. This makes life a lot simpler.

In addition, it's worth noting that when in doubt, give the manufacturer a call to verify the parts list you plan to use. I cannot stress this enough. The more you plan out your build, the easier it is in the long run.

Muncie

One thing you might be thinking is that you'd like to keep your original Muncie. A lot of people want to keep the original console in the car and/or not cut up the trans tunnel. I frankly don't blame you. I do have to caution you before you go ahead with this because although the original M4 rock-crusher is a great transmission, it really wasn't designed to handle the kind of power these LS engines make. Even if you grab a stock LS3, for example, you might just be at the ragged edge of reliability on a stock Muncie M-21 or M-22. That said, there are perfectly good options out there to make your dreams come true.

PACE Performance (PN PAC-1680-TK5) offers a good kit that includes virtually everything you need. While they say this kit is good up to 500 hp, a kit is available for horsepower up to the 600 range (PN PAC-1680-TK6). PACE requires that you specify what spline shaft you have, but that's a given, right? The kits typically include a QuickTime SFI LS 4-speed bellhousing, Ram LS steel SFI flywheel, Ram 12-inch clutch disk, ARP bolts, pilot bearing, Clutch fork pivot ball, and fork boot. For $1,260, it might be the best option for you. You have to provide the mechanical clutch linkage from the pedal to the throwout bearing, but that's pretty standard.

If you have all the necessary parts but just need a bellhousing to convert your Muncie to an LS engine, QuickTime sells them (PN RM-6036) through various vendors.

Refer to the above-mentioned throwout bearing measurement procedure if you choose to run a hydraulic throwout bearing with your manual transmission.

TH400/TH350/700R4/200R4

You can certainly install/mate a classic transmission to your LS engine. There are many reasons to do it. Maybe you have half a dozen lying around your front yard or maybe because TH400s are stout and fairly plentiful. Whatever the reason, you certainly can make it happen with the appropriate spacer, bolts, and a few extra steps.

The major difference is that the LS engine is .400 inch shorter than a typical small-block. The other difference is that the upper right bolthole for the bellhousing is missing. Thankfully, the bolt pattern is the same so you are able to use the same transmission case.

The solution to the shorter length is to use a spacer that can be purchased at places such as Scoggin-Dickey (GM PN 12563532) and Chevrolet Performance. Jeg's and Summit (Hughes PN HP3795) carry their own proprietary brands. You then need to purchase longer bolts to match the spacer (GM PN 11569956). The spacer is bolted to the crankshaft first, between the crankshaft and the flexplate; do it the other way around and you have problems. You also need a flat-faced GM flexplate (PN 12551367). This allows the starter to be engaged in the correct spot by moving it rearward that extra .400 inch (Hughes HP4004X).

Beware that not all flexplates and flywheels are the same. The 1955–1986 crankshafts with a two-piece rear seal has a 3.58-inch bolt circle while the 1987 to present crankshafts with one-piece rear seals have a 3.00-inch bolt circle. The LS crankshafts that have one-piece rear seals have a 3.11-inch bolt circle.

I have heard that you can use the curved or beveled 4.8/5.3 and LS1-style flexplates. This requires ovaling out the torque converter mating holes to make it fit properly. I'm not too keen on this idea as it tampers with something that takes a lot of abuse. Nor can I verify that this is accurate, so it may be worth investigating more fully before diving in. In this setup, you have to use a spacer, but it goes between the flexplate and torque converter to fill that cavity.

The final option may be the easiest, but also the most costly. You can purchase an LS-specific torque converter for your older-style automatic transmission that eliminates the need for a spacer. Currently several companies make a version for your transmission; expect to pay $450 or more.

Crossmembers

A number of crossmembers are on the market, and any of them does just fine. There are different crossmembers for each style of transmission; the most popular is the T56 crossmember. It must be said that it helps to plan ahead and make sure that the headers and engine mounts work with the crossmember. Ask first, purchase second.

CHAPTER 7

ATS

The most popular name in crossmember swaps is ATS. It's a three-piece unit. This piece works well with the stock subframe as well as aftermarket ones. Of course, Speed Tech acquired ATS a number of years ago, so it's only fitting that their subframe comes with a transmission crossmember flexible enough to fit just about every transmission.

G-Force

G-Force is a specialty company that makes a wide range of crossmembers for the first- and second-generation F-Bodies. They have a solid reputation and make crossmembers for almost any transmission. They offer units for older transmissions such as the T10, TH400, TH350, 700R4, and even newer ones such as the T56, 4L60E, and 4L80E.

Hurst Drive Lines

Hurst Drive Lines has a wide variety of parts and price ranges for making the T56 or TKO-5-speed swap or addition. They sell entire kits that take care of everything you need such as the clutch, clutch hydraulics, tubular crossmember, electrical connectors, shifter knob, transmission, driveshaft, flywheel, bellhousing, and speedo-meter cables or wires. These kits can be had for the first- or second-generation F-Body as well as a wide variety of others applications.

The only downside I could find is that each component is not available individually; they only come as a kit. Still, when you purchase a complete kit such as this one, you know that it's designed to work in concert with all the other pieces.

Stock Crossmember

Reusing the stock crossmember is entirely possible; the trick is to modify it to make it fit your swap. I've seen a few reworked stock crossmembers that work perfectly well. The center part of the crossmember needs to be cut out, then careful measurements need to be taken to see how far the drop should be. The driveline angle here is extremely important. A good rule is that the engine needs to be tipped back roughly 3 to 4 degrees and the rear end should be tipped upward about the same amount with no more than a 2-degree difference for typical street driving.

I recommend a thicker plate steel (between 1/8 and 1/4 inch) if you choose to modify your stock crossmember. As with everything the compromise is time versus money. Crossmembers are readily available so you may have to consider which is a better choice: your time or a couple of extra dollars and less effort.

Bellhousing

Regardless of what transmission you want to put behind your LS engine, chances are someone sells a bellhousing for it. QuickTime offers an SFI-certified bellhousing to bolt just about any trans behind an LS engine, including Tremecs, Richmonds, and all the popular GM automatics. Other companies offering transmission solutions are McLeod and Lakewood. If you're stuffing a T56 six-speed behind your LS mill, the low-buck route is to just run an aluminum GM housing, and of course, newer GM automatics have the bell integrated into the transmission case.

Here's a version of a custom transmission crossmember that bolts in from the side rather than from the top. (Photo Courtesy Texas Speed & Performance)

CHAPTER 8

WIRING

As with other LS components, a massive number of computer-control, harness, and electronic equipment options exist for this popular engine platform. Most swappers adapt the factory electronics to the particular F-Body, but installing aftermarket controllers are certainly an option. If you don't want to adapt the EFI and drive-by-wire gas pedal technology to your F-Body, then installing a conventional distributor and carburetor on your LS engine is an option. Many wiring harnesses and installation kits are available for LS engines. For my particular project, I adapted the modern LS EFI system.

For a first-time engine swapper, buying and installing a complete wiring harness and adapter kit is the best option because creating or modifying a wiring harness and adapting the drive-by-wiring controls is incredibly complex. After all, you want to get the car on the road as soon as possible. Typical kits do not require an incredible amount of electrical acumen; in fact, many can be installed by connecting only four wires.

Although wiring may not be your favorite work, it's often necessary to complete a project. One option is to pay a professional to do it, and certainly there is no shame in

For this complete build, I stripped all the wiring and started over with an American Autowire 18-circuit kit. This kit is specifically made for the first-generation F-Body and it adds blade-style fuses, replacing the old barrel style. It also adds a lot of extra slots for accessories such as a banging stereo or even a power converter.

This is an extra feature on the AAW harness. It allows you to power virtually anything with 12-volt power. Some are key-on-only power and some are full-time power. It really beats having to splice into the main harness as in the old days.

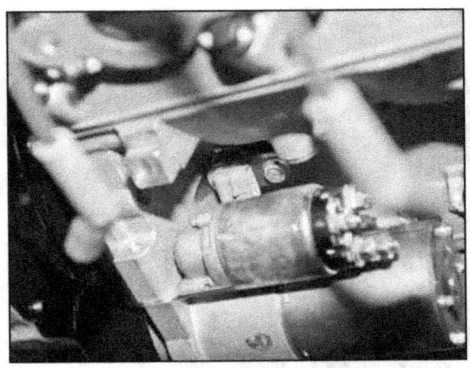

The connector behind the starter tells you what engine you have. The gray one means you have a 58x system; a black connector indicates the older 24x system. Both work equally well to identify which is which for your ECU.

SWAP LS ENGINES INTO CAMAROS & FIREBIRDS 1967–1981   111

that. The LS engine is pretty straightforward when you can get it with a programmed ECU and matching wiring harness. Beyond that, there are a few common issues when performing this swap.

Gauges

The LS engine is a bit of an oddball when it comes to gauges and locations to put them. But the LS wire bundle is a masterful stroke of genius because you don't have to wire anything you don't want to! Since the ECU uses all of the vital parameters that you'd have on the dash to keep the engine running smoothly, you can tap into those systems quite easily using the wiring bundle from the LS harness. Most of these parameters, including RPM, water temperature, oil pressure, voltage, and more, are already coming out of the wiring harness. You need to wire it to the correct corresponding gauge in your gauge cluster. There can be a few exceptions and I cover the ones that you are most likely to need and run into.

Tach Wiring

Tach wiring is fairly straightforward; it is spliced in from the wiring

The injectors and some of the other connectors have a different way of locking. You need to figure out the type of retention system and clip that needs to be pulled. In this case, the green clip needs to be pulled before the plug can be removed.

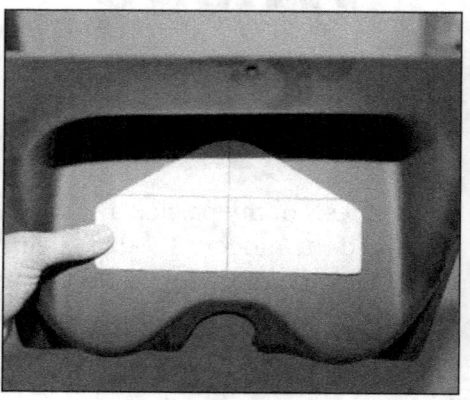

I got this Covan's blank dash from Matt's Classic Bowties. This allows a platform to custom install the Stack gauge cluster in the stock dash hole without having to custom make a dash panel. The Stack cluster comes with its own template. Make sure you really want this in the place you mark it; you only get one shot at it.

Every great journey starts with one small step and a small hole in the dash panel was mine. I went carefully around the perimeter with a variety of cutting tools. First I drilled out the corner and then followed the scribe line with a jigsaw. I went slowly so I could precisely follow the scribe line. I also used a pair of shears to get the shape just right.

If everything goes well, this is what you should end up with. You need to install the four buttons near the cluster somewhere. Below the cluster seemed to be as good a place as any for it.

Two straps and a couple of bolts hold the gauge on the back.

Two adapters are an option for most projects. The PN 2277 (top) is the coolant adapter that plugs into the head converting the M12 x 1.5 fitting to allow you to use a 1/8-inch NPT coolant sensor. The oil pressure adapter (P2268, bottom) comes in at M16 x 1.5 and also adapts to the 1/8-inch NPT fitting. (Photo Courtesy Auto Meter)

WIRING

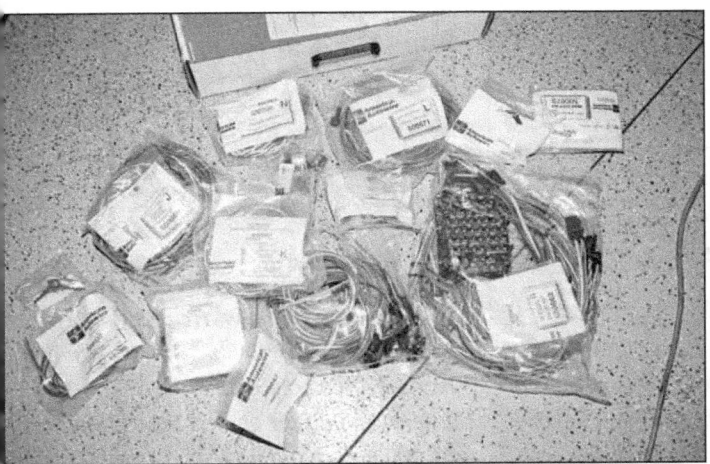

The American Autowire kit comes with everything you need. It even comes with a new ignition lock cylinder and head light switch. They give you plenty of extra wire so if you take your time, it works out really well.

I know this looks intimidating, but if you go slowly and follow the instructions and wiring diagrams, everything will work.

You need an array of tools and hardware to help you in the wiring process. Some shrink tape, wire cutters, and a wire stripper are required to make the necessary electrical connections and complete your wiring job.

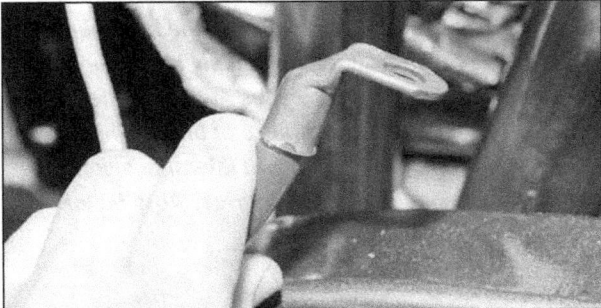

Because I am taking the positive terminal from the trunk I had to bend the terminal to match the bend to the starter.

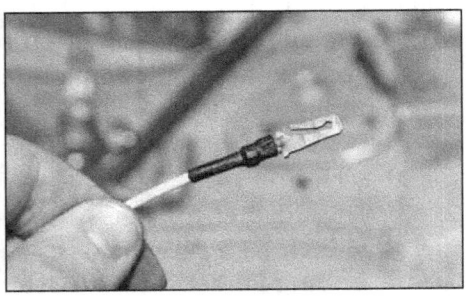

You need to use heat shrink to end up with a properly wired terminal like this.

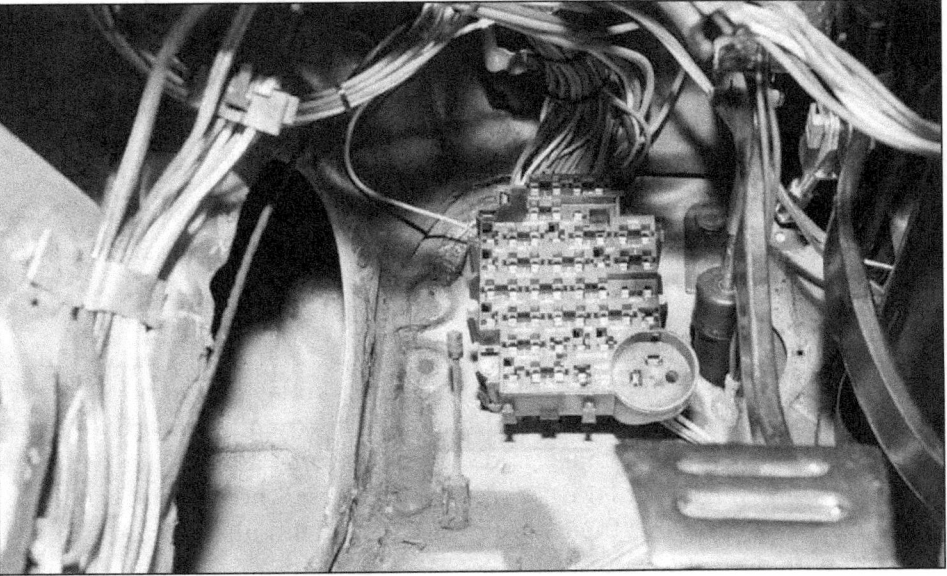

My new 18-circuit fuse block bolts right into place without any modifications, so I didn't have to drill the firewall. The AAW kit is meant to bolt into the stock location, which is a delight. It offers the use of blade-style fuses with larger amperage capabilities and more circuits to work with instead of having to overload the old stock system.

I went through the diagram and located several unused wires, so pulled them from the firewall connector. You need to compress the tabs on the connectors and pull them out of the plug.

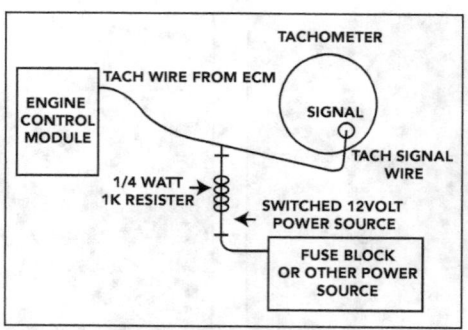

This diagram illustrates the correct wiring for a resistor to go inline for your tachometer. The resister needs a 12-volt key-on source to allow it to work properly.

I am pointing at the water plug that can be used for virtually anything to do with the coolant. This hole measures M12 x 1.5. If you're looking for an adapter, it needs to be this size. Most gauges do not fit this size and need an adapter. Mechanical gauges are usually too big for the adapters, so you have to run an electric gauge or figure something else out. If you're going this far to put an LS engine in your car, don't scrimp on the gauges, they are cheap insurance. (Photo Courtesy Auto Meter)

The smaller of the two sending units is the electrical sweep unit. They are solid state, and therefore Auto Meter claims they are less prone to failure from vibrations like its mechanical cousins. The larger unit can be difficult to fit because it takes up more space. In such cases Auto Meter recommends using a piece of braided hose to relocate the unit to a lateral position. This does not have an impact on the reading of the gauge. (Photo Courtesy Auto Meter)

A smaller and shorter water temperature sending unit (PN 2259) is shown. This allows you to save space when mounting on the head. (Photo Courtesy Auto Meter)

harness and ECU, typically PIN 10 and a white wire (1999 to 2002 have a red connector, 2003 and later have a green connector). In most cases, all that is required beyond the wire hookups is that the tach itself should be set to 4-cylinder or 6-cylinder mode depending on the make and model of your gauge. Sometimes you need to tap the coil wires themselves (usually pink) to run to your tach.

This takes care of most LS tach wiring; however, a few people require a small additional resistor known as a "pull-up" resistor. A wide variance is possible for those who may need to modify the tach signal. You know pretty quickly if you need to do this when you start up the engine and the tach acts erratically or reads inaccurately. Today's aftermarket tachs require a ground wire as well as a 12-volt source and exciter wire. The exciter wire is the one that can necessitate the "pull-up" resistor.

You need a 5,000-ohm 1/4-watt resistor or a 4,800-ohm 1/4-watt resistor. Often a 680-ohm 1/4-watt resistor works; a best practice is to start with the 5,000-ohm 1/4 version and work your way down. Besides, resistors are cheap and plentiful. You need to run this wire from a fuse-protected keyed (only operates when the key is turned to "on") 12-volt source and then spliced into the wire from the harness to the tach. Start it up and see if it's working.

Water Temperature

The LS engine has a variety of ways to measure water temperature. Most notably are the two ports on each cylinder head. On both heads they are at the same location, farthest to the driver's side of the head. You'll find a plug that needs an M12 x 1.5 adapter to run an electric gauge. Because the size of the hole, a mechanical gauge doesn't fit.

Auto Meter has made an adapter for the electric sending unit (PN 2277). This adapter fits right in and has a 1/8-inch NPT port that accepts most sending units. Auto Meter warned me that a smaller sending unit (PN 225) might be needed.

The adapter (PN 2277) is installed in the head. I recommend using a thread sealer to prevent leaks and as the aluminum and brass are soft metals. Be careful not to deform the fitting when tightening it. (Photo Courtesy Auto Meter)

The head is already pre-drilled and tapped to accept an electronic sending unit, which is installed in the head. (Photo Courtesy Auto Meter)

For my Stack cluster, I wasn't able to use the larger fitting because the bore was too tight for the sending unit. I thought I could be clever and bore out the fitting, but that ended in failure. I turned to the heater hoses instead. I used an Auto Meter (PN 2280) to help. It's a 5/8-inch hose adapter that accepts the 1/8-inch port size. I used 5/8 inch because it is the "feed" side of the heater box, meaning that hot engine coolant enters the heater core through this hose and exits out the 3/4-inch hose.

Oil Pressure

The LS engine has an oil pressure plug similar to the small-block in the respect that they are in the same vicinity. That's about where the similarities stop. This plug requires a special adapter to run 1/8-inch NPT sending units. Auto Meter sells a brass fitting (PN 2268) that allows you to use this pressure port for the cockpit gauge. Auto Meter reports that you can run a short piece of pipe or braided hose from the oil pressure side and it does not diminish any readings you get from the gauge!

I had to use an inline water temperature gauge for the stack unit as the sending units are too large to fit any of the regular places without drilling and tapping a very expensive cylinder head.

The oil filter port is used to adapt the pressure gauge. It is located just above the oil filter on a stock LS engine. (Photo Courtesy Auto Meter)

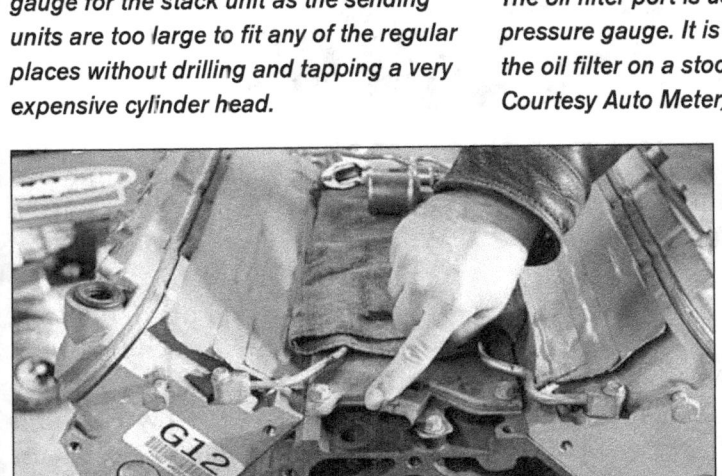

Just as on the small-block Chevy, the oil pressure port is located at the back of the engine. (Photo Courtesy Auto Meter)

The adapter (PN 2268) was installed on the engine. Be sure to thread the fitting as far in as you can to flatten the washer. Do not over-tighten as these fittings can snap off. (Photo Courtesy Auto Meter)

Here's where a few things get tricky. The engine harness needs a port to tell the ECU how much oil pressure is being generated. That typically is the back slot behind the intake in the traditional location. If you use this for your gauge, you have to figure out something else to make the ECU happy.

The solution is a modification to the oil cover plate located right above the oil filter. The oil pan from Mast doesn't have this option, but I show you how to solve that problem. Drilling and tapping this plate gives you an excellent way to add a gauge without making any unsightly changes. You need to keep everything away from the heat since the headers are directly in front of this piece.

Oil-Pressure Sending Unit Installation

You need to cut off the excess material to make room for the NPT tap, which is tapered. Don't cut off so much that you have nothing left to thread to. However, you need to remove roughly 1/2 inch to fit the sending unit. (Photo Courtesy Auto Meter)

Use a 5/16-inch drill bit to enlarge the center. (Photo Courtesy Auto Meter)

Chase the drilled-out section with a 1/8-inch NPT tap. You need to go slow and steady to properly clean metal shards out of the oil filter port. You obviously don't want metal debris flowing through your engine. (Photo Courtesy Auto Meter)

You can now screw the oil-pressure sending unit into place; snuggly so as not to leak but not too tight to cause a crack.

For my oil pan, I had to be a bit creative. I quickly noticed that the oil pan doesn't have the typical plate that can be modified. It only has two -10AN ports that are meant for an oil cooler (I mentioned that Mast doesn't mess around when they build engines, right?). I called Mast and they informed me that the rearward-most port is the "feed" line and provides accurate oil pressure readings. Just as with the stock oil plate, I was able to drill and tap the aluminum -10AN fitting to accept the 1/8-inch NPT sending unit. I added a 90-degree elbow to clear the side of the block to allow the sending unit to clear and not interfere with the hot header. I plan to take the advice from Mast and add an oil cooler.

Oil Temperature

The good news about the oil temperature gauge is that it doesn't need any pressure; it only needs to be submerged in hot oil to work properly. There are several ways to get the proper oil temperature. You can branch off the oil-pressure sending unit with a T-fitting or you can make its own special slot. Chances are, your wiring harness isn't using the low-oil-level sending unit. On the passenger's side of every LS pan is a plug that the stock harness uses for an oil level warning light.

I was able to find the right fitting for my 1/8-inch NPT sending unit. I used a specialty pre-tapped aluminum fitting from Speedway Motors (PN 481201). It allows me to use the sending unit and not make any major modifications. Typical operating temperatures for the LS engine are roughly 195 to 210 degrees F. If you plan to track your car and start seeing temperatures above 275 consistently, you need to add an oil cooler.

WIRING

I tapped into the right side of the Mast oil pan to access the pressure side to get an oil pressure reading.

After drilling and tapping the appropriate 1/8-inch NPT hole, I reattached the oil pressure–sending unit.

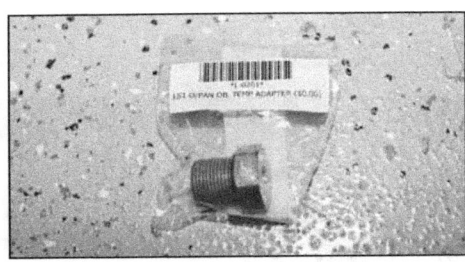
This is a Speedway Engines adapter (PN L-0201). The oil pan temperature replacement plug allows you to have a port for the oil temperature with a 1/8-inch NPT tapped port.

You might have to remove the sensor to get the fitting in. Remember to use a little Teflon tape to seal any air leaks. Thread it into the head by hand until it is snug.

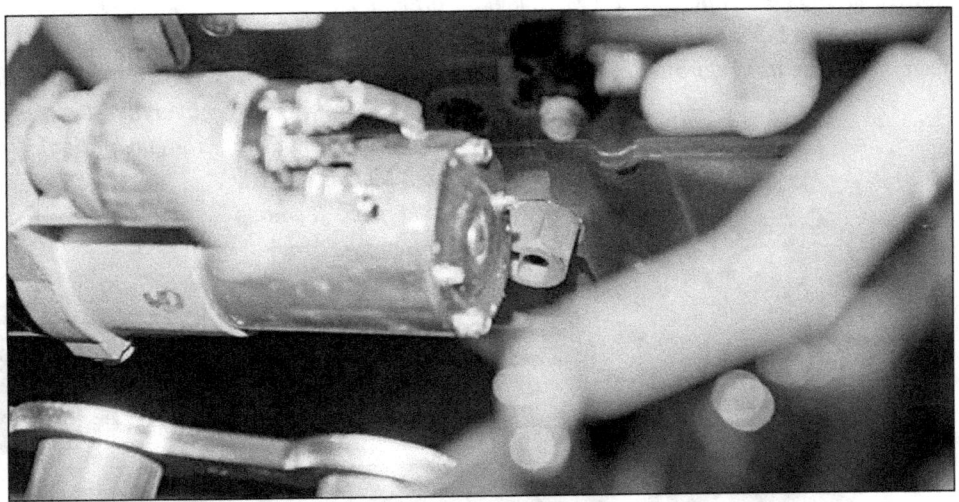
The brown port behind the starter is the oil level sensor. Removing it with a socket or wrench allows the adapter to monitor the oil temperature.

Fuel Pressure

You must maintain the correct fuel pressure of 58 psi at all times in an LS engine to realize maximum performance. I used an -8AN adapter from Earl's that allows me to run a 1/8-inch NPT solid-state sending unit that matches the stack EFI injection stack unit (PN AT100196ERL).

To check the fuel pressure, insert the key into the ignition and turn it to "on" so the EFI system primes itself. It should turn the fuel pump on for 2 to 5 seconds and shut off if the car is not running. This allows you to check the gauge and fuel system leaks.

Wiring Harnesses

A number of automotive businesses, including Painless Wiring and American Autowire are more than happy to build a wiring harness for you. It will be more costly, but it's an option if you don't have a lot of time. You can, of course, build your own wiring harness as I have shown you.

Both companies make great kits to suit any need and in many cases make kits that far supersede anything that came from the factory on the first- or second-generation F-Bodies. I chose the American Autowire kit because I've had experience working with their systems and felt comfortable using them again. The best advice I can give you is to go slowly! Take your time and work with the components one at a time. It can be a bit daunting when you see all the wires in one giant bundle, but if you look at each circuit individually the bigger picture tends to take shape.

You need to know a few things up front before you order a harness: the transmission needs, whether you are sending a harness to be reworked or purchasing one, the length of extra harness (crucial if you want extra to mount the PCM under the dash), the oxygen sensor requirements, and the fuse/relay box needs.

Wiring Harness Installation

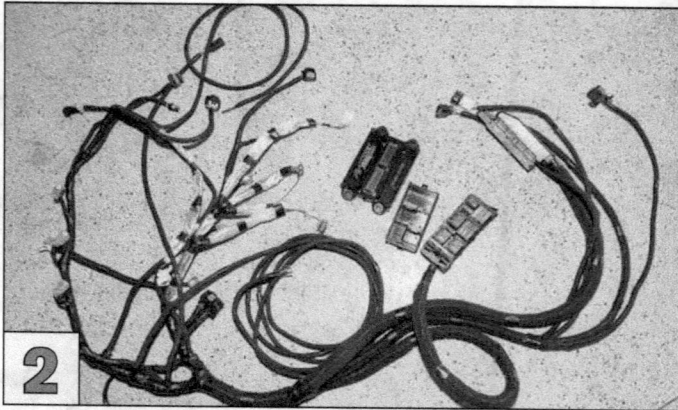

The Mast wiring harness comes pre-labeled with many of the popular connectors already marked. It's nice when things are so easy. Since the Mast harness is customized and pre-routed for the particular engine, connecting the wires is a no-brainer. Decisions about the fuse box and ECM are crucial. Those need to be free from heat, free from vibrations, and in an easy-to-access area.

Here's the Mast wiring harness that came with the engine. Everything is well laid out and fits to the block (doing its best to remain hidden).

The M-90 DBW ECU from Mast is a pretty solid piece. It comes with rubber grommets. It's up to you to find a good place for it away from vibrations, heat, and excess moisture.

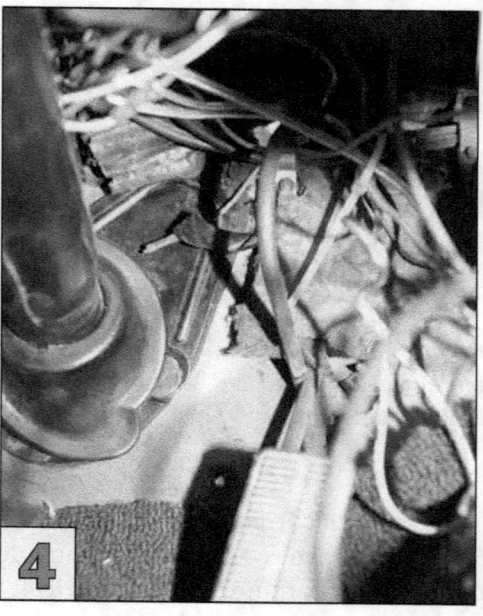

This is the original gas pedal; it has to go. The drive-by-wire pedal will be mounted to the firewall.

This jumble of wires is not as confusing as it looks. Everything has a place and there is a place for everything. Go slowly and it will make sense very quickly. Because each wire has only one way to be routed and only one specific counterpart to be plugged into, routing/connecting the wires is a simple procedure. After it's clicked into place, tuck the wire behind anything close, such as the injector.

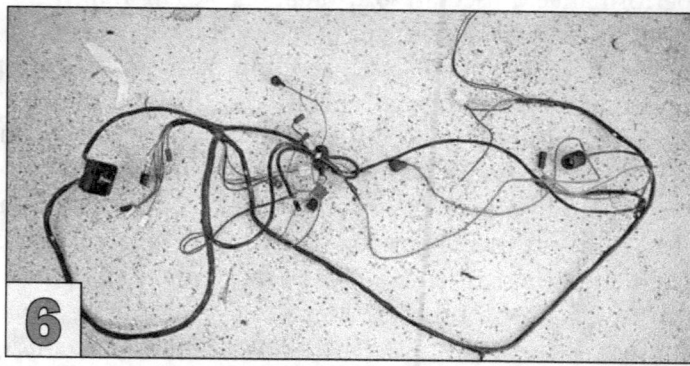

The American Autowire (AAW) kit replaces the old front body harness further along in the build.

Removing the old wiring harness can be difficult but if done carefully I can probably resell it at the swap meet and maybe recoup some of the cost. Many of the wires from the factory are held in with bent tabs or clamps. It pays to follow each wire cluster until you get to a junction then gently remove it.

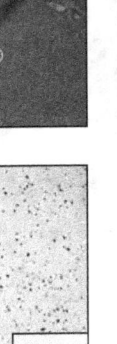

Here are the original gas pedal (left) and the new DBW gas pedal (right) side by side.

Once all the wiring has been removed, you can start to plan your wiring setup more carefully.

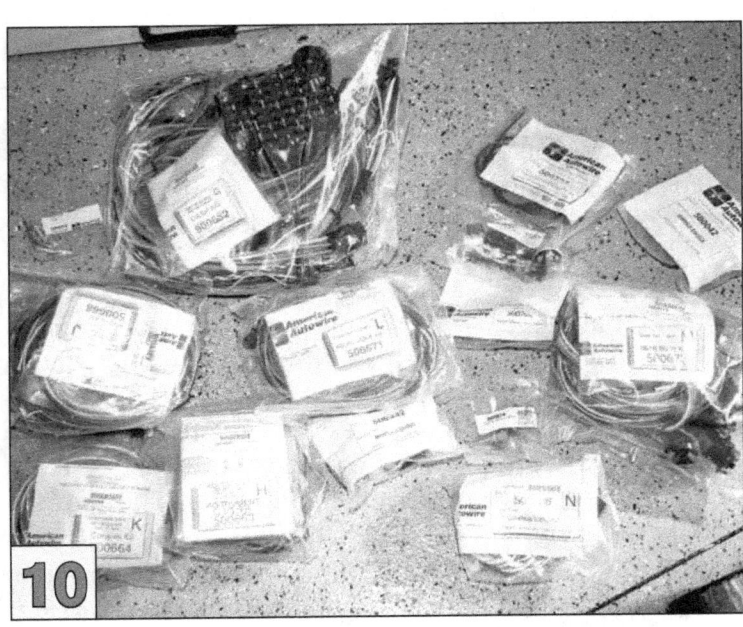

Here's everything you get in the AAW wiring kit: a new ignition switch, bright-beam switch, and headlight switch.

The idle air temperature sensor is an easily missed connection. This one just plugs directly into the K&N air filter.

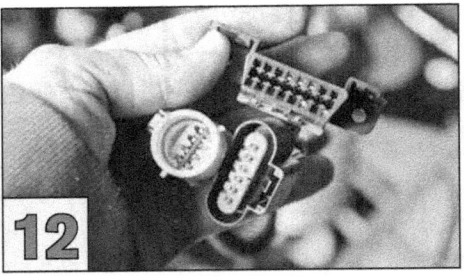

The Mast harness comes with three connectors under the dash in addition to the main wire bundle. They are: OBD-II port (upper right), drive-by-wire port (right), and ECU interface (left). Determine the location in the foot well to mount it, drill two pilot holes, and then screw the plug down with sheet-metal screws. Your wiring harness most likely only has the OBD-II port and drive-by-wire plug.

To get all these wires in the dash, I had to cut a 3-inch access hole in the firewall. I use a 3-inch rubber grommet to make sure air and gases don't enter the cab. Placement of the hole depends largely on what you want to do. If you want a hole closest to the gauges for ease of wiring such as I did, this is a good location. Others have put a hole behind the engine to hide the harness. The choice is up to you.

CHAPTER 8

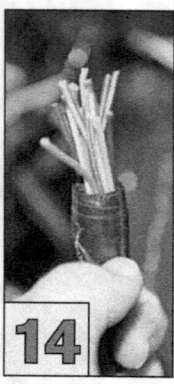

This is the bundle that comes out of the Mast wiring harness. Most of these wires aren't necessary for the entire wiring. Some go to gauges while others are crucial, such as ignition and key-on cycling. Wires that are not used are capped. It helps to have the wiring diagram handy to make sense of it all because each wiring harness is slightly different. This harness came with a set of instructions. I pulled back a good part of the sheathing to reveal the wire markings to determine which was which.

A ground strap can be found at any local auto parts stores, and you need to be sure your electrical system is properly grounded. Because this frame was powder coated I had to scrape some off to make sure the ground strap had excellent metal-to-metal contact.

You can use a wiring harness from a junkyard or you can have one made out of whole cloth but you should be prepared for some extra cost.

Fabricators usually ask questions about your particular build. You need to determine which computer you are going to use and specify which transmission will be installed. If it's an automatic, you need to program the ECM's shift points and transmission functions or you'll have to use an external stock ECM or aftermarket version. You also need to determine if you are going to be running A/C. In addition, you need to decide whether to use a speed-density system or a mass air system.

The final consideration is the length of your harness. To figure that out, you need to decide on the mounting location of the computer because that dictates the length of the harness. You can mount the ECM in the passenger's compartment and run the wires through the firewall. If you choose this placement, you need a longer harness than if you mount the ECM in the engine compartment.

Wiring Harness Hookup

Don't let this giant bundle of wires intimidate you. I like to call this type of automotive work a "process of elimination." Once the engine arrived at my place, I promptly removed the wiring harness and started working on the engine accessories and other pieces. After a while, the harness had to go back on and I couldn't remember the right way to install it. Thankfully, the weather pack plugs and configuration allowed me to figure it out quickly. It's pretty hard to mess this up when everything has a specific place and corresponding connector. If you organize them, everything should go smoothly.

Length of Harness

Any wiring harness company worth anything asks you how much "extra" length you want in your harness. The extra length allows you to mount the ECM and the fuse block in a suitable location. The location

Chances are that your wiring harness is original and looks a lot like mine. While it's entirely possible to put an LS engine in your car and get it working well, installing an updated kit, such as the AAW kit, can make life a lot easier.

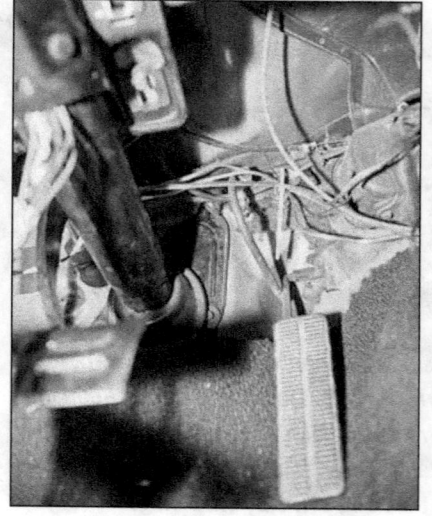

To remove the original gas pedal, remove the two bolts holding the pivot arm in place. A simple socket does the job even though it can be a bit of a pain and the plastic holder can easily break. Remove the cable from the pedal and it should fall right out after removing the bolts located on the firewall that hold the pedal lever in place.

determines how much extra length you need. I've seen extra lengths range from ultra-short (where the components are mounted in the engine bay), to super-long, as in 3 feet or longer (to accommodate mounting inside the passenger compartment). This extra bit determines where you can put your ECM in the vehicle. It might be worth figuring out where you want to put your computer well before you order a harness.

OBD-II Port Location

Any wiring harness should come with an OBD-II port. This is a standard port for all newer vehicles. It allows you to plug in a scan tool or laptop to "talk" with the PCM to program it further or troubleshoot codes that are being thrown.

The wiring harness side is a female 16-pin J1962-type connector with two rows of 8 pins. The government standards mandate that this must be within 2 feet of the driver's position. This is the best position because it allows you to use the scan tool or laptop while in the driver's seat to turn the car on or off with the key.

I located it under the dash within easy reach and away from the pedals. Of course you can position it anywhere you like. People who want the clean look put it in the glove box.

Drive-by-Wire Pedal Installation

Because I have a drive-by-wire setup I need to fabricate the housing for the electric pedal. I built a simple box out of 1/8-inch plate and will weld it onto the floorboard of the car.

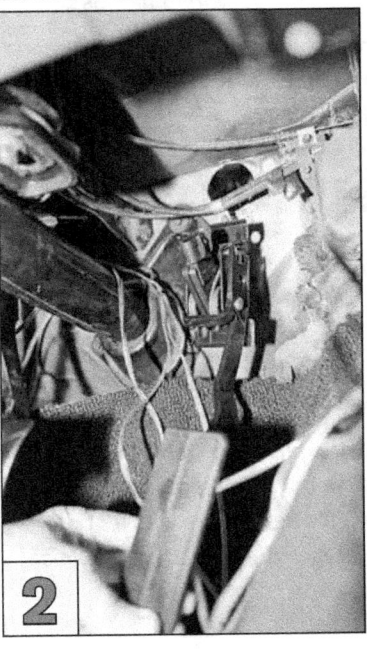

I found a good spot for the pedal, not too close to the transmission hump and not too close to the brake pedal. I also made the gas pedal a few inches closer to the floorboard than the brake pedal to allow for better heel-toe braking and revving.

First, I matched the mating plate to the pedal. Then I drilled a couple of holes so I could mount it to the bracket. I welded a couple of anchoring nuts on the backside because I want to be able to remove the gas pedal if something happens.

After finding a decent place to mount it, I tack welded it in place, making sure it goes to full throttle without hitting the floor. I also looked carefully at the brake pedal height to see where it is in relation to the gas pedal. I plan to drive the car aggressively and will be doing a lot of heel-toe braking and gassing. A simple MIG welder is sufficient if you make sure the welder is on a low-amp setting and you're using the correct rod for the job. You don't want to burn through the thin sheet-metal floorpan.

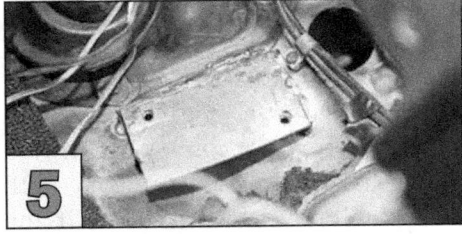

I removed the pedal to finish welding the box. I added a couple of support areas due to some flex in the box as I articulated the pedal. A full box weld isn't necessary. Make sure nothing on the other side is near it; it could start a fire to burn something important.

CHAPTER 8

To hide the main harness wire, I cut a hole in the firewall, added a grommet, and fed it through. A lot of people like to put the hole directly behind the engine to clean it up even more. You need to avoid routing the wiring harness too close to the exhaust or other hot engine parts. Routing the harness behind the engine is fine because there is not excessive heat in this area.

After I put the pedal back on the bracket, I connected it to the wiring harness.

Oxygen Sensor Requirements

Many states (including California) have pretty strict emissions standards so it might be worth keeping the front and rear oxygen sensors. Some states have looser emissions standards, so you don't need them. Either way, make sure to communicate this to the harness builder. Also, keep in mind that you need to communicate your oxygen needs to the person who is going to reprogram your PCM.

If you live in a state with tough emissions standards, it might be worth looking into the E-Rod line of products from General Motors. These are emissions-legal exhaust systems that meet many state requirements.

Fuse Box and Relays

If you have a stock harness, chances are that you won't have a relay and fuse block to work with and you'll have to be creative. If you chose a premade wiring harness, a fuse block can be integrated into it.

You need a 12-volt power source leading to the relay, a trigger for it, a ground wire, and the power wire to whatever it is you need to power. In some cases, you can pay a little extra

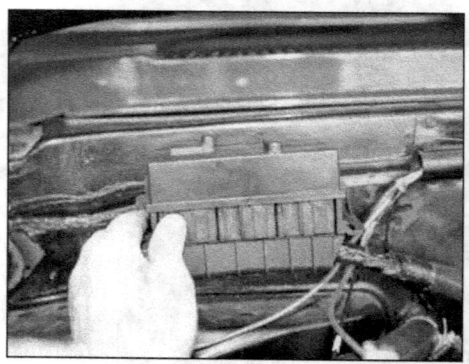

This Mast wiring harness comes with a relay and fuse box. I felt that mounting it just above the heater box was a good place as it makes it accessible and almost looks factory.

The relay and fuse kit for the wiring harness makes life nice. It allows you to run a lot of the components including the fuel pump and electric fans without any extra wiring. That's a good thing.

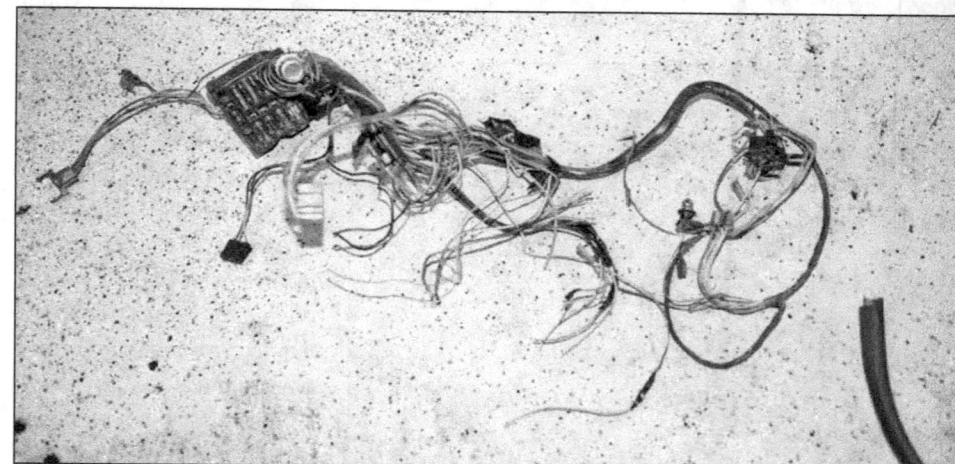

The original main fuse block has certainly seen better days. I will replace it with an 18-circuit version from American Autowire that can handle more juice and more connections.

SWAP LS ENGINES INTO CAMAROS & FIREBIRDS 1967–1981

For better weight distribution and to clean up the engine bay, I mounted the battery in the trunk. A popular battery for pro-touring cars is Optima.

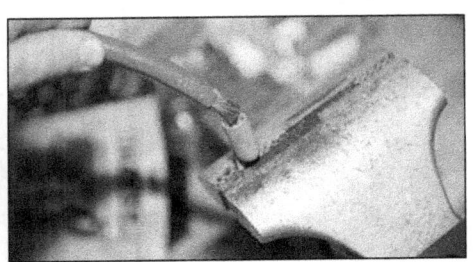

A good and easy way to make a perfect positive battery terminal is to fill the terminal end with solder and heat it up with a torch. While it's still hot, shove the wire in and let it cool for a few seconds. This usually makes a pretty strong bond.

Wiring Harness Sources

Part	Part Number	Source
LS Truck Wiring Harness		Junkyard
(1) OBD-II connector/ port 829-12110250	GM 12129373	Mouser Electronics
(4) OBD-II terminal 829-12129373	GM 12110250	Mouser Electronics
(2) Terminal lock 829-12160437	GM 12160437	Mouser Electronics
(8) Relay terminals 571-42238-2*		Mouser Electronics
(1) Universal 30-amp relay and socket**	Summit DAK-RLY-1	Dakota Digital
PCM Terminals (pack of 100 for extras)		
18-gauge wires	GM 12084912	Mouser Electronics
20- to 22-gauge wires	GM 12084913	Mouser Electronics
Fuse block	Dorman 85668 Summit RNB85668	

* These are replacement terminals for the relay sockets so you can use your own wires if desired.
** One powers the whole engine harness. Additional relays are required for fuel pumps, fans, etc.

for the ease of an incorporated fuse/relay box.

I found this extra feature in the Mast harness to be a wonderful lifesaver. Not only did it come with fuses for things such as the fan control, but it came with a fuel pump relay that allows me to run a wire directly to the fuel pump and keep things ultra-tidy.

Transmission

Because various transmissions require different setups, you must determine which transmission to install. If you are using an older automatic or manual transmission, and want the ECU integrated into the harness, you need to specify the transmission and that you want this extra feature.

Adapting an LSX Wiring Harness

Many LS owners are on a limited budget and don't have the funds to construct a custom harness for a major rewiring job. You may think that wiring is too challenging and difficult to tackle yourself. If you go slowly and carefully you can adapt a truck wiring harness to your particular application. You simply break each sensor down into its individual components and wires.

For most enthusiasts, the mechanical part of building a car is second nature while electrical wiring is more of a challenge. I was a complete novice when it comes to anything wiring so I went to my local LS guru and custom fabricator of all things GM LS, Nate Shaw of One Guys Garage. Nate has made many custom-length wiring harnesses. He strives for a virtually invisible wiring harness that is completely functional but leaves car show visitors wondering where it is when looking under the hood.

I bought an inexpensive wiring harness from a GM truck equipped with an LS engine. I combined it with a few off-the-shelf parts to build a custom wiring harness for less than $100. Be prepared to spend anywhere from 8 to 12 hours on the build. However, this is a great way to get into the LS engine family for the person who has a lot of time but not a lot of wallet.

You need to work slowly and methodically because this is intricate and detail-oriented work. The list of pin outs for the typical 1998–2002 Corvette wiring harness is long but they haven't changed much over the years. If you completely strip the PCM connectors and only plug in the parts you need, this part of the project will be completed in no time.

Blue (C1) PCM Connector

Pin	Wire Color	Circuit No.	Function
1	BLK/WHT	451	PCM ground
2	LT GRN	1867	Crankshaft position sensor B+ supply
3	PNK/BLK	1746	Injector 3 control
4	LT GRN/BLK	1745	Injector 2 control
5–6	—	—	Not used
7	GRY	596	Engine oil pressure sensor 5v reference
8–10	—	—	Not used
11	LT BLU	1876	Knock sensor (KS) 2 signal
12	DK BLU/WHT	1869	Crankshaft position sensor signal
13	ORN/BLK	463	Requested torque signal
14	TAN	800	Throttle actuator control serial data
15	ORN/BLK	1061	Throttle actuator control serial data
16	—	—	Not used
17	DK BLU	1225	Transmission range signal B (automatic transmission only)
18	RED	1226	Transmission range signal C (automatic transmission only)
19	PNK	239	PCM ignition supply
20	ORN	340	PCM battery supply
21	YEL/BLK	1868	Crankshaft position sensor ground
22	—	—	Not used
23	GRY	720	Sensor ground
24	—	—	Not used
25	TAN	1671	HO2s signal low bank 2 sensor 2
26	TAN	1667	HO2s signal low bank 2 sensor 1
27	—	—	Not used
28	TAN/WHT	1669	HO2s signal low bank 1 sensor 2
29	TAN/WHT	1653	HO2s signal low bank 1 sensor 1
30–31	—	—	Not used
32	BLK/WHT	771	PRND A input signal (automatic transmission only)
33	PPL	420	TCC brake switch (automatic transmission only)
34	WHT	776	PRND P input signal (automatic transmission only)
35	GRY	48	Clutch switch (manual transmission only)
36	BLK	1744	Injector 1 control
37	YEL/BLK	846	Injector 6 control
38	PNK/WHT	1101	Powertrain induced chassis pitch signal (if so equipped)
39	—	—	Not used
40	BLK/WHT	451	PCM ground
41	—	—	Not used
42	DK GRN	335	Engine cooling fan relay 1 control
43	RED/BLK	877	Injector 7 control
44	LT BLU/BLK	844	Injector 4 control
45	GRY	474	A/C refrigerant pressure sensor 5v reference
46	GRY	598	Fuel tank pressure sensor 5v reference
47	—	—	Not used
48	GRY	416	Map sensor 5v reference
49–50	—	—	Not used
51	DK BLU	496	Knock sensor (KS) 1 signal
52	—	—	Not used
53	ORN/BLK	1057	Transmission temperature sensor ground
54	ORN/BLK	469	Map sensor ground
55–56	—	—	Not used
57	ORN	340	Pcm battery supply
58	DK GRN	1049	Serial data
59	—	—	Not used
60	BLK	407	A/C refrigerant pressure sensor ground
61	PNK/BLK	632	Camshaft position sensor ground
62	GRY	847	Extended travel brake switch signal
63	BLK	452	Engine oil pressure sensor ground
64	—	—	Not used
65	PPL	1670	HO2s signal high bank 2 sensor 2
66	PPL	1666	HO2s signal high bank 2 sensor 1
67	—	—	Not used
68	PPL/WHT	1668	HO2s signal high bank 1 sensor 2
69	PPL/WHT	1665	HO2s signal high bank 1 sensor 1
70	BRN	1174	Low oil level switch
71	—	—	Not used
72	YEL	772	PRND B input signal (automatic transmission only)
73	BRN/WHT	633	Camshaft position (CMP) sensor signal
74	YEL	410	Engine coolant temperature (ECT) sensor signal
75	—	—	Not used
76	BLK/WHT	845	Injector 5 control
77	DK BLU/WHT	878	Injector 8 control
78	—	—	Not used
79	GRY	587	2nd and 3rd gear block out solenoid control (MM^)
79	WHT	687	3–2 shift solenoid control (M30)
80	BRN	718	Engine coolant temperature (ECT) sensor ground

WIRING

Red (C2) PCM Connector

Pin	Wire Color	Circuit No.	Function
1	BLK/WHT	451	PCM ground (automatic transmission only)
2	BRN	418	TCC control solenoid (automatic transmission only)
3	—	—	Not used
4	PPL	421	Air solenoid control
5	TAN/BLK	464	Torque delivered
6	RED/BLK	1228	Transmission fluid pressure control solenoid high (automatic transmission only)
7	—	—	Not used
8	LT BLU/WHT	1229	Transmission fluid pressure control solenoid low (automatic transmission only)
9	DK GRN/WHT	465	Fuel pump relay control
10	WHT	121	Engine speed (tach) output signal
11–13	—	—	Not used
14	RED/BLK	380	A/C refrigerant pressure sensor signal
15	RED	225	Alternator l terminal
16	—	—	Not used
17	DK GRN/WHT	762	A/C request signal (C60 only)
18	DK GRN	59	A/C status signal
19	—	—	Not used
20	PPL	401	Vehicle speed sensor (VSS) reference low
21	YEL	400	Vehicle speed sensor (VSS) signal
22–24	—	—	Not used
25	TAN	472	LAT sensor signal
26	PPL	2121	Ignition control 1
27	RED	2127	Ignition control 7
28	LT BLU/WHT	2126	Ignition control 6
29	DK GRN/WHT	2124	Ignition control 4
30	—	—	Not used
31	YEL	492	MAF sensor signal
32	LT GRN	432	MAP sensor signal
33	DK BLU	473	Engine cooling fan relay 2 and 3 control
34	DK GRN/WHT	428	Evap canister purge valve control
35	—	—	Not used
36	BRN	436	Air pump relay control
37–38	—	—	Not used
39	RED	631	Camshaft position sensor B+ supply
40	BLK/WHT	451	PCM ground
41	—	—	Not used
42	TAN/BLK	422	TCC enable circuit (automatic transmission only)
43	DK GRN/WHT	459	A/C clutch relay control
44	LT GRN	1652	Reverse inhibit solenoid control
45	WHT	1310	Evap canister vent valve control
46	BRN/WHT	419	Malfunction indicator lamp (MIL) control
47	WHT	375	1 to 4 up-shift lamp control (MM6)
47	YEL/BLK	1223	Transmission shift solenoid B (M30)
48	LT GRN	1222	Transmission shift solenoid A
49	—	—	Not used
50	DK GRN/WHT	817	Vehicle speed output circuit
51	YEL/BLK	1227	Transmission temperature sensor signal
52	GRY	23	Alternator F terminal
53	—	—	Not used
54	DK BLU	1936	Fuel level sensor signal
55–56	—	—	Not used
57	PPL	719	LAT sensor ground
58	TAN/WHT	331	Engine oil pressure sensor signal
59	—	—	Not used
60	BRN	2129	Ignition control reference low bank 1
61	BRN/WHT	2130	Ignition control reference low bank 2
62	GRY	773	PRND C input signal (automatic transmission only)
63	PNK	1224	Transmission range signal A (automatic transmission only)
64	DK GRN	890	Fuel tank pressure sensor signal
65	—	—	Not used
66	PPL/WHT	2128	Ignition control 8
67	RED/WHT	2122	Ignition control 2
68	DK GRN	2125	Ignition control 5
69	LT BLU	2123	Ignition control 3
70–72	—	—	Not used
73	LT BLU	1937	Fuel level sensor signal (secondary)
74–80	—	—	Not used

SWAP LS ENGINES INTO CAMAROS & FIREBIRDS 1967–1981

Wiring Harness Installation

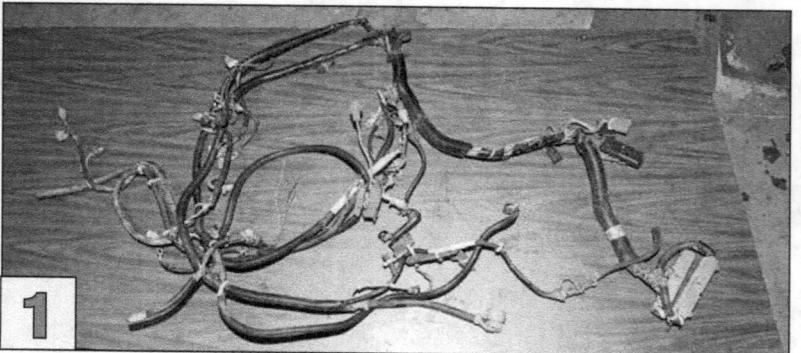

1. I started with the wiring harness out of a 2000 Chevrolet Suburban truck that cost $25 from a local junkyard. It was such a bargain that I bought two! It originally came wired for an automatic. More specifically, this was designed to fit with a 4L60E transmission, but I am going to upgrade it to use the 4L80E for its robust strength, as I am looking for something that can handle more than 600 hp. For a build like this, you may use whatever port you wish to match the transmission you're going to use.

2. If your wiring harness came from a manual transmission car, you don't have this plug; that's something important to look for when planning your wiring project.

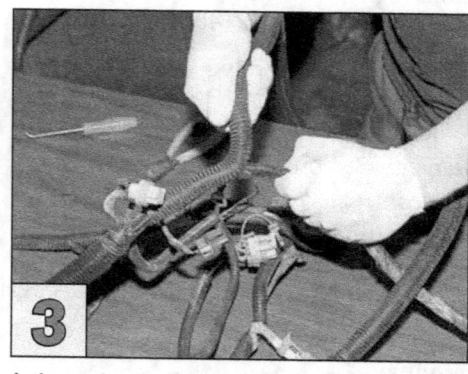

3. I cleared out all the wiring coverings and plastic retainers. This helps get a visual of the harness and get it down to the basics so I can route every wire exactly where I want it to go.

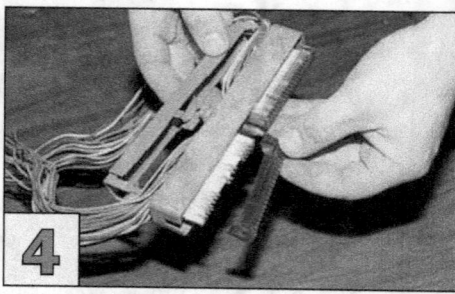

4. Take apart the PCM connectors to get at the wires; they slide right off without much effort. The back cover just clips into the metal holder. Make sure to take care and not snap off the clips so it can go back together smoothly. The front cover (blue or red) slides off easily with a small pick.

5. An easy trick to removing the wires is to use your fingernail and pry up slightly on the tab. Label your PCM connectors so you don't get lost.

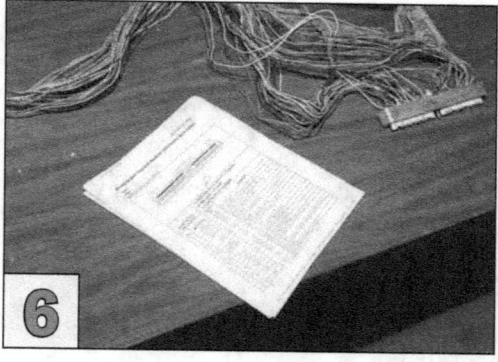

6. Pull out your wiring diagram and follow along. Going on from this point takes a fair amount of concentration and attention to detail. Each plug designates one of the sensors corresponding to the ECM. If one of the plugs is not in the right location, the ECM does not know what to look for and what is wrong. If done correctly, you will have taken the mystery out of wiring.

7. Laying out the harness allows you to see where wires, connectors, and terminals need to go. It also keeps everything organized.

WIRING

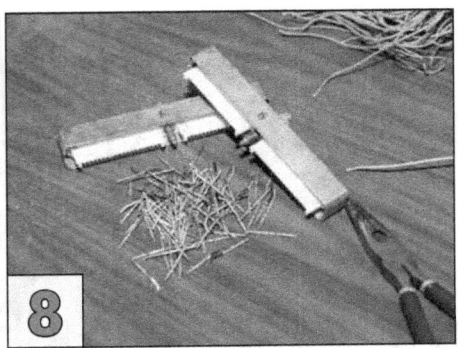

You need to cut or remove all the wire terminals and label the PCM connectors to help you later. Typically, when you find a pink wire in the harness, it's used when the key is on or "key-on" type wiring; when you see an orange wire that is usually for 12-volt full-time power.

Pay attention to how each of the PCM connectors are numbered. On each side, the red and blue look similar but are numbered with each pin to do a very specific job. Be sure all the connections have been made and are correct. Follow the diagrams and wiring locations that were provided, General Motors used a lot of them and they are fairly universal.

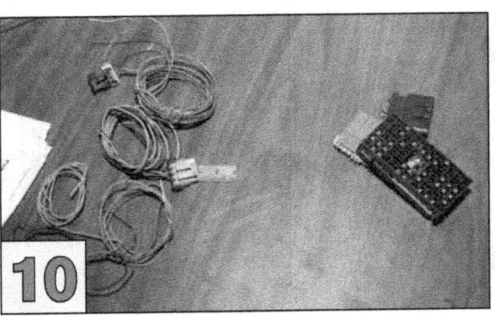

Separate things into two piles. One is a wire bundle of things you need later and the other is the throwaway pile. You often need to wire in the post-converter oxygen sensors, EGR connectors, and mass airflow sensor, particularly if you are converting to a speed density setup. In addition you often need to connect for the A/C compressor, clutch, and transmission wires if you are going to convert to a manual transmission.

The fuel injector connectors need to be replaced because I plan to use standard LS1 injectors (right connector). If you are using truck injectors (left connector) you can skip this step.

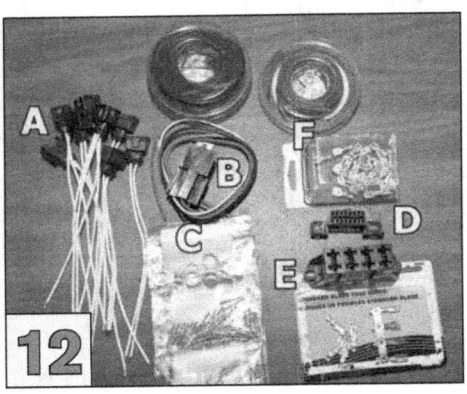

To complete the job, you need the following:
A. Correct connectors for the EV1 fuel injector.
B. Relay to power the harness, sensors, and injectors.
C. Hoop connectors for the ground wires in the system (top bag), an 18- and a 20- to 22-gauge wire terminals to rewire the PCM connectors (middle and bottom bag).
D. OBD-II connector (usually from the junkyard); replacing it is necessary and straightforward.
E. Fuse block to protect the circuits in the wiring harness. The factory harness typically incorporates this in the main fuse block. Since I can't take the entire fuse block out of the truck I have to bypass it; this is a crucial component to the life of your wiring.
F. Extra wire (top) to extend a couple of pieces and female blade-style connectors (bottom) for other connections.

I had to purchase an injector driver box to help run low-impedance injectors. Here, I am installing large high-capacity injectors so it was cheaper in the long run even with purchasing the injector box. This step isn't necessary if you are going to run high-impedance injectors. I just wanted to include it as a less-expensive alternative to fancy injectors.

The closest wires are the ones I plan to throw away and the tightly bundled wires in the back are the wires and pigtails I am going to reuse.

SWAP LS ENGINES INTO CAMAROS & FIREBIRDS 1967–1981

CHAPTER 8

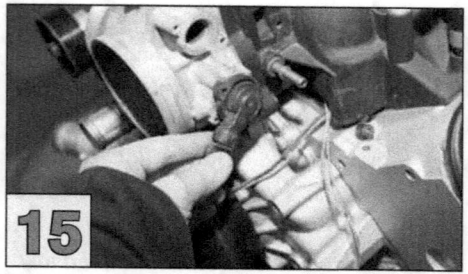

15 Next, I need to run the wires to each of the respective items. Then I'll run each wire back to the simulated PCM position. You can be judicious with your placement because you are in control of the length of the wire.

16 I trial-fitted the PCM connectors behind the engine. I measured the placement in the car and determined the location. This step is critical in getting a harness that fits well. Depending on where you decide to mount the ECM you may have varying lengths of extra wire. I measured the distance from the engine to the location of the ECM on the donor car.

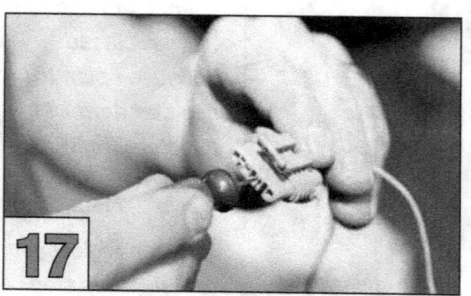

17 Here's a good look at removing terminals from a weather-pack connector. You need a very small implement to stick inside to remove the wire. This is a truck alternator plug-in; I removed one of the wires because the LS1 alternator only requires one exciter wire. I used a small-bladed screwdriver to gently remove the extra wire. A small tab on the inside of the connector releases the wire.

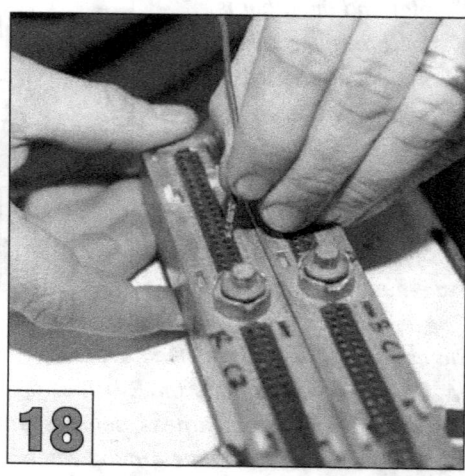

18 After studying the wiring diagram I found the correct hole for the alternator wire. It was located on the red (C2) PCM connector in slot 15.

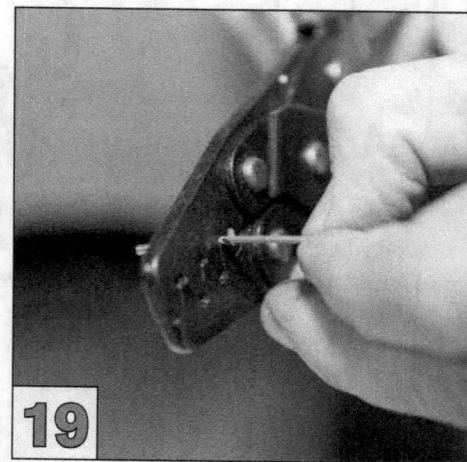

19 This Matco wire crimper (PN TCT1028) is a useful tool. It has all the correct crimps and allows you to breeze through the tedious work of crimping all new connections.

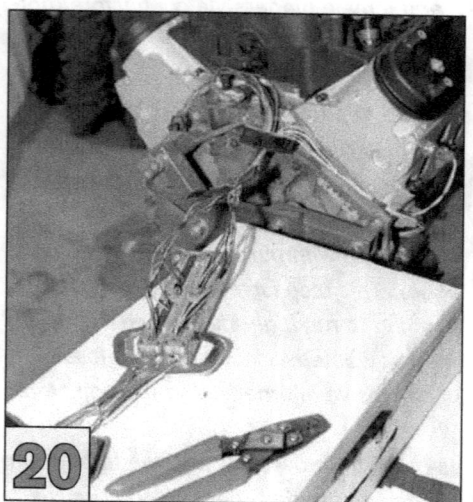

20 After a few sensors, your wiring harness should look similar to this. Go slowly and do one sensor at a time; this reduces errors and ensures a perfect fit. Connect the wiring one at a time. This reduces any issues around the ECM block and also reduces chances of tangling or mismatching any sensors. Make sure to follow the diagram for best results.

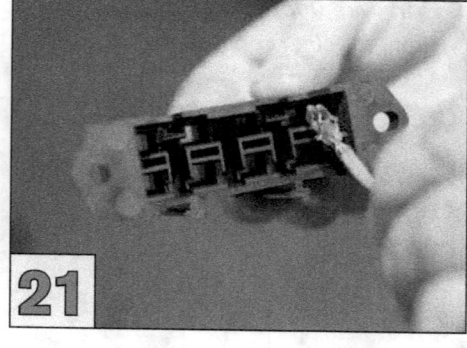

21 I'm attaching the coil power wire to the fuse block, and the other end is attached to power from the battery through the relay. One fuse provides full-time power for the PCM, but the rest requires the ignition switch to be turned on. The other fuses are used to power the transmission connector, oxygen sensors, and injectors. The wire must first be stripped and the appropriate end put on for each type of connector.

WIRING

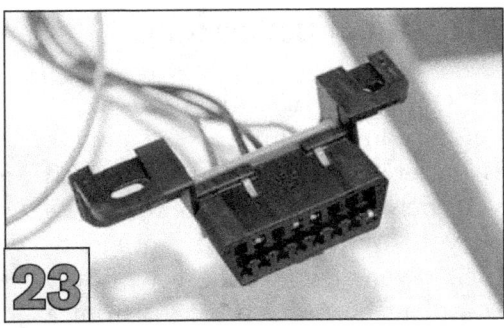

All of the pink wires from each injector run to the fuse block, and are spliced together. The other wire at each injector triggers the injector to supply fuel to the head. The pink wire provides the power.

All the information comes off the PCM connector. Combine that wire with the 12-volt power wire and two-ground wires and the installation is complete. To wire the OBD-II sensor, you need the green wire from the PCM in the upper-left position. Two ground wires are found in the two middle positions (shown). Finally, you need a constant power source that comes from the orange wire (lower right). You can tap into a constant power source from the battery or even the back of the alternator.

After you've collected all of your power wires from your injectors, you should have something that looks similar to this. Remember, orange is constant power and pink is "key-on" power.

I have run each wire to each connector and kept the wires as inconspicuous as possible. I recommend putting them close to the intake and routing them tightly. The process was repeated for each sensor on the engine and for the transmission.

You can use any type of sheathing you wish. You may even use the original GM sheathing. A number of sheathing products are on the market. I used Bentley Harris Roundit 2000 braided sleeving from Cableorganizer.com. This stuff is a bit pricey and puts me over the $100 mark for this project, but it looks totally killer. Remember, it's the little details that really make a car stand out.

ECM Calibration

One of things you need to do before you can fire up your engine is to get it programmed to fit with your new setup. Make sure to discuss all your options with the programmer. (Even if you choose to buy a complete harness and ECM from a junkyard, you still must reprogram the computer.) Most GM donor cars and trucks you're most likely to run into have the VATS system. You will have to calibrate that factor out of the tune. Also, since most of these swaps aren't subject to emissions standards (see your local state laws for compliance) you may want to eliminate the two rearward oxygen sensors because you won't be running catalytic converters.

Here's a short list of things that need to be changed when you send your ECM to be programmed or when you purchase one:

- Fuel type
- VATS disabling
- Transmission (shift points, stall converter, manual versus auto, converter lock up, etc.)
- Changes to the engine (for example, cam swaps, displacement changes, forced induction, etc.)
- Power versus economy tunes
- Speed limiters
- VIN
- Pedal engagement, if you're using a drive-by-wire system

One nice feature of buying a completed and dyno'd engine (like mine from Mast) is that you get a fully programmed engine right from the builder, with no guesswork. Mast provides the tuning software free of charge on their website; a proprietary data cable that costs extra if you want to fiddle with the tune.

You can mount your ECM in almost any location but you don't want it exposed to moisture or extreme heat. Make sure the harness is the proper length for the intended mounting location. This is a vital component so make sure it is properly protected. I placed mine under the front fender, so it's away from any moisture (the Mast ECM comes with mounting pads). It's important to create a small space under the ECM for airflow to avoid overheating. Other popular places are under the dash and at the firewall. It's best to create an open area for the ECM wherever you decide to mount it. Solidly mounting it means bolting it through a rigid structure with a vibration dampener such as rubber pads, by far the most common and best practice.

MSD makes a series of products for the F-Body builder who wants to keep it carbureted. You need a controller, trigger converter, and distributor. (Photo Courtesy MSD)

The main plug for the Mast harness is this trick little connector. It allows me to place the connector on the ECU; the bar does all the work snugging the connector into place and locking it without having to force it.

CHAPTER 9

EXHAUST AND INDUCTION

Often the exhaust portion of a build is left to the very end when everything is bolted up; it's often quite literally an afterthought. As I stated in Chapter 2, a sound strategy is to select the engine mounts, transmission crossmember, headers, and related parts as a kit. The header routing and clearance of the brake booster, steering rod, and other components are common problems. You have to take all of the components into account when making a decision.

I want to remind you again that this needs to be planned out. If you do it correctly, you won't run into any major snags. If you are going to have a problem, it will most likely be when you bolt the headers up when the engine is already between the frame rails.

The reason that companies sell complete kits that include engine mounts, oil pans, and headers is that they are designed to work in concert. I have seen many combinations of mounts, pans, and headers that work just fine. On the other hand, I've seen plenty of setups with the headers hitting something they shouldn't be hitting and that's never a good thing.

So, once again, I feel the need to repeat that if at all possible get the engine mounts, oil pans, and headers from the same place. Why settle for "making it work" when you can just "have it work."

Headers

Headers have come to be the defining purchase after the engine is acquired. However, the purpose of headers is to maximize exhaust flow while providing optimal scavenging. The result is the best-performing exhaust for your particular application. You should select headers for your type of driving.

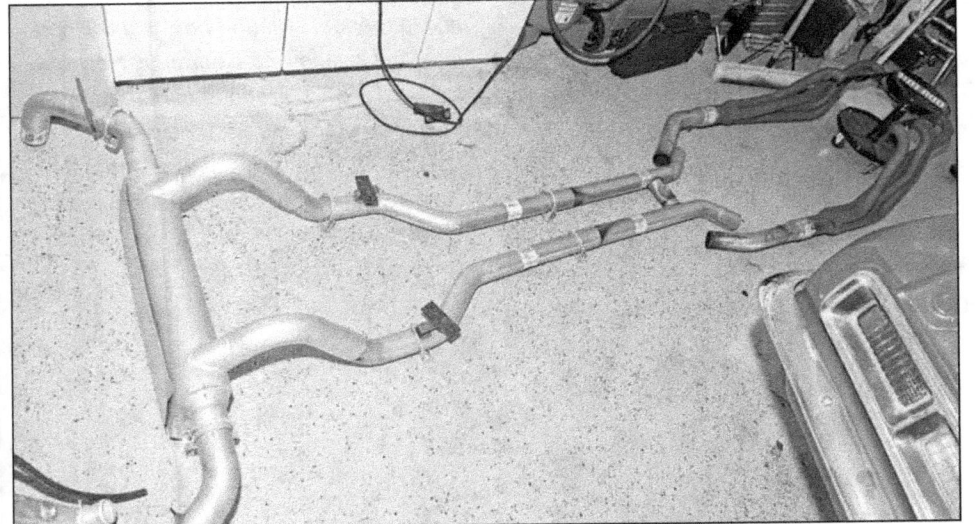

This is the original exhaust that I pulled out of the 1968 Camaro test vehicle. This system would probably work pretty well but because I installed a sophisticated rear suspension the exhaust system had to be suitably rerouted. This is a custom kit from Jegs that's compatible with my rear suspension system. Exhaust systems like this are fairly inexpensive and can be installed in less than a day. I liked the rumble, but I had to get rid of it because of size constraints.

CHAPTER 9

In broad terms, a street engine benefits from optimized torque because the car operates at lower RPM and lower speeds. You want your F-Body to launch quickly from a stoplight and accelerate quickly. On the other hand, a road-race engine needs to produce high-RPM horsepower to be competitive because many road-race engines live at 6,000 to 9,000 rpm all day long. Therefore, you need to need to define the application of the car and common operating RPM so you can select the best set of headers.

As with other LS parts, you have many header choices, but you need to select headers that match your application and are compatible with your total engine package. Hooker, Hedman, Street & Performance, and others make LS exhaust systems for first- and second-generation F-Body swaps. You can buy the pieces separately from different manufacturers; this may entail more problem solving and fabrication work. Or you can buy a complete system for your particular F-Body. Jegs offers several Hooker Header swap kits, which include a direct-fit aluminum radiator, engine mount kit, and hooker headers.

The benefits of buying the engine mounts and headers together in a package is that these items are engineered to work as a unit and provide the necessary clearance. After all, you're trying to package your engine and related parts in a particular F-Body car, so you need to be sure the headers clear the steering box and the frame. The two major areas of concern for clearance issues are the steering box and the frame. There's no real process for figuring out how these fit together other than trial and error. I can say that if you buy all your components from the same place you are likely to run into fewer errors and interference.

A variety of headers are on the market, from the stock iron manifolds from the factory to the typical long-tube headers that are purpose-built for performance. Headers for this swap aren't what anyone would call cheap. Prices typically start around $400. Some specialty headers can cost as much as $2,000. Choose wisely.

Stock

Let's just get this out of the way: Stock F-body and Corvette LS1 headers do work on first- or second-generation F-Body cars. There, I said it.

Most, if not all, LS swap headers you find on the market now have a slip-on cover that allows you to place the oxygen sensor at virtually any angle. This is a simple slip-and-slide add-on that is held on with a pressure clamp. I pointed mine straight in toward the transmission for maximum clearance to the road and floorpan.

When planning any build, you may run into a problem like this where the header touches something it's not supposed to. In this case, you have a few options: You can dimple the headers, replace them, or swap in a newer and smaller steering box. If you have a manual steering box, you will not have any issues with clearance. However, I've seen a 50/50 ratio of cars that have clearance problems with the power steering unit. This just proves once again that using a system of complementary parts removes most of the guesswork. (Photo Courtesy Ryan Barichello)

Options are available for tight spots too, such as these block hugger headers. (Photo Courtesy Street & Performance)

EXHAUST AND INDUCTION

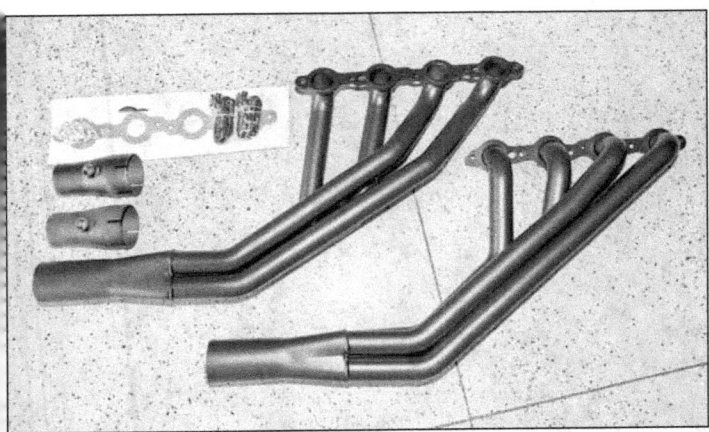

These are the Hooker headers (PN 2288) that I used to mock up a set. You get everything in the kit you need: bolts, gaskets, headers, oxygen sensor, wiring, plugs, and collectors with bungs welded in for the sensor installation. Mocking up headers is a simple procedure in which all components are installed on the car and then clearances are checked. Steering components, hoses, etc. are kept away from the head and, of course, routing of the exhaust manifolds is crucial.

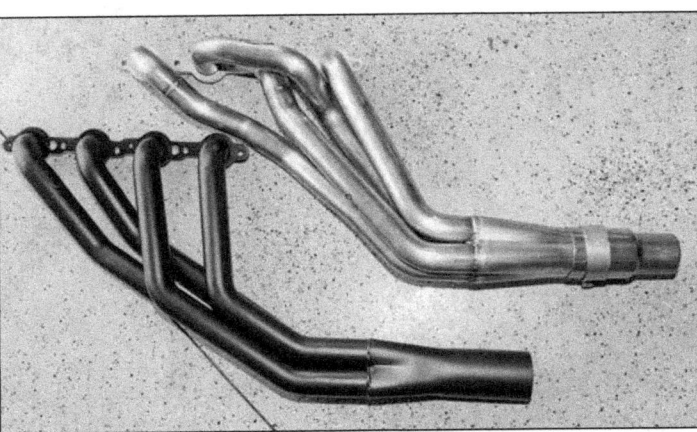

Most passenger-side headers are similar and do not have component clearance issues. Therefore, I only show you a driver-side comparison because often there are steering rod and other component clearance issues. Stainless Works specifically makes a version for the Speed Tech subframe (top). A universal version (bottom) is made by Hooker (PN 2288). Notice how the number-3 cylinder exhaust port is placed up and away from the steering components.

A few nuances may be tricky but if you have an LS2, LS3, or LS7, you should be fine. If you have an LS1, you are golden in my estimation. For a budget build, these suffice until more funds become available.

These stock manifolds weren't really known for making better power numbers, so it's best to upgrade them now while you have the engine out of the car and have easier access. I have found that the better-fitting stock manifolds currently on the market are the 2010 and later F-Body headers; be aware that people have run into steering box interference on the driver's side.

Aftermarket

Well before the current LS swap craze, enthusiasts were forced to custom fabricate or "Frankenstein" their own headers to fit into first- and second-generation F-Body cars. Fortunately, a number of companies now offer a variety of shorty, mid- and long-tube headers for various applications. These swaps have become so popular that there is little guesswork required for installing and fitting the exhaust. Proving yet again that if the trends are there, the aftermarket figures out a way the rest of us can join in and play. The following are the most popular header manufacturers.

Hooker: The Hooker headers that I test fit in my stock subframe worked quite well. A little tip here might be to install them from the bottom for

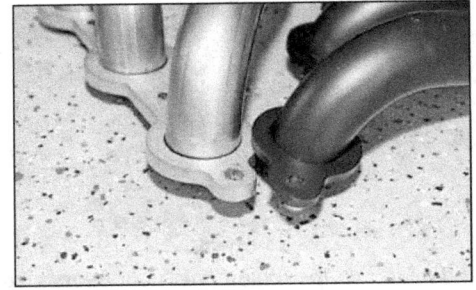

Another header variation is the gasket mating surface thickness. The general rule is that the thicker they are, the less likely they are to warp and cause header leaks. Either of these versions has a sufficient amount of material thickness.

the driver's side; it just seems to work a lot better. The Hooker LS engine swap headers have laser-cut flanges, flat-finished TIG welded port sealing and are made of 18-gauge steel. The tuned-length primary tubes deliver a healthy horsepower bump, the 5/16-inch head flange offers excellent sealing for increased horsepower, and all the hardware is included with the headers. This particular kit fits both first- and second-generation F-Body cars.

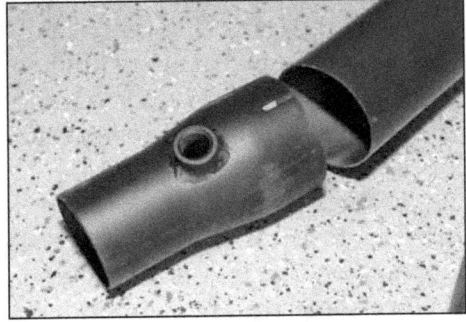

My Hooker headers came with step-down bungs for oxygen sensors. You're killing two birds with one stone: a 3- to 2.5-inch reducer and a welded-in bung!

CHAPTER 9

The Hooker header had plenty of clearance to the steering box, but it was quite tight. If you're running a power steering box (not like mine), you might have to dimple the header or find another solution. Most folks just use a ballpeen hammer to make that indentation.

Sometimes fitting the headers can be difficult. I raised the engine an inch with a hoist. You can also use a jack supported by a board under the oil pan and then bring the headers up from the bottom.

Hooker's black-painted headers are a good alternative for those who are budget conscious. They come with the obligatory 3- to 2.5-inch reducers with oxygen sensor bungs welded in for good measure. The headers come with gaskets, bolts, and oxygen wiring connectors if you need them. Overall, it's a pretty good little package for the price.

Hedman: Hedman has built headers specifically for F-Body swaps in its Husler's Muscle Rods Hedders and LS Conversion Kits so you can complete the install and avoid many fitment problems. Designed for 1970–1981 F-Bodies, these have a black ceramic coating and are available in a range of tube lengths and diameters. Long-tube headers are also offered but for correct fitment and ground clearance you also have to buy the conversion kits.

Stainless Works: Stainless Works likes to boast that they don't do any sort of metal work that doesn't involve some type of stainless steel, as their name suggests. I opted to go with a set of Stainless Works headers for this build for a number of reasons. The most important reason was

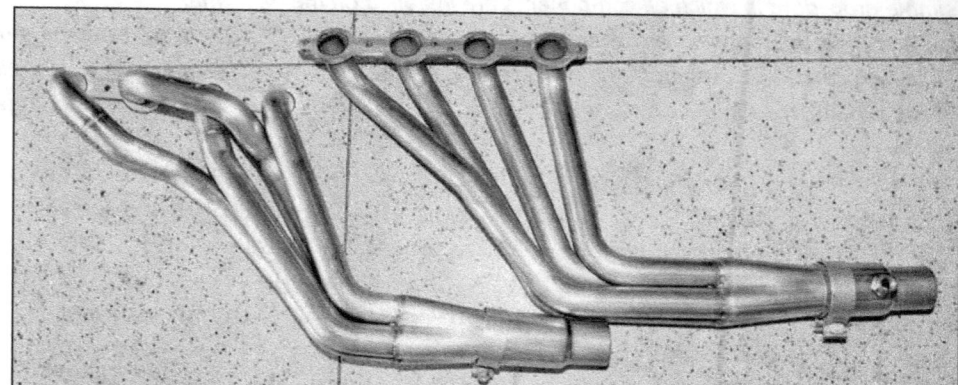

The Stainless Works headers have excellent fit, finish, and performance for LS engines.

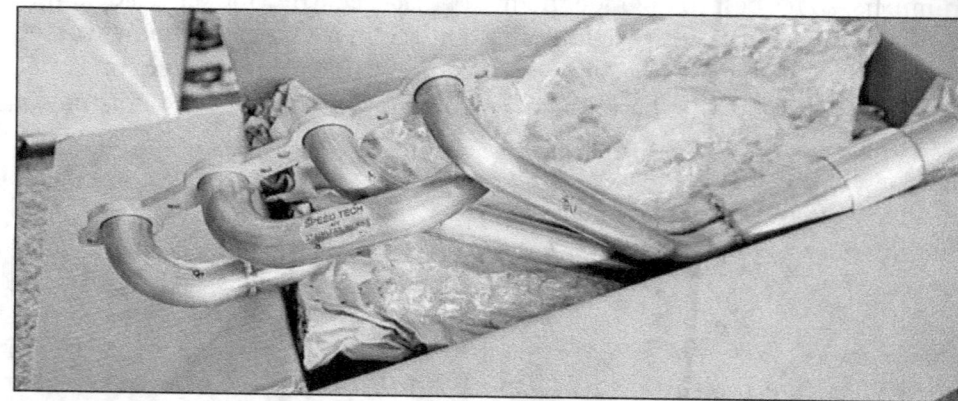

I decided on the milled finish of headers from Speed Tech and Stainless Works. Since they are made specifically for the subframe, I knew that they were the best bet for the build. You need to do your research and plan carefully for your particular project. That means asking around at many places and finding the best system for the application. When using parts designed as a system, you eliminate a lot of headaches down the road. Do most headers fit your application? Most likely; however, it's a crapshoot if you don't do your homework.

EXHAUST AND INDUCTION

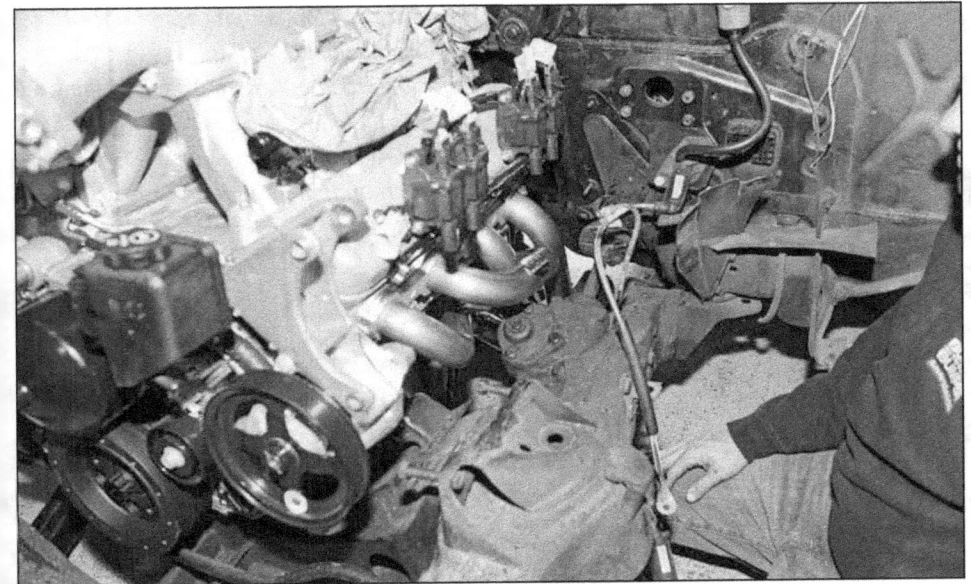

The Stainless Works headers worked just fine in the stock subframe clearing the steering box and other major components.

that the headers were custom-built to work with my Speed Tech subframe and engine mount combination. I opted for a milled finish, but they also offer polished.

I was impressed with the headers and liked the weld quality. They came with 3- to 2.5-inch reducers and band clamps with welded oxygen sensor bungs for easy installation. They come loose so you can clock them in any position that fits best; I pointed mine inward to avoid hitting anything and keep wiring away from the hot pipes. I did have to supply my own gaskets and longer bolts to accommodate the massively thick flanges. I also had to snip off a bit of the dipstick.

The headers fit the other side equally well.

All of your stuff should play nicely with everything else. I had to modify the dipstick tube to fit the new thicker flanged headers. I used a cutoff wheel on a grinder to cut a notch in the bracket for the dipstick tube to match the header.

Don't forget the gaskets. They go in a particular direction, so pay attention to the orientation. These aren't like some header gaskets that you could drop in from the top. These need to be installed with the header and gasket as one unit.

SWAP LS ENGINES INTO CAMAROS & FIREBIRDS 1967–1981

CHAPTER 9

You can see the amount of clearance I have on each side of the headers. It's important to keep vital stuff out of the way, such as fuel lines, brake lines, and in this case, battery cables, because I plan to remote mount the battery.

Oxygen Sensors

On newer style engines, the PCM uses oxygen sensors to balance the ratio of the air/fuel mixture. This, with a combination of engine temperature, ambient air temperature, and a few other parameters, allows the engine to run at its peak performance at any given moment. Oxygen

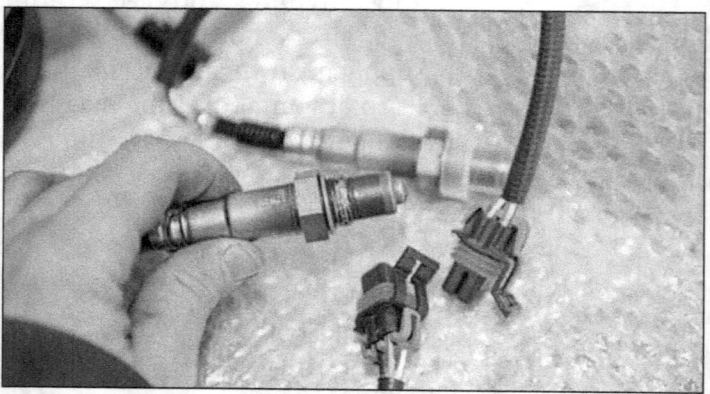

Mine are standard oxygen sensors; just make sure you use a little anti-seize. They are difficult to remove if they've been through many heat cycles.

I found this little factory wire clip. It seemed like a great place to hang the oxygen sensor wire and make sure the sensor doesn't melt.

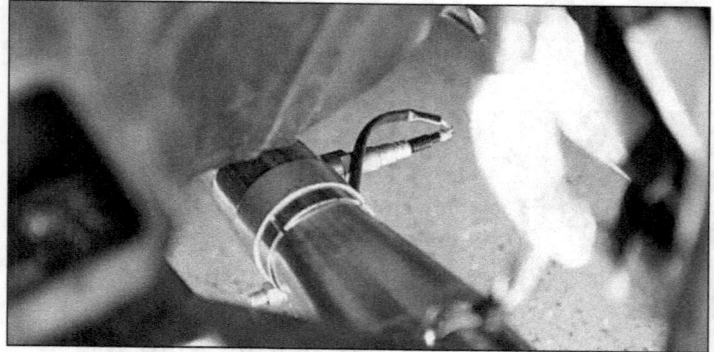

Installing oxygen sensors is pretty easy; just make sure you keep the wires away from header heat. If you don't have sensors already in your headers you can mount them anywhere after the collector in any orientation. Just make sure that the welds are clean and have no leaks.

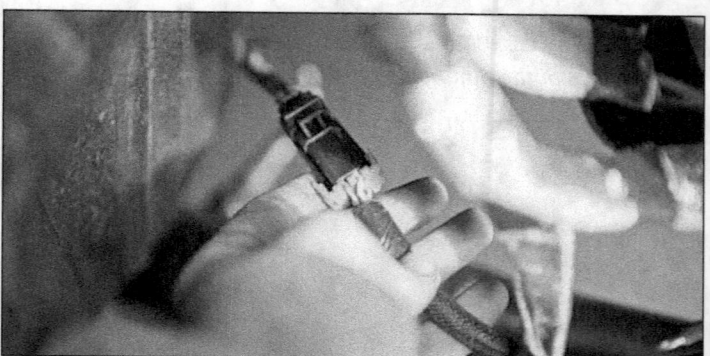

Make the connection at the wiring harness and you are pretty much good to go. The matching oxygen wiring connection is made specifically for the wiring harness so you are just about guaranteed to get these connections correct. Just make sure you connect the driver's side and passenger's side to the right connector.

EXHAUST AND INDUCTION

sensors are crucial to your engine running smoothly. Do not remove them if you are running an EFI LS engine; not only does it throw a code constantly, but it doesn't make anywhere near the power you want.

Now, here's where it can get kind of tricky. Since the late 1990s, the government has mandated that cars get a certain gas mileage among other things. One of those standards was to adopt the OBD II system that has two oxygen sensors per bank of cylinders, one before the catalytic converter, and one after. If you pull an engine from the boneyard that has four oxygen sensors and four plugs, don't be alarmed; that's perfectly normal. For all intents and purposes, all LS engines are OBD-II compatible.

Catalytic Converters

If you live in a place that doesn't require emissions tests for older first- or second-generation F-Bodies, this section probably isn't for you and you don't have to run any type of catalytic converter or submit to any emissions standards. However, if you live in a state that requires those tests for your F-Body, there are a few options you can consider for your car to be emissions legal.

E-Rod

General Motors has come up with the E-Rod package (PN 19244805); the newest version is the E-Rod LS3. The engine is rated at 430 hp with 424 ft-lbs of torque. The package comes with an engine, ECM, wiring harness, exhaust manifolds, catalytic converters, oxygen sensors and bosses, fuel tank evaporation canister, fuel pedal, and air filter. Similar packages are available for the LS7 and LSA.

Other options are always available for completing an exhaust system, such as this 100-percent food-grade stainless-steel custom setup that was made to fit around the massive torque-arm rear suspension. (Photo Courtesy Speed Tech)

There's no different strategy for exhaust after the headers on an LS swap for your F-Body. You only need to contend with the suspension in your imagination or go the normal route as shown here. (Photo Courtesy Stainless Works)

Everything else is up to the owner to provide or fabricate. You have to source a set of engine mounts, which can be easy to find and are relatively inexpensive. You also need to find a stout fuel system. General Motors recommends using the 4L60E automatic transmission (PN 19156260) with the matching GM controller (PN 12497316). If you want to go with a manual transmission, you have to order E-Rod package PN 19256487. At the time of this writing, both versions are priced at $9,375. Not bad considering it comes with a 12-month/50,000-mile warranty.

The package is CARB legal (California Air Resources Board), which makes it legal in all 50 states. You could think of this as a smog-legal version of the basic Corvette and Camaro SS engine. It doesn't get any easier than this if you want something legal and almost plug-and-play.

Stock Systems

Another option, albeit a time-consuming one, is to grab all the smog parts required to make your car legal. That means you have to get the catalytic converters off the car or purchase new ones. In addition, make sure your ECM and wiring harness are set up for the extra two oxygen sensors. In addition, a part that everyone forgets about is the evaporation canister from the fuel tank. This is typically a black box that allows the recirculating gas vapors to return to the fuel tank. This is a critical piece that you have to source before becoming 100-percent smog legal. You can put in a set of aftermarket headers, but you have to figure out how to mount the dual catalytic converters. You need to route the exhaust pipes beneath the car and then bolt or weld the catalytic converters between the pipes and the mufflers.

A good thing about many LS variants is that they do not use EGR systems because they have camshaft overlap, much like LT engines. The C5 and C6 Corvette systems and F-Bodies don't need the EGR for this reason and the same goes for 2003-and-later trucks.

After the Oxygen Sensor

If you aren't forced to use a catalytic converter system, you're pretty much free to come up with any system you want after the oxygen sensors. If you went with a long-tube header, you can pretty much bolt up your old setup, assuming you have the current reducers (if you need them). This isn't a book on exhaust, so you're on your own from the header back, but pretty much any aftermarket kit fits. It's all a matter of brand loyalty and which sound you like.

In the case of my 1968 build, the rear-torque arm setup made life a bit more complicated and I was forced to be more creative. A well-meaning friend convinced me to install a Trans Am–style exhaust with each pipe dumping out on the driver's and passenger's sides before the rear tire. And this reinforces my point that after the oxygen sensors, you're free to be as crazy as you want. Typically, many people install a dual muffler system with a crossover pipe in the middle and a rear-exit exhaust.

Induction

One of the last things you probably think of is the induction system. Regardless of whether you choose to use the mechanic throttle body or the drive-by-wire version, you need to figure out some way to deliver air to the new engine. You have to bring the intake tube out of the throttle body at a 90-degree angle and then to the air filter.

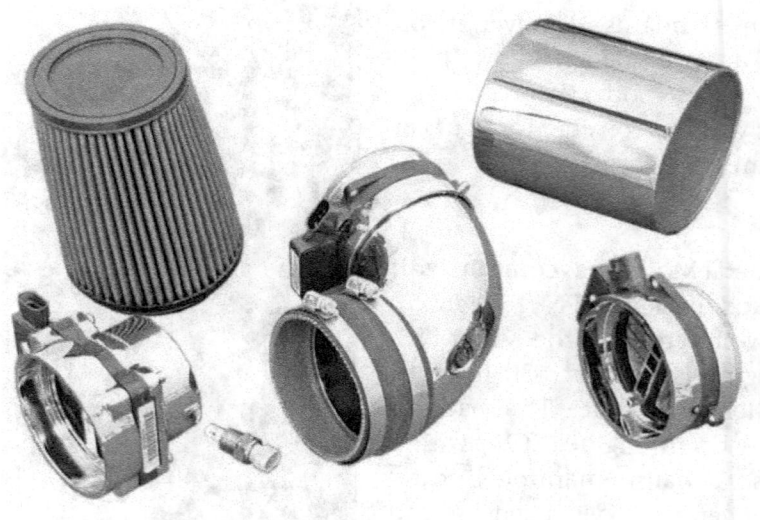

A few places, such as Street & Performance, make kits like this that even work with a MAF sensor, thus eliminating the need to fabricate anything on your own. (Photo Courtesy Texas Street & Performance)

EXHAUST AND INDUCTION

Easier options are out there, such as this quick 90-degree bend to get it over with fast. (Photo Courtesy Texas Street & Performance)

On the LS9 intake, it's easier to cut off the collar and remount it so that the intake tube can run more efficiently. (Photo Courtesy Mark Stielow)

The best way to do this is to first figure out where you want the air filter to go. I wanted to route the air filter to the driver-side inner fender. Remember, the cooler air is farthest away from the engine; cooler air means more power and that's a good thing.

For example, Nate Shaw fabricated my tube out of 4-inch aluminum tubing. He took several pre-bent forms (that can be purchased through a number of sources) and pieced them together by cutting and splicing. He worked with them until he had the correct bends. In this situation I couldn't take it out the passenger's side because the upper radiator hose gets in the way, so I had to route it out the driver's side. Unfortunately, I had to snake the intake hose around the catch-can for the radiator since it protruded more than I thought.

With a tube this long, you have to find a place to mount it rigidly to the engine. I found the closest was the lower alternator bolt. Later, I TIG-welded the pipe pieces together and matched the finish of the engine.

If you choose to make a tube or use something stock (such as a tube from Spectre), you have to remember to mount and hook up your IAT (idle air temperature sensor). If you're running a MAF setup, it's best to place it in a straight piece of pipe with some silicone elbows to make it fit properly.

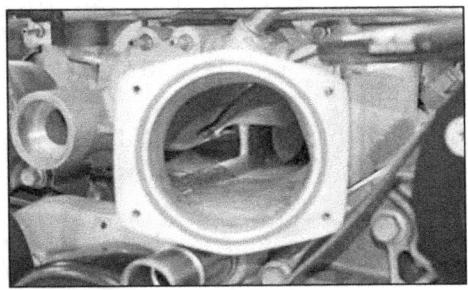

After the new intake collar is on, the air flows straight into the intake, rather than making a sharp bend immediately. (Photo Courtesy Mark Stielow)

After mocking up the block-off plate and intake tube, you can get a better picture of what you're making. (Photo Courtesy Mark Stielow)

SWAP LS ENGINES INTO CAMAROS & FIREBIRDS 1967–1981

CHAPTER 10

INITIAL START-UP

I am pretty sure that by now you are ready to turn the key and fire up the engine. Now take a deep breath and slowly walk away from the car. Yes, that's right. Walk away. This may sound counter intuitive because you're itching to get your LS-powered F-Body car on the road. However, the last thing you need is a half-cocked initial failure to set you back another month in your project. Clear your mind and relax. Then review the pre-start-up checklist and make sure everything has been done correctly.

You have transformed a common stock F-Body into a high-performance muscle car, and as such, you need to carefully inspect and monitor the systems during first start-up. If you have installed a new crate engine with a warranty or a freshly rebuilt engine pulled from a junkyard, you need to pay particular attention to the engine when it is started for the first time. If you have installed a used engine, it has run before; it should do so reliably now and you do not have to break it in.

First, you need to be alert and sharp so you can identify problems. You need to be prepared to shut the engine down immediately if a problem is discovered; you want to avoid doing any damage to it.

Be sure that all of the fluids are topped off. Make sure your oil pan is filled to capacity, which is 5 or 6 quarts. I recommend that you use actual break-in oil that contains ZDDP (such as Joe Gibbs "driven oil"). But before you actually fire up the engine, you should pre-lube it, so oil adequately coats all internal surfaces, including rocker arms, lifters, and main bearings.

If you don't pre-lube the engine, you take a chance on damaging vital components because some areas may be starved of oil while the oil pump works up to full pressure. You invested a tremendous amount of time and money in your LS swap so you don't want to cut corners because it could result in a fatal mistake. Goodson sells an air-pressurized pre-lube tank system (PN PL-40) used with an air compressor that sends oil through the engine, but it costs $200.

Another method is to build your own pre-luber and that's easily done. You can install a small-block Chevy oil pump in a 5-gallon plastic bucket and puncture it with an electric drill so that oil is drawn out of the bucket, routed through the engine, and returned to the bucket. Doing it this way ensures the engine is properly protected for first start-up.

Be sure to mount an oil pressure gauge on the engine so that you can

My 1968 Camaro is now complete and ready for first start-up. It is fitted with a Speed Tech front subframe and rear suspension and a myriad of other parts. This fade-away shot shows the MAST Motorsports LS3 beneath the hood.

INITIAL START-UP

verify oil pressure when you're circulating oil through the engine.

Safety should always be paramount with any automotive project and this one is no different. Make sure the transmission is in "Park" or "Neutral" (that is, not in gear) and that the emergency brake is set. You should also chock the wheels so the car cannot roll.

Systems Checks

This section prepares you for many of the common missteps folks make when rushing into starting their car for the first time and somehow fouling it up. Worse yet is when you've invited everyone over for the grand unveiling. The first celebratory beers are cracked, you hear a fizzle when you turn the key, and look like a dope when you ask everyone at the party to, "just hang on . . ."

VATS

The vehicle anti-theft system (VATS) is pretty standard on most GM vehicles. This means that the key is matched to the lock cylinder; the engine does not run if they are not harmonized. The easiest fix is to have the company that reprogramed your ECM and wiring harness edit this part out of the code. If you have full power to the car but no starter engagement, you just might have a VATS problem.

Park/Neutral or Clutch Switch

The lockout for the clutch or park/neutral switch is in the wire bundle of the LS-engine ECM. If the computer doesn't recognize that the clutch is depressed or that the car is in Park or Neutral, the computer does not send the signal to the starter of the vehicle. Double-check that this is installed properly or as a last resort (and I don't recommend this) you can ground the wire from the ECM to fool it into believing that the switch is depressed. This is clearly a safety item and should be wired to engage this feature whenever possible.

Clutch Engagement

The LS engine typically uses hydraulics to actuate the clutch. Most, if not all, of the setups around have a fully hydraulic clutch, meaning the system uses a master and a slave cylinder. If you haven't bled the system yet, you need to do it before you start the engine for the first time because the clutch's default position is "engaged." (See Chapter 7 to bleed your system effectively.)

An easy way to tell if the clutch has adequate engagement is to support the rear wheels securely on several jacks so they can spin freely. Have a helper push the clutch pedal down (disengaged) and try to turn the rear wheels with your hands. If they don't move, you have a problem.

Oil Pressure

You should have an oil pressure gauge on your car, no debate. If you don't, get one now! The single greatest thing that kills an engine faster than your quarter-mile times is oil starvation.

Be sure to prime the system first. General Motors recommends that you fill the engine with oil and disconnect the engine control system. Then, using an oil pressure gauge, crank the engine in 10-second bursts until oil pressure is achieved. You can remove the spark plugs to help relieve pressure in the system.

When you start the car for the first time, oil pressure should be instantaneous. If you do not get any

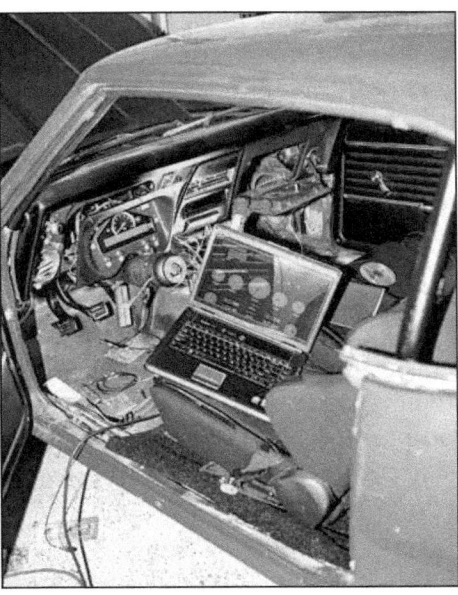

Your setup might look like this for a while if you plan to tune it yourself. I used the tuning software that came with the Mast engine to reprogram the system after an intake swap.

reading on your gauge within 5 to 10 seconds, shut the engine down and start diagnosing the problem. A lack of oil pressure can be many things, such as major malfunction in the oil pump. Be sure that the oil pick-up tube is matched to the oil pan before you install it in the car so you don't have to take it apart later.

Leaks

I've seen it more often than not that people get a little over zealous and start pounding on things unnecessarily. I once even got a little ahead of myself and forgot to put the lower power-steering hose on the build. I finally realized it after half a quart of fluid spilled all over the floor.

It helps to make a checklist of fluids that could possibly leak and simply make a mess or be a symptom of a much larger problem. Fuel leaks are the most common followed by leaks of radiator fluid, power steering fluid, brake fluid, transmission fluid, rear-end housing fluids, and engine oil.

Fuel

You need to verify that your fuel system provides between 58 to 60 psi. This can be checked via an external gauge or in my case, a fuel pressure gauge that is part of the gauge cluster in the dash. The easiest way to check this is to turn the key to the on-position, but do not engage the starter. You should hear the pump whine a little and this means it's turned on. Keep in mind that the pump is designed to only turn on for 5 seconds before shutting off in the key-on position.

If you do not have pressure or can't hear the pump prime, it needs to be corrected. Most often it is simply an easily corrected wiring issue. (This would be a good time to double-check your other wiring connections and make sure they are secure as well.)

When you are testing fuel pressure it's usually a good idea to bleed the system of air. If you have AN fittings, a small crack with a wrench sometimes gets most of the air pockets out. Otherwise, the engine may need to be cranked and run for a short time to get all the air out of the system. This is a great time to double-check for leaks while the system is under pressure; you should be able to spot them rather quickly.

Nut and Bolt the Car

I cannot stress this point enough; you need to double- and sometimes triple-check your work. I highly suggest that you put the car on jack stands or up in the air and "nut and bolt" the car. This means going through the car systematically to make sure that every nut and bolt is tight and ready for service. Nothing would stink more than to find a crucial loose bolt when you're 50 miles from home. Even Mark Stielow has said that he finds loose nuts and bolts from time to time after driving his hand-built rolling works of art.

Engine Break-In: First Firing and Test-Drive

Some people jump right in their newly built ride and take off. This may be fine for some, but I like to keep my stuff in one piece for as long as possible. The best option is to break in the engine on an engine dyno so you can control all aspects of the engine break-in. If that's not possible and you have to break in the engine in the car I have several recommendations.

If this is your first fuel-injected engine you may be pleasantly surprised at how easily and quickly these engines start up. They self-regulate instantly. I do not recommend using the gas pedal at all while starting the engine because it can confuse the throttle position sensor; let the engine and ECM do all the work.

The engine idles relatively fast at first, roughly 800 to 1,200 rpm until it goes into "closed-loop" operation, which means that the computer has recognized that the engine is ready for normal operation. This usually means that the engine has good oil pressure, the coolant is at a safe temperature, fuel pressure is good, and there are no obvious issues with the fuel/air mixture or any sensors malfunctioning. This is a good time to monitor your gauges to make sure that they are accurate and that they are reading safe numbers for each engine statistic. If all seems well, look for leaks such as in the high-pressure power-steering line. Many leaks don't show unless the car is running.

If no leaks are detected it is time for a test drive. There are many ways to truly break in an engine and drivetrain components. The following procedure has worked well for me for many years.

First, cycle the fuel pump a few times. It's entirely possible you have air in the system, so I suggest cracking the system open at the fuel rail to let the air bleed out.

After the start-up it's important to let the piston rings seat in the bores. Long gone are the days of letting the flat-tappet cams and lifters mate over time. LS engines have fixed that little problem for all of us. I recommend hitting the city streets; piston rings love a variable-RPM range during the break-in period. I also suggest keeping the RPM below 3,500 and no full throttle accelerations. Engines also hate long constant-RPM drives right away. Several engine builders have told me that this plan should be followed for the first 500 to 1,000 miles of the engine.

After the first drive, monitor the fluid levels and top off any that need it. Lunati often recommends changing the oil after 100 miles to get rid of the initial bearing wear, then at 500 miles, and then at 1,500. It has also been recommended that for LS engines, conventional oil should be used for the break-in process as it promotes piston ring and cylinder wall seating. After the 1,500-mile oil change, you should stick to the manufacturer's recommendations for oil change intervals.

The final step is to enjoy the car! Keep an eye on all the vitals and have fun. That's the name of the game!

Source Guide

Abbott Enterprises
901 W. Fourth Ave.
Pine Bluff, AR 71601
870-535-4973
shiftworks.com/tailhousing.htm

American Autowire
150 Heller Pl. No. 17W
Bellmawr, NJ 08031
800-482-9473
americanautowire.com

ARP
1863 Eastman Ave.
Ventura, CA 93003
805-339-2200
arp-bolts.com

Autokraft
5020 W. Folsom St.
Eau Claire, WI 54703
715-874-5921
autokraft.org

Auto Meter
413 W. Elm St.
Sycamore, IL 60178
866-248-6356
autometer.com

AutoRad
4647 Jim Hood Rd.
Gainesville, GA 30506
770-983-1345
autoradradiators.com

Baer Brakes
2222 W. Peoria Ave.
Phoenix, AZ 85029
602-233-1411
baer.com

Bear's Performance
5060 O'Neil St.
Oldcastle, ON Canada N0R 1L0
519-737-9333
bearsperformance.com

Cable X
901 W. Fourth Ave.
Pine Bluff, AR 71601
800-643-5973
abbott-tach.com

Chevrolet Performance
800-450-4150
gmperformanceparts.com

CJ Tunes
651-224-0267
cjtunes.com

Dirty Dingo Motorsports
541 E. Juanita Ave., #2
Mesa, AR 85204
480-824-1968
dirtydingo.com

Eddie Motorsports
11479 Sixth St.
Rancho Cucamonga, CA 91730
888-813-1293
eddiemotorsports.com

Edelbrock/Russell
2700 California St.
Torrance, CA 90503
310-781-2222
edelbrock.com

Forgeline Motorsports
1-800-886-0093
forgeline.com

General Motors
GM.com

G-Force
330-753-5300
crossmembers.com

Holley/Earl's
1801 Russellville Rd.
Bowling Green, KY 42101
270-782-2900
holley.com

Jegs
101 JEGS Pl.
Delaware, OH 43015
800-345-4545
jegs.com

KWiK Performance
417-955-1467
kwikperf.com

Mast Motorsports
330 N.W. Stallings Dr.
Nacogdoches, TX 75964
866-551-4916
mastmotorsports.com

Matt's Classic Bowties
7114 Village Pkwy.
Dublin, CA 94568
888-628-8746
mattsclassicbowties.com

MSD Ignition
1350 Pullman Dr.
El Paso, TX 79936
915-857-5200
msdignition.com

SOURCE GUIDE

Norm's Tire
2767 Long Lake Rd.
Roseville, MN 55113
651-483-4591
normstire.com

One Guys Garage LLC
8802 250th St. W.
Lakeville, MN 55044
763-221-1755
one-guys-garage.com

OPTIMA Batteries
5757 N. Green Bay Ave.
Milwaukee, WI 53209
888-867-8462
optimabatteries.com

OptiShift
Baumann Electronic Controls
207 Mistr Ln.
Pickens, SC 29671
864-646-8920
optishift.com

PACE Performance
50 Karago Ave.
Boardman, OH 44512
800-748-3791
paceperformance.com

QuickTime Bellhousings
10601 Memphis Ave., No. 12
Cleveland, OH 44144
216-688-8300
lakewoodindustries.com

Ram Clutches
201 Business Park Blvd.
Columbia, SC 29203
803-788-6034
ramclutches.com

Rick's Tanks
228 E. Sunset Rd.
El Paso TX, 79922
915-760-4388
rickstanks.com

Rockland Standard Gear
150 Route 17
Sloatsburg, NY 10974
1-877-774-4327
rsgear.com

Scoggin-Dickey
5901 Spur 327
Lubbock, TX 79424
800-456-0211
sdparts.com

Shift Works
200 Air Park Dr., Ste. 10
Rochester, NY 14624
585-436-0139
shiftworks.com

SpearTech
3574 East State Rd. 236
Anderson, IN 46017
765-378-4908
speartech.com

Speed Tech Performance/ATS
888-467-1625
speedtechperformance.com

Speedway Motors
800-979-0122
speedwayms.com/

Street & Performance
1 Hot Rod Ln.
Mena, AR 71953
479-394-5711
hotrodlane.com

Summit Racing
P.O. Box 909
Akron, OH 44398-6177
800-230-3030
summitracing.com

Tanks
260 Welter Dr.
Monticello, IA 52310
877-596-3842
tanksinc.com

Texas Speed & Performance
5619 FM 1585
Lubbock, TX 79424
806-698-0365
texas-speed.com

TPiS
4255 Creek Rd.
Chaska, MN 55318
952-448-6021
tpis.com

Tremec
800-401-9866
tremec.com

Turn One Steering
7436 E. Holland Rd.
Saginaw, MI 48601
877-GO-TURN1
turnone-steering.com

VaporWorx
vaporworx.com

Vintage Air
18865 Goll St.
San Antonio, TX 78266
800-862-6658
vintageair.com

www.ingramcontent.com/pod-product-compliance
Lightning Source LLC
Chambersburg PA
CBHW081452070526
44586CB00019B/2318